THE POWER OF THE BLOOD COVENANT

Uncover the Secret Strength in

God's Eternal Oath

MALCOLM SMITH

HARRISON HOUSE
Tulsa, Oklahoma

Unless otherwise indicated, all Scripture quotations are taken from *The New King James Version*. Copyright © 1979, 1980, 1982, Thomas Nelson, Inc.

Scripture quotations marked (KJV) are taken from the *King James Version* of the Bible.

Scripture quotations marked (AMP) are taken from *The Amplified Bible, Old Testament* copyright © 1965, 1987 by The Zondervan Corporation. *The Amplified New Testament,* copyright © 1958, 1987 by the Lockman Foundation. Used by permission.

Scripture quotations marked (RSV) are taken from *The Revised Standard Version of the Bible,* copyright © 1946, Old Testament section copyright © 1952 by the Division of Christian Education of the Churches of Christ in the United States of America and is used by permission.

Scripture quotations marked (NASB) are taken from the *New American Standard Bible.* Copyright © the Lockman Foundation 1960, 1962, 1963, 1968, 1971, 1972, 1973, 1975, 1977. Used by permission.

Scripture quotations marked (MESSAGE) are taken from *The Message.* Copyright © 1993, 1994, 1995. Used by permission of NavPress Publishing Group.

Scripture quotations marked (PHILLIPS) are taken from *The New Testament in Modern English,* (Rev. Ed.) by J.B. Phillips. Copyright © 1958, 1960, 1972 by J.B. Phillips. Reprinted by permission of Macmillan Publishing Co., New York, New York.

22 21   15

The Power of the Blood Covenant —
Uncover the Secret Strength in God's Eternal Oath
ISBN 13: 978-1-57794-816-5
ISBN 10: 1-57794-816-2
Copyright © 2002 by Malcolm Smith
7986 Mainland Drive
San Antonio, TX 78350
www.malcolmsmith.org

Published by Harrison House Publishers
P.O. Box 35035
Tulsa, Oklahoma 74153

Printed in the United States of America. All rights reserved under International Copyright Law. Contents and/or cover may not be reproduced in whole or in part in any form without the express written consent of the Publisher.

Table of Contents

1	What Is Missing?	1
2	Welcome to the World of Covenants	11
3	The World of the Living Dead	23
4	The Lovingkindness of God	41
5	The Core of the Covenant	55
6	The Representative Man	73
7	The Story of Mephibosheth	91
8	The Blood of God	99
9	The Oath of God	117
10	Entering the Covenant	137
11	The Covenant Meal	155
12	Sin Is Remembered No More	173
13	I in You, You in Me	191
14	The Summation of the Christian Life	209
15	How To Walk in the Spirit	227
16	The People of the Spirit	251
17	The Friend of God	269
	Afterword	287
	Endnotes	291
	References	295

Chapter 1

WHAT IS MISSING?

Before they actually saw it, astronomers were aware that the planet we now know as Pluto was in the solar system because of the gravitational influence it exerted on other planets. My journey into the contents of this book was much the same.

As I read through Scripture and studied its characters, I became aware that they knew something that I did not know. That "something" exerted a tremendous influence over the way they understood God and His salvation. The bold faith they exercised with authority was in response to that "something."

As I studied the Psalms and the prayers of the men and women of God recorded in the Scripture, I became aware that their praying and worshipping was in response to a revelation that they had of that "something." It became obvious to me that whatever it was, was the foundation upon which the people of God built their lives. That "something" was the secret of their life and walk with God and the basis of their exploits done in His name.

It showed up the most in the New Testament, where again I was aware that the believers were responding to something that I did not know was there. They seemed to look at salvation through a different lens than the one I was using.

I had been reared to see my salvation through the model of a courtroom where I was the condemned prisoner under the sentence of death, and the Judge took my place and paid my penalty, and I was justified, declared righteous. That was a quite useful model, but it lacked something I could not put my finger on.

A few weeks after my accepting Christ, I had an experience of the Holy Spirit that dramatically changed my life; but as I read and reread the pages of the New Testament, I realized that the Spirit was the writer's very life. This very Spirit was the way they defined and understood their salvation. They knew Him not merely as an ecstatic experience but as the entire context of their lives.

It was obvious that they did not have a second or third experience that catapulted them into this dimension of life. There was "something" they knew by which they interpreted the cross, the blood-shedding of Jesus, His resurrection, His ascension, and the giving of the Holy Spirit that I knew nothing about. That same "something" gave the definition to the work of the Spirit in their individual lives and in the community of believers that was light-years beyond my experience of the Spirit.

THE COVENANT CORE

I discovered that the "something" I did not know about was the covenant God had made with His people. It is difficult for me now to remember how I looked at the Scripture before I came to see and understand the covenant. I certainly did not see that everything was working out from the hidden core of the covenant. I had a belief system that was incoherent; each part stood by itself as an island in a sea called Christianity, no part having any real relation to the other parts. I believed God created the universe, but I did not see how that related to our salvation. Salvation was the act of God's love, but it just happened without any connection to certain commitments He had made. My experience of the Spirit was a glorious add-on to being saved from sin; I did not see it as vitally part of everything else.

It all lacked the "something" to tie it all together. The promises of God were the Word of God and utterly reliable, but again hung in their own space with no relationship to a commitment in blood that God had made.

Faith was a mystery to me. I pondered the authority with which the heroes of Scripture spoke, and I wondered whence came the authority for them to speak such wonders and for God to honor their words. I did not realize they were speaking out from a prior commitment God had made to them.

Prayer fell into the same category: What did it mean to pray in the name of Jesus? It seemed limiting and liberating at the same time. I did not know that His name was at the heart of the covenant. Even the praise, thanksgiving, and worship in the Psalms were thanking Him for "something," which I did not realize was His covenant and loyal covenant love.

The discovery of the new covenant made in the blood of God, shed from the wounds of the Lord Jesus, gave to me a new Bible. My vague sea of Christianity gave way to solid land, and the islands of truth and experience came together as a whole. I was introduced to a rest in Christ and an understanding of the place of the Spirit in my personal life and of the church that I had never known prior to my discovering the covenant.

A GOSPEL WITHOUT POWER

The tragedy is that a vast majority of believers entering the twenty-first century are blind to the fact that the Gospel announces and empowers them to be included into such a relationship with God. Not realizing such a breathtaking calling, they settle for the weekly round of church services, attempts at prayer and Bible study, and the keeping of rules that deal for the most part with the physical life.

I am not mechanically minded. In fact, I could be described as illiterate in things mechanical. In my late teens, I was the pastor of a small church in a farming community in Northern Ireland. I visited my congregation at their farms on my bicycle; and to make my task of visiting the flock easier, one of the farmers gave me a small motorbike that had belonged to one of his sons. I had never owned or dreamed of owning such a machine and took to it with fear and awe. No one told me how it worked or what I had to do to make it work, and no instruction book came with the old bike.

I dressed the part with helmet and riding gear and set out savoring the new experience of being taken to my destination. Gone were the days of pedaling myself to exhaustion against a headwind.

The second day out, though, the bike sputtered and died. I sat sad and confused without a clue as to what might be wrong. I began pushing the machine along the road. I sweated under my heavy gear and longed for the old days of a predictable bicycle. I trudged mile after mile under the sun. I was tempted to trash the wretched machine in the ditch but did not want to offend the farmer who had given it to me.

My thoughts of disgust at my gift and despair that so soon it was broken beyond repair were interrupted by the voice of a friendly farmer. He had seen me dragging my load along the road and called out, "You can have some of my gas, son!" I stopped in delighted wonder: My bike was not broken, but out of gas!

I have met many Christians who push their lives along the highway, about to throw it into the ditch because, although they have the outward trappings of a Christian, they do not know the powerful energy that is the heart of the believer's life. They are pushing themselves to exhaustion, when they should be propelled by the energy of Another.

What Is Missing?

What is the Gospel? If what we believe to be the Gospel is not the power of God unto salvation, then we need to ask if we understand it at all.

What is biblical faith? For many, it is the religious version of the faith spoken of by the writers of self-help books.

How do we stop being terrified of God and begin to truly love Him? Is it possible to be His friend as well as being His servant?

What is true holiness? It surely must be more than keeping a list of external rules.

What did Jesus mean by the phrase "I in you and you in Me?" It sounds like a lot more than going to church twice a week!

How do we overcome temptation? Is it a matter of strong willpower and determination?

How is it possible to love unlovable people? How can we love one another as Jesus loved us? How can we forgive the unforgivable?

Tragically, there are millions of believers who are as educated in the answers to those questions as I was in how the motorbike works.

Let me share a letter with you that I received the other day:

Dear Malcolm,

You do not know who I am, and I have never met you, but a friend of mine told me he has been greatly helped by your teaching and he gave me your address and urged me to write. I trust you will read this letter and give me some answers.

I am writing to you because my Christian life is a disaster and I have nowhere to turn. I am in a position of leadership in my church, and if I shared with the pastor or any of the deacons the way my life is, I do not know what would happen. I know I would no longer be welcome in the church. I pray that you will read this and be able to help me.

Let me say upfront that if you saw me in the context of the church, in the weekly meetings, in social gatherings with other church members, or teaching my adult Sunday school class, you would never imagine that I am not the person you see. I did not set out to be a hypocrite. From the very first, I gave my very best to live for Jesus. I have disciplined myself to pray every day and read and even memorize the Scripture. I honestly set out every week to live for Jesus. But I fail every time. The life that my family and the people I work with see is very different from the one that is portrayed before the church. I have a terrible temper that I cannot control, however much I try. I wrestle every day with lustful thoughts, and when I am out of town on business I watch pornographic movies in the hotel room. I have a brother I have not spoken to in twenty years and cannot bring myself to forgive because of a betrayal of confidence that deeply hurt me. If Christianity is loving as Jesus loved, then count me out.

But above all, I do not love God; I do not find joy in my prayer or Bible reading—it is something I do because I have been told that it will nurture my Christian life. But my heart is not in keeping His commands and being with Him; in fact, there are times I have to admit that I envy the world—they look a lot happier than I ever feel.

Maybe I have continued to live this way for the last ten years because in the church I can get by with a veneer that satisfies my peers and leaders. You know what I mean by veneer—the rules of the subculture we evangelicals are part of. I went over them the other day. We are the people who do not do certain things; we do not go to certain places; we do not smoke or

What Is Missing?

drink liquor, nor do we dress like the world, especially our poor women! As long as I keep those rules, everyone thinks I am a great Christian.

But in the last weeks I have faced myself and realized that the Bible primarily addresses my thoughts, motives, and relationships, not so much the lists that I spend my life trying to keep that have been given by the church. Above all, it commands me to love God and delight in Him, to obey His commands out of love for Him.

I miserably fail. Malcolm, the truth is I do not love God. It would be more correct to say that I am afraid of Him, and go to church and pray because I am afraid if I do not, I will go to hell. I look around at the others in my church, even my friends, and wonder if they are living in the same craziness that I am—and why not? They do not know what I am really like. Do they scream at their kids and sneak pornography when no one is watching? Do they go through all the words and motions on Sunday while their hearts are untouched and without love for God? Is their religious life like mine, just a millimeter-thick mask over the real person underneath?

There have been times when I think that I have had an experience of God. At special meetings when hands have been laid on me, I have felt a warm glow inside, the flickering of a joy that has lasted for a couple of weeks, and I have wondered if that is how real Christians feel all the time. At times I have heard a message that lays out a formula for living as a victorious Christian, and I have tried it, but it feels artificial when I try to live it out with the guys in the office. All my spurts of hope that I can live this life are dead ends and leave me in greater despair than before.

In the last weeks, I have looked at myself and evaluated what my life is really like. It has left me in utter *despair. This letter is my last attempt to ask someone I can trust if the Christian life can be lived by ordinary people like my friends and me. Tell me honestly, Malcolm, is it for a few unusual people who do not have the desires that we have, who really do hate the world and love God? And if it is for everyone, then is there something I have missed, is there a level of dedication or an experience I need to have that will finally get me into living the Christian life? Or is my life as I have tried to describe it to you as good as it gets?*

If my experience of Christianity is as good as it gets, then I will quietly walk away from it all. I can no longer live a life that is so incredibly shallow and meaningless. Please be honest with me, Malcolm—if you tell me that this is the way Christianity really works out in practice, I will not tell anyone you said so; I will burn your letter and drop out. There is a Bible study and prayer meeting at the church tonight, and I do not want to go; in fact, I have no interest in being there. If I go, it is because I do not want to go through the hassle of being asked by the pastor why I was not there or of having my friends think I am backsliding. But I think I will stay home because I am sick of this game. Please answer me and be honest with me, whatever the answer is.

Thank you,
Bob

I receive many letters that reflect the same despair that Bob describes. Tragically, he is correct in assuming that many of his friends who sing hymns beside him in church live in the same hopeless confusion he is in. They are hiding behind a mask of Christian activity, going through the motions and keeping the surface rules that give the appearance of loving God. A life of loving God and honestly and joyfully wanting to do His will from the heart is a mirage in the spiritual desert wilderness in which they live.

Many in despair have given up all hope of living the kind of Christian life they see reflected in the New Testament. Why is this? Most of these people are as sincere as Bob in giving their best and trying to do what they believe God demands of them. As best they know how, they believe the Gospel. So why are their lives so shallow and empty?

Is it possible that these people have not grasped what the Gospel is really about? Is it possible they have heard only parts of the Gospel, while missing the vital ingredient?

When I was speaking in a church in Hong Kong, the pastor asked my advice. He told me that so many of the church members who regularly attended the Sunday services and midweek Bible study also would go to the Buddhist temple during the week. Whatever he would say and teach made no difference. He was frustrated and asked if I had an answer.

During the week, I went to the temple to see if I could find out why these believers would go there. The answer was in the vast courtyard filled with little tables of fortune-tellers. Each table had a line of men and women seeking an answer to a problem, advice on business or marriage, direction for the best time to take a journey, and so on.

I questioned the pastor regarding the subject of his sermons. There was a great emphasis on heaven, the second coming, hell and judgment, as well as teaching concerning the Trinity and the work of Jesus on the cross.

His people came to church to be taught about the transcendent God who had worked in history, far above them, far removed from their daily grind. Salvation, as the congregation had been taught, focused on a Jesus who would save them from hell and take them to heaven and the fine-print details of the events that would herald the end of the world, but they went to the fortune-teller for advice on living today! They needed to know the God who walked through life with them and in them, the source of wisdom and the power to live.

Returning to the United States, I realized that it was much the same situation here. The weekly diet of many Christians is a call to escape hell and get to heaven after death, and many of the best-selling Christian books deal with the intricate details of end-time prophecy. But how to live in the power of the Spirit, to walk as Jesus walked, and to love as He loved are questions rarely talked about.

This book is my answer to the many believers who are asking the same questions Bob did. I am seeking to introduce many believers to a Christianity that works in the here and now, that empowers us to live in heaven on the way to heaven.

The answer is to be found in understanding that the Gospel is the announcement of God's covenant and how we can walk in its authority and power in the midst of the darkness of the world's system. Let me warn you: It is possible that what I am about to share with you may turn your present understanding of the Gospel and the way the Christian life should be lived on its head. If your present understanding of the Gospel is not producing fruit in your life, then it is time to say, "Maybe I have missed something, and it is time to radically reexamine my faith."

Chapter 2

WELCOME TO THE WORLD OF COVENANTS

This book unfolds the amazing story of the Gospel, looking at it through the eyes and ears of those who first heard it. Words that we are familiar with through reading the Bible were pregnant with a meaning to the original audience that we who live in the twenty-first century are ignorant of. They understood the Gospel as the working out of a covenant.

Through my years of studying the Bible I had missed it, mainly because the concept of covenant is almost unknown in the Western world today. However, this concept of covenants is known and documented in ancient societies and among peoples of the Third World to this day.

The people who populate the pages and stories of our Bible lived in the atmosphere of covenants as the air they breathed. All relationships were linked in some way to covenant, whether in the union of nations or clans or individuals. The family unit was understood as a covenant, each family member being tightly knit to the others with a sense of covenant responsibility.

The Bible contains two documents that have been unfortunately named the Old Testament and the New Testament. The word "testament" is not adequate to describe what these two documents are. The correct naming of these two documents is the old covenant and the new covenant.

The old covenant is the covenant that was made with Israel at Mount Sinai through Moses, their representative. It was the covenant of the law of the Ten Commandments, the sacrificial system of offering up lambs, bulls, and goats to cover the sins of the people; the mark and seal of membership in the covenant was the circumcision of the male.

The new covenant is called new because it made all that went before it old and of no more use as a means of salvation. It was not just another covenant that improved on the previous one, as this year's automobile model is an improvement over last year's. The word "new"[1] means new in kind, that which has never been thought or dreamed of before. This covenant is mediated by the Lord Jesus and established in His blood. Membership is in being sealed by the Spirit of God, who writes the law on the heart and in the desires of men and women. He is the power of the covenant enabling those within it to live its promises.

A BINDING OBLIGATION

The English word *covenant* comes from the Latin *convenire*, which literally means "to come together or agree."[2] The Hebrew word is *berith*, which literally means "to bind or to fetter; a binding obligation." In the Scriptures, it is the ultimate expression of committed love and trust and was usually made to define, confirm, establish, or make binding a relationship that had been in the making for some time.

We need a working definition of a covenant that we can explain in detail as we proceed through our study. So here is our definition of a covenant that we will use throughout the book: *A covenant is a binding, unbreakable obligation between two parties, based on unconditional love sealed by blood and sacred oath, that creates a relationship in which each party is bound by specific undertakings on each other's behalf. The parties to the covenant place themselves under the penalty of divine retribution should they later attempt to avoid those undertakings. It is a relationship that can only be broken by death.*

In the Bible, we see covenants that for the most part are unequal covenants. That is, they are made unilaterally, initiated by a person who is vastly superior in power and authority, and graciously imposed on a person of lesser power and position for one's greater good.

In the making of covenants between clans and tribes and people, certain ingredients were always present. We will see that in making covenant with us, God used the pattern of human covenant-making. By having a working understanding of the ingredients that made human covenants, we can better understand the covenant that God has made with us in Jesus Christ.

THE REPRESENTATIVE

When a group of people prepared to enter into covenant with another party, they selected a man from among themselves to represent them in the covenant-making. The word "represent"[3] means to present again, to re-present the will of another, to speak and act with authority on the part of another; to be a substitute or agent for. Knowing the needs and desires of those he represents, the representative *re*-presents their case, speaking as and for them to the other party of the covenant.

The representative had to be of the same blood and family as those he represented. As representative, he gathered the tribe, clan, or family into himself and made the covenant as and for them. The representative is also known as the guarantor of the covenant, the one in and through whom the covenant is made and who is the guarantee that its terms and promises will be kept.

This can be difficult for us in the West to understand, for we think of life as beginning and ending with the individual.

The Bible introduces us to a different way of thinking, in which people are "in" a representative person whose actions and achievements become the actions and achievements of the whole family, clan, or tribe.

The familiar story of David and Goliath from 1 Samuel 17 perfectly illustrates this way of thinking. The Philistine armies had declared a war of aggression on Israel, and King Saul mustered his troops to halt them. The Philistines were a tall people, trained warriors striking terror in their enemies' minds. They wore brass armor and tall-feathered headdresses atop their helmets that made them appear taller than they really were. There were some among their ranks who were massive, gigantic men towering up to nine feet tall. Goliath of Gath was such a giant and was the hero champion of the Philistine army.

Before the fighting began, Goliath stepped out and bellowed a challenge across the valley. It sounds strange to our ears, certainly unlike we conduct our wars today!

> **Then he stood and cried out to the armies of Israel, and said to them, "Why have you come out to line up for battle? Am I not a Philistine, and you the servants of Saul? Choose a man for yourselves, and let him come down to me. If he is able to fight with me and kill me, then we will be your servants. But if I prevail against him and kill him, then you shall be our servants and serve us." And the Philistine said, "I defy the armies of Israel this day; give me a man, that we may fight together."**
> **1 Samuel 17:8-10**

He was saying that he represented the Philistines, in a sense had become them, so that their history was wrapped up in him. When he would fight a similar representative of Israel, it would be the end of the war. The whole issue would be settled in two men who embodied their people.

Saul was the tallest man in Israel but secluded himself to his tent and offered prizes to the man who would accept the

Welcome to the World of Covenants

challenge that Goliath reissued every morning and evening. But no one accepted the giant's challenge or the prize of the hand of the princess in marriage or lifetime freedom from taxes.

As the weeks passed, the monstrous man became bold and lumbered across the valley to hurl his challenge in the faces of the cowering Israelites. The Israelites had lost the war by default; all they had to do was to formally surrender and get out of their shameful position.

After six weeks of humiliation for the Israelite army, back in Bethlehem, old Jesse, father of some of the soldiers at the front, called for his young teenager David, who was too young to be called to the army and was left at home to care for the sheep. He instructed David to find out what was happening in the battle and gave him some gifts to give to his brothers.

David arrived in time to hear the morning challenge along with oaths and curses directed at the men whom Goliath called the yellow cowards of Saul. David did not know this had been going on for six weeks and looked expectantly at his brothers to see who would be the first to answer the challenge. Then they reluctantly told him the shameful story of their army that did not have a representative champion.

David immediately volunteered. King Saul could not really refuse. David was an Israelite and therefore was qualified as one who could take the place of Israel. He was given permission to go and fight the monstrous man.

Understand how the army of Israel looked at this when the news was shouted through the trenches that a representative had been found and Israel had a champion. He didn't look like much of a threat to Goliath: a slip of a shepherd lad without armor and with only a slingshot in hand. But he exuded a notable confidence in God.

As he left the ranks of the army to follow the enormous figure weighted with armor, he ceased to be simply a private citizen of

Israel. Fully aware of the needs of Israel, he was representing them, as they, because of cowardice, were unable to present themselves. He summed Israel in himself, embodying its people; what happened to him this day happened to the entire nation. His victory or defeat would be felt not only by the army, but also in every village and city of Israel in the lives of people who were not there at the battlefront. At that moment, the history of an Israelite as yet unborn was being decided. In David, present and future Israel went to face Goliath.

Goliath had not yet reached his own front lines when David danced behind him, issuing his challenge:

> **Then David said to the Philistine, "You come to me with a sword, with a spear, and with a javelin. But I come to you in the name of the Lord of hosts, the God of the armies of Israel, whom you have defied. This day the Lord will deliver you into my hand, and I will strike you and take your head from you. And this day I will give the carcasses of the camp of the Philistines to the birds of the air and the wild beasts of the earth, that all the earth may know that there is a God in Israel. Then all this assembly shall know that the Lord does not save with sword and spear; for the battle is the Lord's, and He will give you into our hands."**
>
> 1 Samuel 17:45-47

He danced around the massive man, his slingshot whirling in his hand. There was a very small hole in Goliath's helmet that David aimed for, and with his expertise and the grace of God the stone went through it and sunk into the Philistine's temple. The man staggered and fell, and David took the giant's own gigantic sword and hacked off his head.

Behind him, a shout of triumph went up from the watching Israelites. They shouted the victory and poured down the sides of the valley to route the stunned Philistines. They shouted of a victory to which they had contributed nothing except six weeks of cowardice. Yet they were correct. It was their victory, for

Welcome to the World of Covenants

they had been "in" their representative and shared his victory as if it were their own. But without him there would be no victory, for he was the guarantor of it.

THE COVENANT OATH

We may feel strange with the word "covenant" and the concepts attached to it because the word is rarely used in modern society; and even when it is used, it is confused with a contract.

Let us get the concept of a contract out of our heads right away. A contract is a vehicle whereby properties and goods are conveyed from one person to another.[4] Contracts are negotiable by both of the parties and can be changed or even canceled. In a contract, promises are made that are as good as the character of the contracting parties whose signatures seal the document; therefore, they are easily broken.

A covenant is totally different. A covenant is far above the exchange of properties and things. It is the giving of one's whole person and life to another and the wholehearted receiving of that other person and his or her life.

A covenant is made with an oath. An oath is a solemn affirmation, a binding of oneself to the fulfillment of the words spoken while appealing to God. The covenant partners of Old Testament times called upon God to be the witness of the truth of their words. They also called upon God to be their strength in the keeping of the covenant terms. Finally, they called upon God to keep an ever-present watch over the parties to ensure that the covenant was indeed being kept. By calling on God while making an oath, the two parties made God the third party to the covenant. Once made with the oath, a covenant was nonnegotiable and could not be altered.

We demand an oath from persons giving testimony in court or those in whom we are placing a great deal of trust, such as representatives entering public office. When such oaths are taken, the expression "So help me, God" is used. The phrase means that if the words given in testimony are false, or if the person betrays them, then God will be the person's judge.

THE COVENANT BLESSING OR PROMISES

Every covenant of Old Testament times contained the promises each party made to the other and the responsibilities each took with the benefit of the other party in view. In 1 Samuel 20, in a covenant made between David and Jonathan, David swore to bless Jonathan.

"And you shall not only show me the kindness of the Lord while I still live, that I may not die; but you shall not cut off your kindness from my house forever, no, not when the Lord has cut off every one of the enemies of David from the face of the earth."

1 Samuel 20:14,15

Years later, David blessed Mephibosheth with the blessing he had sworn in covenant oath to Mephibosheth's father, Jonathan.

So David said to him, "Do not fear, for I will surely show you kindness for Jonathan your father's sake, and will restore to you all the land of Saul your grandfather; and you shall eat bread at my table continually."

2 Samuel 9:7

Such promises, terms, and responsibilities were often written down and read at certain specified times in remembrance of the covenant being made.

THE COVENANT SACRIFICE

At the making of a covenant, there was always the shedding of blood. An animal was slain and its carcass split down the middle into two halves. The parties making covenant walked through the bloody path between the pieces of the divided animal. In vivid symbolism, they proclaimed that they were entering into a death and were journeying into a new life. They were dying to living for their self-interests alone and passing through that death to a new relationship of union with the other party to the covenant.

They also shed their own blood, usually drawn from the right arm or hand. They would raise their bleeding right arms, calling upon God to be their witness. The combination of bloody sacrifice and their own bloodshed combined to give the powerful statement that each was implicitly making: "I will keep this covenant even if my blood has to be shed in order to do so. If I break this covenant, may my blood be shed and my dismembered body be thrown to the scavengers."

Genesis 31:43-54 describes a covenant between Jacob and Laban. Neither of them trusted the other, and at best it was a shaky agreement. However, in verses 48-49, they attach an oath to it:

>...Therefore its name was called Galeed, also Mizpah, because he said, "May the Lord watch between you and me when we are absent one from another. ...although no man is with us—see, God is witness between you and me!"

Having called upon God to witness and watch over the covenant, they both knew that they could never break the promises of covenant and get away with it.

THE COVENANT SEAL

The scars from the wounds in their arms were the seals in their bodies of the participants' declaring that they were parties to the covenant. They were carried in pride, identifying them as covenant partners. Often the names of the covenant makers were joined to make a new name announcing that they were joined as one by covenant blood.

COVENANT FRIENDS

From the making of the covenant, the two parties would be described as friends. The word *friend* has been greatly cheapened in the language of our Western society; but in societies where covenant-making is practiced and understood there is no higher honor than to be called a person's friend, for it announces a covenant relationship.

This explains why Abraham is called the friend of God in the Scripture; it is a title that is the constant reminder that God made covenant with Abraham.

> **Are You not our God, who drove out the inhabitants of this land before Your people Israel, and gave it to the descendants of Abraham Your friend forever?**
>
> **2 Chronicles 20:7**

COVENANT MEAL

Every covenant ended in a meal that declared the covenant now valid and in effect, functioning in the lives of the parties to it. This was a very important part of covenant-making. To eat with someone at any time was a kind of covenant, and it had a far greater meaning when placed at the end of the making of a covenant. The meal declared the covenant, as the two representatives would eat of the same bread and drink of the same wine telling the world that they were one, partaking one of another. We have illustration of such covenant meals being eaten in the context of covenant-making between men:

> **But they said, "We have certainly seen that the Lord is with you. So we said, 'Let there now be an oath between us, between you and us; and let us make a covenant with you, that you will do us no harm, since we have not touched you, and since we have done nothing to you but good and have sent you away in peace. You are now the blessed of the Lord.'" So he made them a feast, and they ate and drank. Then they arose early in the morning and swore an oath with**

one another; and Isaac sent them away, and they departed from him in peace.
Genesis 26:28-31

We have already looked at the covenant that was made between Jacob and Laban. Take note that it was sealed with a meal at the place of the covenant.

> "Now therefore, come, let us make a covenant, you and I, and let it be a witness between you and me." So Jacob took a stone and set it up as a pillar. Then Jacob said to his brethren, "Gather stones." And they took stones and made a heap, and they ate there on the heap.
> Genesis 31:44-46

THE MEMORIAL OR PLACE OF THE COVENANT-MAKING

The place where the covenant was made was hallowed as the memorial site of the two parties' becoming one. Sometimes there was an enduring memorial set up to remind succeeding generations of what had taken place. Sometimes the name of the place would be changed to reflect the covenant that was made there.

LOVINGKINDNESS

To become part of a covenant was to enter into a new situation, becoming part of a relationship that is best understood as a family—not based on birth ties, but on a commitment of love freely given and bound with a sacred oath. The oath created a new kind of family bound together with an unbreakable life-and-death relationship.

Among the Arabs to this very day is the saying "Blood is thicker than milk," meaning that those bound by the blood of covenant are held in a stronger bond than those who have drunk of the same mother's milk.

The covenant made was to be worked out for the duration of the two parties' lives under all circumstances. *Hesed*[5] is the Hebrew word used to describe the ongoing relationship of the parties in covenant who worked out the commitment made in covenant, the keeping of its promises and responsibilities. *Hesed* is a difficult word to translate into the language of the Western world, for we are a society that knows very little of the commitment involved in being part of a covenant. In various translations of the Scripture, different words are used to catch aspects of the meaning of the word or to try to encompass its whole meaning. It is translated as "mercy," "goodness," "steadfast love," "loyal love," "covenant love," "lovingkindness," or simply "kindness." Most of the time in this book, we will use the English word "lovingkindness" to translate the Hebrew word *hesed*.

The most amazing news to be announced to the human race is that God, in His unconditional love for us, has called us to participate in the most intimate relationship and unbreakable bond known among humans or capable of being expressed in any language. He has called us to covenant relationship with Himself, to come into the circle of friendship in which God and humanity are bound together in an intimate love union.

This covenant is the content of the Gospel. It is called the new covenant. It consists of the everlasting oath of God, the shedding of the blood of God in the death of Jesus Christ and His resurrection and ascension to the Father. The Holy Spirit was sent to make the covenant a reality in the lives of men and women who surrender their lives to Jesus Christ.

Chapter 3

THE WORLD OF THE LIVING DEAD

We were created for covenant union with God, to be in the circle of His friends. We are made in His image and in His likeness, uniquely fitted to interact with Him in love. This is the meaning of our existence: to live by the life of God, enjoying the privilege of being His friends.

We are the unique ones in creation: spirits who are able to commune and be the intimates of God that are in bodies of flesh made from the dust of the earth. The flesh body—that it should not merely house the spirit but be the way the spirit is expressed—is the genius of God. Men and women are creatures that are created to be at home in the heavens in communion with God, while in the same moment to be at home in the world of the created matter. We were created to live from our spirit center, conscious of the heavenly world, and from that center order our flesh and physical world.

But an interaction of love such as God intends between Himself and humanity must be by choice. Love cannot be legislated. Robots do not make covenant partners! Before Adam, and the human race that was in him, could embark on the path for which he was made and find the reason for his being, he had to choose to trust God, to freely obey Him, and so to take the first steps of loving Him.

We stand amazed that God, the only free will that existed, with no necessity within and no pressure from without to bring about another creature with free will, freely chose to create a being who had free will, who was capable of saying no to Him. We might look at the chaos in the world and, above all, the death and suffering of the Son of God because of it, and ask why God would create a being with free will.

The only answer possible is almost too incredible to think. He chose to create us because His love desired to share itself with free beings that could partake of His life and join Him in His unspeakable joy. What makes this so incredible is that He did not purpose this out of a need within Him for company. He is the infinitely fulfilled One. He created men and women because His love must share and be given away. He loves you not only because you are here, but also you are here because He loved you into existence.

All that would happen because of what men and women would do when their free will sinks into insignificance in the light of the glorious end in view. The goal that made it all worthwhile was that these men and women would be conformed to the image of the Son of God and would share His life for eternity. For that goal, the Son of God would take on flesh, suffer and die and rise again, and God the Spirit would come and bring men and women to the goal.

THE CHOICE

But that is anticipating the end! In order for the man and the woman to make the deliberate choice to believe Him and begin the journey of loving Him and walking in His love, there had to be something about which a free choice could be made. God placed the man into the Garden of Eden (or Delight), a park designed and planted by God for His infinitely loved creatures, man and woman. In the midst of the Garden, He placed the Tree of Knowledge of Good and Evil, which would be the place of choice.

> **And the Lord God commanded the man, saying, "Of every tree of the garden you may freely eat; but of the tree of the knowledge of good and evil you shall not eat, for in the day that you eat of it you shall surely die."**
> **Genesis 2:16,17**

The response of the man and woman to the tree would either be one of obedience or of disobedience. Obedience would develop into trust and love toward God. Disobedience, unbelief that rejected God and His love and the result of such a declaration of independence from God, would be death.

The tree was not poisonous but was the divinely appointed place for man and woman to choose to obey. They were warned that in the day that they ate of the tree, they would surely die.

It must not be looked on as an exam that, had they passed, they could have moved on to the next grade. It was the very necessary opportunity they had to have to become the freely choosing humans they were created to be.

But why would they even consider eating of a tree that guaranteed their death? What bait would lure them to even consider it?

Adam had everything and needed nothing. He lacked only one thing; and because he was a creature, he would always lack it. He was owner of all the earth, having all that he needed, knowing no lack. But all that he had, from the breath in his lungs, to his dominion over all of creation, was all the free gift of God. With every breath he took, he was reminded that he was not God but a dependent creature and that the meaning of his life was to be submitted to his Creator.

It was on this point that the devil came to tempt him. He dangled before him as a possible possession the one thing a creature could never have—divinity.

The heart of Adam's sin was that he envied God. He could not be tempted to envy what God had, for he shared that in abundance. He could, however, be tempted to envy who God was; and that could be fired into the desire to dethrone Him and take His place. Sin in its ultimate desire wills to remove God, kill Him if it could, and crown the creature human in His place.

Satan began by portraying God as a liar not to be trusted. He then told the woman that in eating the tree and thus announcing before God and creation their self-sufficiency and declaring independence from God, they would possess that one thing they did not have: They would become as God. He assured them that God had lied: Eating of the tree would not bring death but was instead the doorway to total, self-directed freedom.

Then the serpent said to the woman, "You will not surely die. For God knows that in the day you eat of it your eyes will be opened, and you will be like God, knowing good and evil."

Genesis 3:4,5

This is the *lie* and will be referred to as such throughout the following chapters. From that original lie, all the sin of humankind has flowed.

Who exchanged the truth of God for the lie, and worshiped and served the creature rather than the Creator, who is blessed forever. Amen.

Romans 1:25

...the devil...does not stand in the truth because there is no truth in him. Whenever he speaks a lie, he speaks from his own nature, for he is a liar and the father of lies.

John 8:44 NASB

They believed Satan and made the choice to disobey and declare their independence from God, to sever themselves from the One who was the source of their life and the meaning of their existence. In that moment, their universe came crashing down around them.

DEAD IN SIN

We can only understand the necessity of the death and blood shedding of the Lord Jesus when we have understood what happened in that moment of disobedience. It was the act of disobedience from which all other disobedience and sin flowed. It was the Great Disobedience and is the response to the Primal Lie.

It was not a simple falling out among friends. In that case, each goes one's own way and licks one's wounds, either to get on with life without one's friend or to seek reconciliation.

There is life after a falling out among human friends. But in this case, one of the parties was the Creator, the giver and sustainer of life. To rebel in an act of disobedience that declared independence from Him was to disconnect with the source of life and plunge into death. This must be understood in its magnitude. It was not the breaking of a pointless rule. They were not caught talking in class and given detention with a hundred lines to write. This was a deliberate act of unbelief in the basic law of the universe.

This is not to be likened to talking in class; it is likened to defying gravity, only infinitely more so! Apart from causing creation to cease, there was nothing God could do to suspend the results of their sin. "In the day you eat of it, you shall surely die" was not a punishment, but the announcement of a fact: You are dependent upon God for your life; you are created to live in His love, and if you walk away from Him a law will be triggered that cannot be reversed—you will certainly and unquestionably die.

They were created to say yes to God and to choose to trust His love. Instead, they said no to God and yes to the lie of Satan and, in so doing, became the enemies of God. They denied the meaning of their existence as creatures and rejected their God-given glory of submission and obedience to the Creator. They said no to the covenant union with Him, for whom they were created, exchanging it for the dead-end street of independence that results in death.

Man and woman died in the moment they ate of the tree. But what do we mean by death? After all, they continued to live for many years and the human race is still here. Granted, everyone dies in the end; but the warning was that in the day they ate, they would die.

The problem with defining death is that those who are in the state of death are doing the defining and are convinced that they are alive! From their perspective, they are alive now and death is what happens at the end of physical life; but the Bible plainly says that outside of Christ, they are not alive now! This is the world of the walking dead who do not live but exist.

There are many dimensions to what we mean by life.

First, God is life and the source and upholder of all life. No life exists outside of Him, and nothing is independent of Him.

Then there is the life of the human, the most complex of all living creatures but, most importantly, created to share in and participate in the divine life. This incredible human is created to live in God's world and in the physical creation simultaneously.

Next, there is animal life, which has a graded scale of complexity from the primates all the way down to the amoeba.

The amoeba is alive, my dog is alive, I am alive, and God is life. Life and living mean something different at each level.

The human is the only creature whose life was intended to go far beyond the natural life by sharing in the divine life. The Hebrew word for life or to live is *hayah*,[1] which means simply to be alive but always assumes that for a human to be alive is more than one's possessing a beating heart and lungs filled with air.

Moses explained that the troubles in the wilderness were intended to point the people to the fact that their life consisted of more than physical characteristics.

> **So He humbled you, allowed you to hunger, and fed you with manna which you did not know nor did your fathers know, that He might make you know that man shall not live by bread alone; but man lives by every word that proceeds from the mouth of the Lord.**
>
> **Deuteronomy 8:3**

The word he uses for "live" is *hayah*, indicating that in men and women *hayah* is a quality of life that is more than the keeping of body and soul together; it is living on the life of God in His Word.

Moses, speaking to the people, defined life *(hayah)* in terms of walking in obedience to the words of God:

> **In that I command you today to love the Lord your God, to walk in His ways, and to keep His commandments, His statutes, and His judgments, that you may live and multiply; and the Lord your God will bless you in the land which you go to possess.**
>
> **Deuteronomy 30:16**

In the Greek language, the word *zoe*[2] is used to describe life as God knows life. *Zoe*, then, becomes the foundation of all life; but it specifically describes that quality of life that is unique to God, translated in the New Testament as everlasting life.

The New Testament abounds in references to *zoe*, assuring us that it is the purpose of God that we should receive *zoe* life as the addition to our natural life and so truly live as we were always intended to.

> The thief does not come except to steal, and to kill, and to destroy. I have come that they may have life *(zoe)*, and that they may have it more abundantly.
>
> John 10:10
>
> For God so loved the world that He gave His only begotten Son, that whoever believes in Him should not perish but have everlasting life *(zoe)*.
>
> John 3:16

In each of these verses, the word *zoe* is used for "life" and "everlasting life." We were created to partake of the life of God. Sin stole it, and Jesus came to return it to us.

Therefore, we must define death as including, but so much more than, what occurs to the body at the end of physical life. Death must be understood as separation from, of being unaware and unresponsive to, the dimension that one is dead to. The physically dead human is conscious in another dimension but separated from the physical world and therefore unaware and unresponsive to it.

Using this definition, we can say that the animal world is dead to the human world. Do not be upset with me but, according to this definition of death, your cat is dead to the fullness of human life. It lives in a human world but is unaware and unresponsive to everything that is essentially human. It responds to our providing food, water, and shelter and has an awareness of our being there. But it is unaware and unresponsive to a Beethoven symphony or the reading of a passage from a book, nor does a joke have any effect on it. It does not ponder the meaning of its existence or discuss life with other cats. It may see two humans kiss but has no reference point for the love that the kiss expresses or, in fact, what a kiss means. It only has cat life, which cannot relate to human life.

In that sense, through the great disobedience, the man and the woman plunged into the state of being dead to God and alive only to human awareness of their physical world, which was light years above animal life but light years below what they were created to enjoy.

There is an awful finality in both spiritual and physical death. Once dead, only God can bring a person back to life. In the realm of the physical, He does that in the resurrection; and spiritually, He accomplishes it in the miracle of the new birth.

The human lives on the edge of awareness of God, enjoys His providential care, but is hardly aware that it is He who cares for him. Humankind is oblivious to the love of God and is unresponsive to His approach. Men and women are alive in the physical world, the world of the creature, of flesh; but they are separated from God and unaware of Him, deaf to His words, and thus unresponsive.

The human spirit is like a radio that is no longer able to pick up or transmit a clear signal. But, importantly, men and women know they have a radio even though it doesn't work. They are lost but not so lost as to not know that there is something missing. They exist out on the edge of an awareness of God, haunted by the uneasy feeling that He is there and some moral responsibility to Him is demanded. The race has a memory that cannot be recalled, a dream that cannot be remembered of the glory they were created to enjoy and once had.

There is a longing to be loved unconditionally that cannot be satisfied by another human. They are surprised by unexpected surges of longing within for something above and beyond the prison walls of sin, selfishness, and satanic domination.

Men and women are aware of a vast emptiness within, which sends them searching after something higher than their human existence. There is a hole inside each one of us that is bigger than the universe, but left to ourselves we have no tools for discovering who can fill the hole.

There can be no contact with God from the human side; God is not known by the logic of the human intellect but by revelation in the spirit from the God side. The groping after God within the categories known by the human intellect and imagination creates a God made in the image of man, which reduces Him to a superhuman and leaves the human in a greater darkness than ever. Such groping into the unknown inevitably leads to the spirit world of darkness, deception, and the demonic.

Jesus defines for us the biblical meaning of the word "dead" in the parable of the lost son. (Luke 15:11-32.) The father announces, **"This my son was dead and is alive again"** (verse 24); that is, he was separated from the father's love, unaware of it and untouched by it and unresponsive to it, finding his existence far away from it. For him to come "alive" was to become aware of that love, be touched and embraced by it, responding by opening himself to it.

Our first parents, Adam and Eve, did not become "as God," as Satan had promised them, but instead became the slaves of the one who had lied to them and promised ultimate freedom and independence. Life now was lived on the meaningless treadmill of trying to make the lie of Satan work in life. They were doomed to fail at meeting their goal of being as God, yet in a blind and insane belief have been spurred on to attempt to achieve it in every succeeding generation of humankind.

Dead while physically, mentally, and emotionally alive, the sad parade of humanity moves through existence toward physical death, the dissolution of the body, being separated even from the physical existence. Created to rule the universe, humankind has ended up being absorbed back into the dust from whence he came. And the first man and woman believed that they would become gods!

Unlike lower creatures, men and women know that physical death is inevitably coming, which makes their existence meaningless. Whatever they may do, whatever they may achieve or aspire to, whatever their hopes and ambitions, men and women are acutely aware that all is being swept on toward inevitable death. Life itself becomes pointless and meaningless.

THE COSMIC ACT

Adam's act of the great disobedience was also the cosmic disobedience, for Adam was lord of the creation and head of the human race. His act brought death to the whole creation and brought the race that was in him into a state of living death. The entire human race was in Adam when he sinned; therefore, his was not a private sin but a cosmic act that involved the entire cosmos and all of future history and people.

The human race outside of Christ is called "in Adam" or "the old man(kind)." We are not isolated individuals but are locked in to one another.

For example, some of my far off ancestors were Vikings. When my ancestor came in his longboat to the shores of eastern England, I was in him; I was potential in his life. If he had been killed in the raid, I would have died in him—like it or not, that is the way it is.

Likewise, if Adam had died before his first child was conceived, none of us would be here today. When he disobeyed he carried us, the entire race of humankind, into the darkness. That does not excuse us, for we have all willfully chosen the same path he did. Every generation believes the lie and votes by its actions that Adam was right. We are personally responsible for our sin.

THE FUTILITY OF LIFE IN THE FLESH

Humankind has become something other than what we were created to be. Men and women were created to be spirit persons, living from their spirit centers, where they were to be submitted to God and share in His life. From that center, they were to live in and through their physical bodies and rule the universe.

But dead to God they became flesh persons, living from the created flesh as the source and center of their life. That was inevitable, for that was all that was left! The spirit was not functioning and the lie told every man and woman that within themselves, independent of God, they could find the meaning of life and happiness.

Let me make it very clear that the body and all its cells and organs are good. God created the human body and pronounced it good, and Jesus took to Himself a human body made like ours in every way.

What happened when the first couple died to God in Eden was that they now looked in the realm of their created physical existence for the meaning of life. In that physical arena, they would live out their rebellion to God. There is nothing wrong with flesh; the evil is in fallen men and women's making the flesh the source and meaning of existence.

It would appear that before sin and death entered, the couple lived in an acute awareness of the spirit dimension—so much so that they were hardly aware of their bodies except as the vehicles of their spirits. It would seem that the glory of the life of God shone through their bodies, clothing them in glorious light, much as it did Jesus in His transfiguration.

The entrance of sin and death turned everything upside down. After they sinned, they were suddenly acutely aware of their bodies stripped of the glory of God, while paralyzed and confused in terms of the heavenly dimension.

The shock of the new awareness that their flesh had become the center of their existence was vividly portrayed by their reaction. It is significant that the first act after their sin was a total focus on their bodies and a frantic effort to cover them. They had no horror of their sin, but were obsessed by the shame of bodies stripped of glory and now stark naked.

From then on, this was where they would find their life and the meaning of their existence—in the realm of creature flesh. Men and women would now spend their lives searching for meaning within their magnificent brains, intellects, emotions, feelings, and passions, which all exist in the organs of their bodies.

But for every human being, the questions regarding the meaning of existence will not go away. Men and women cannot forget the dream they cannot remember! The human is plagued by "Why am I here?" "What is the point of my existence?" "What is the meaning of my life?" Midlife crisis is due to looking at life and realizing that the elusive meaning has not been found and time is running out. Humans explore all possible reasons for existence within the physical, material universe in which they find their entire existence.

Men and women outside of Christ are flesh persons living with their flesh bodies at their center, with only a dim awareness of the spirit and its function. For the human created to know and walk in love with the Creator, there is no ultimate meaning to life in the flesh.

I once owned a very beautiful painting that hung on the wall of my office in a frame carved with leaves and overlaid in gold leaf. One day, I decided to sell the painting. The empty frame stood against the wall, and I remember thinking how I needed to put it in the attic until I could find another picture that would fit the frame. It never occurred to me to hang the frame on the wall, however beautifully it was carved. Frames are for pictures, and apart from the pictures they have little meaning.

Our flesh existence is the frame around the picture that is our spirits joined with and participating in the life of God. Our meaning is living in the love of God in the frame of our creature existence. Without the picture, there is no point to the frame except to wait for its fulfillment in having a picture placed in its heart.

The Scripture uses the word "futile" to describe the life lived in the flesh. It is a word that means going nowhere, dead end, aimless, and bringing nothing to fruition or harvest.

Knowing that you were not redeemed with corruptible things, like silver or gold, from your aimless conduct received by tradition from your fathers.

1 Peter 1:18

This I say, therefore, and testify in the Lord, that you should no longer walk as the rest of the Gentiles walk, in the futility of their mind.

Ephesians 4:17

Our pursuit of false meaning is sin because we were created to find our meaning in living in the love of God. Our looking for that meaning elsewhere is a slap in the face to God.

I once saw a group of young boys playing street baseball. I was shocked to see that they were using a violin for their bat. Its strings were broken, and it was dirty. Some of the veneer had stripped away, and a boy held its neck and swung it like a bat. I am sure the boys had found it trashed by someone and were using it creatively, but there was something very wrong with what I was seeing. I do not know much about violins, but this one had obviously not been purchased in a dime store; even in its dilapidated condition, it was beautiful. It had been lovingly made, fashioned, and lacquered by a craftsman with the one purpose in mind of filling a music room or concert hall with music to delight the ears of the listeners. Now broken, dirty, its strings flying in the wind, it was used as a baseball bat. I felt that what I was seeing was an insult to its maker and an affront to music and beauty.

We were created to delight in being the object of God's love and to fill the creation with the music of His love by our lives lived in union with Him. The great disobedience is trashing the purpose of our creation and seeking, on an endless, futile quest, another meaning to life. In so doing, we insult our Maker and shame our very existence.

ALL HAVE SINNED

The major Greek word that sums up the condition of humankind is *harmartia*,[3] which the New Testament translates as sin. Its basic meaning is "to miss the mark" and describes the action of human beings in missing totally the reason they were created. This must not be thought of as missing the mark like the little boy at summer camp who can't hit the bull's eye with his arrow but keeps trying in hope of success. Humankind misses the mark deliberately, having set up an alternative target, which in fact is the lie and an illusion.

But in the New Testament the word, while retaining its original meaning, takes on the much broader meaning of separation from God that is rooted in the principle of independence from Him, which is contained in the lie, which has become the source of all action and behavior.

> **Therefore, just as through one man sin entered the world, and death through sin, and thus death spread to all men, because all sinned.**
>
> **Romans 5:12**

Harmartia is described as a ruling power. In Romans 6:6, it is spoken of as the body of sin, enslaving the members of the body.

> **Knowing this, that our old man was crucified with Him, that the body of sin might be done away with, that we should no longer be slaves of sin.**

Again in Romans 6, Paul speaks to believers who have been delivered from sin, describing it as a master that had ruled them as a tyrant through the members of the physical body. Although sin is an action taken by the will, it is the body that is the instrument by which sin is expressed in concrete behavior.

> Therefore do not let sin reign in your mortal body, that you should obey it in its lusts.
>
> For sin shall not have dominion over you, for you are not under law but under grace.
>
> Do you not know that to whom you present yourselves slaves to obey, you are that one's slaves whom you obey, whether of sin leading to death, or of obedience leading to righteousness? But God be thanked that though you were slaves of sin, yet you obeyed from the heart that form of doctrine to which you were delivered.
>
> Romans 6:12,14,16,17

Paul often speaks of sin personified as a tyrant master. In Romans 7:8,11 he writes,

> But sin, taking opportunity by the commandment, produced in me all manner of evil desire. For apart from the law sin was dead.
>
> For sin, taking occasion by the commandment, deceived me, and by it killed me.

RECONCILIATION AND RESURRECTION

Although humankind is dead, men and women can still hear when God speaks, even as Lazarus heard the voice of Jesus and came forth from the tomb. The true person lies buried within each of us, awaiting the Gospel call of the Son of God that summons him or her to resurrection to true personhood.

> And you He made alive, who were dead in trespasses and sins, in which you once walked according to the course of this world, according to the prince of the power of the air, the spirit who now works in the sons of disobedience, among whom also we all once conducted ourselves in the lusts of our flesh, fulfilling the desires of the flesh and of the mind, and were by nature children of wrath, just as the others.

The World of the Living Dead

> **But God, who is rich in mercy, because of His great love with which He loved us, even when we were dead in trespasses, made us alive together with Christ....**
> *Ephesians 2:1-5*

Humans are hostile to God and neither in a covenant nor are in a position to initiate one. They are not only hostile to God but are the covenant breakers, for the first sin was the breaking of the covenant that was their destiny to enjoy; and as covenant breakers, they are under the penalty of death. The Bible is the fascinating story of how God has achieved the reconciliation of men and women to Himself, bringing them into covenant with Him.

> **God was in Christ reconciling the world to Himself, not imputing their trespasses to them....**
> *2 Corinthians 5:19*

Chapter 4

THE LOVING-KINDNESS OF GOD

One reason that I did not initially discover the covenant in the Scripture was that the word "covenant" is not to be found very often. It was the discovery of another word that led me right into the heart of the covenant. That word in the Hebrew language is *hesed*;[1] it is the word of the covenant in Scripture.

The word is translated in our various versions of the Bible in a number of different ways. In our older versions of the Bible, it is translated as "mercy," and we will explain why below. The modern versions attempt to get to the heart of its meaning as the word of the covenant, translating it as "steadfast love," "covenant love," "unfailing love," or simply "loyalty."

The word is found approximately 250 times in the Hebrew Old Testament and probably ranks among one of the most important words of the covenant. It is a word rich with meaning, but at its heart it describes the mutual responsibilities that each party to a covenant has to the other, and the rights that each enjoys in the covenant relationship. This is daily lived out in mundane tasks, as well as in self-sacrificing decisions that sometimes have to be made in order to carry out the covenant blessings and promises given to each other at the making of the covenant.

Hesed is the word that describes the working out of the expressions of love that were potential in the original covenant commitment. *Hesed* describes the relationship of the covenant partners, but more, it describes that relationship being worked out; it is the covenant in action. So when Scripture is speaking of God's lovingkindness, it is often in the context of His *doing* and *showing* and *keeping* the covenant when every word that has been sworn to is put to the test. "Lovingkindness" is the word that describes the covenant when it takes to the streets and simply does it every day. It is God's keeping every word and giving every blessing He has promised.

The word has three ideas that must be present in order to fully grasp its meaning. The three ideas are *strength, steadfastness,* and *love,* each to be understood in the context of a covenant's having been made. If we have only one of these ideas, the word will lose its meaning. If we emphasize love to the exclusion of strength and steadfastness, it will tend toward the romantic and sentimental and lack the vital element of commitment. If we leave out love and emphasize strength and steadfastness, we will be left with a cold, legal faithfulness to the covenant and the ability to perform it, without passion or desire to do so. But at the heart of *hesed* are love, warm-hearted generosity, and goodness, not merely loyalty and legal obligation.

Hesed is a word that is often related to marriage, and that is certainly a legal matter attended with solemn vows and the taking of obligations and responsibilities. Yet at the heart of the relationship is committed love that transcends the legalities even as it fulfills them. With that in mind, maybe the word "devotion" is a better translation.

The Lovingkindness of God

The word *hesed* was used by the Hebrews to describe the ideal family love, the love that binds people together relationally. In seeking to understand its meaning, we must include all the elements of belonging to a circle of love, of mutual caring, of providing and protecting love. It carries with it the assurance that the other party to the covenant will be there in the day of need or trouble.

To emphasize the idea of the steadfastness of the relationship, *hesed* is often linked with *faithfulness* in the Scripture. Behind His *hesed* is His *faithfulness*, a word that means that God is infinitely reliable and can be counted on at all times; He is constant and unchangeable. It arises directly from the covenant oath of God, which is the foundation of our faith.

> **Your mercy** *(hesed)***, O Lord, is in the heavens; Your faithfulness reaches to the clouds.**
> **Psalm 36:5**

> **It is good to give thanks to the Lord, and to sing praises to Your name, O Most High; to declare Your lovingkindness in the morning, and Your faithfulness every night.**
> **Psalm 92:1,2**

> **I have not hidden Your righteousness within my heart; I have declared Your faithfulness and Your salvation; I have not concealed Your lovingkindness and Your truth from the great assembly. Do not withhold Your tender mercies from me, O Lord; let Your lovingkindness and Your truth** (or faithfulness) **continually preserve me.**
> **Psalm 40:10,11**

GOD IS HESED

When humans make a covenant oath, it is in order to create the bond of lovingkindness and to hold it in place. But we must understand that God makes covenant with humans not to lock Himself in to acting in love toward us lest He should be tempted to fail in so doing! He makes covenant not to create lovingkindness, but in order that we might see that His heart is lovingkindness from eternity.

> And the Lord passed before him and proclaimed, "The Lord, the Lord God, merciful *(hesed)* and gracious, longsuffering, and abounding in goodness and truth."
>
> **Exodus 34:6**

> ...But You are God, ready to pardon, gracious and merciful *(hesed)*, slow to anger, abundant in kindness, and did not forsake them.
>
> **Nehemiah 9:17**

> The Lord is merciful *(hesed)* and gracious, slow to anger, and abounding in mercy.
>
> **Psalm 103:8**

> So he prayed to the Lord, and said, "Ah, Lord, was not this what I said when I was still in my country? Therefore I fled previously to Tarshish; for I know that You are a gracious and merciful God, slow to anger and abundant in lovingkindness *(hesed)*, One who relents from doing harm."
>
> **Jonah 4:2**

> Therefore know that the Lord your God, He is God, the faithful God who keeps covenant and mercy *(hesed)* for a thousand generations with those who love Him and keep His commandments.
>
> **Deuteronomy 7:9**

Our very existence arises from His *hesed*. Psalm 136 states that the creation and the laws that cause the universe to continue arise from His lovingkindness, here translated as mercy:

> To Him who by wisdom made the heavens, for His mercy endures forever; to Him who laid out the earth above the waters, for His mercy endures forever; to Him who made great lights, for His mercy endures forever—the sun to rule by day, for His mercy endures forever; the moon and stars to rule by night, for His mercy endures forever.
>
> **Psalm 136:5-9**

The Lovingkindness of God

The entire history of Israel, the people of God of the Old Testament, in their relationship to God is summed up in this word. Whatever they are going through, whether they are at the high peak of walking with Him or plunging into the depths of sin in their turning away from Him, always there is the presence of His lovingkindness delighting and yearning over the covenant people. His continual unfailing presence with His people to achieve His purpose is at the heart of this word *hesed*. When this word is understood, the Psalms are seen as the delighted response to covenant love. The Prophets come alive as covenant documents addressed by God to His people. The history of Old Testament Israel is of His lovingkindness meeting the need of His people for redemption from sin, their enemies, and troubled times.

Because He is *hesed* and is not bound to it only because of a covenant's being made, His covenant love is greater than the covenant. It explains when the human breaks covenant that His heart of lovingkindness still reaches after them and will not let them go.

> **With a little wrath I hid My face from you for a moment; but with everlasting kindness** *(hesed)* **I will have mercy on you," says the Lord, your Redeemer.**
>
> **"For the mountains shall depart and the hills be removed, but My kindness** *(hesed)* **shall not depart from you, nor shall My covenant of peace be removed," says the Lord, who has mercy on you.**
>
> **Isaiah 54:8,10**

Even after Jerusalem fell and the people were led away captive to Babylon because of their many sins, Jeremiah could find peace in the covenant loyalty of God to His wayward people.

> **Through the Lord's mercies** *(hesed)* **we are not consumed, because His compassions fail not. They are new every morning; great is Your faithfulness.**
>
> **Lamentations 3:22,23**

When David committed adultery with Bathsheba and then arranged for her husband to be killed in battle, he knew that there was no forgiveness under the Law of Moses, which stated that he must be stoned to death. He appealed beyond the law to the covenant heart of God:

> **Have mercy** *(hesed)* **upon me, O God, according to Your lovingkindness; according to the multitude of Your tender mercies....**
>
> **Psalm 51:1**

We may sum up the covenant love of God in the Old Testament by saying that it is the eternal covenant love of God committed to keep every word of His covenant promises. It is seen in His commitment to be there for us, His covenant people, every day and every hour to save, keep, protect, and care for us. *Hesed* tells us that God passionately loves us, longs for us, and pursues us even when we walk away from Him.

THE STORY OF GIBEON

Perhaps one of the most amazing stories in the Bible, the story of Gibeon illustrates the strength and steadfastness of covenant love, or *hesed*. The story is found in chapters 9 and 10 of the book of Joshua.

Joshua had led Israel into Canaan, the land of promise, to conquer and take it as their homeland. The people who then lived there were idolaters practicing vile immoral acts as part of their worship of their false deities, and the command of God was plain: His people were to have no treaties or covenants with the inhabitants of Canaan.

One of the Canaanite tribes, the Gibeonites decided to trick the leaders of Israel into entering into a binding covenant with them. They were only a few hours from where Joshua was camped, but they put on worn and ragged clothes and sandals that were falling apart and put crumbling and moldy bread in their packs. They arrived at Joshua's tent looking as if they had traveled many miles over a period of weeks.

They sat and told the elders of Israel that they had come from a land far away and had traveled the great distance because they had heard of the wonders God had done for the Israelites in Egypt and in their trek through the wilderness to Canaan. They presented themselves as the representatives of their people who desired to enter into covenant with such a God-blessed people.

Foolishly, the elders of Israel, although suspicious, did not check out the story the Gibeonites told, and most foolishly they did not consult with God. They were gullible and believed every word the men of Gibeon told them and entered into covenant with them, invoking the Lord with a solemn covenant oath.

> **So Joshua made peace with them, and made a covenant with them to let them live; and the rulers of the congregation swore to them.**
>
> **Joshua 9:15**

The fact that Israel was in covenant with God made the Gibeonites not only partners with Israel, but also with their God. With beaming smiles and great inner rejoicing, the men of Gibeon left the following day to trek a few miles over the hills to their people with the great news. They had pulled it off! They were in covenant on the basis of a lie that the leaders of Israel had never bothered to check out.

But three days later, Israel discovered the truth that the Gibeonites were their neighbors. What would Israel do? The leaders realized that they had been deceived and, worse, had involved themselves and God in a covenant with a people that God had expected them to subjugate.

They confronted the Gibeonites. Here we face the unchangeable nature of *hesed*. How would they treat these liars who were their sworn enemies but now, by false testimony, were in covenant with them? The leaders of Israel knew that they could not go back on their covenant oath, even though there was complaint against the leadership from the people. *Hesed* held, and they spared the people of Gibeon.

> **But the children of Israel did not attack them, because the rulers of the congregation had sworn to them by the Lord God of Israel. And all the congregation complained against the rulers. Then all the rulers said to all the congregation, "We have sworn to them by the Lord God of Israel; now therefore, we may not touch them."**
>
> **Joshua 9:18,19**

They punished their deceitfulness by making them the servants of Israel, specifically servants to the priests and Levites, but the covenant oath was honored.

It was not long before the surrounding tribes heard of the deceitful union with powerful Israel that the tribe of Gibeon had brought about. They were angry with them, not because they had deceived Israel but because they had betrayed them, their Canaanite brothers. Five Canaanite tribes united to attack the hopelessly outnumbered Gibeonites.

The elders of Gibeon sent an urgent message to their covenant partner Israel and, through them, to the God of Israel. They were, in fact, calling upon *hesed:* "Help! Your covenant partners are being attacked, and you are covenant-bound to fulfill *hesed* and come and help us."

The steadfast covenant love of God, even to such deceitful liars, never shows up better than in this little story. God gave His full blessing to Joshua to go and defend those who were now His covenant partners. He promised Joshua that the five Canaanite tribes would fall before him.

> **And the Lord said to Joshua, "Do not fear them, for I have delivered them into your hand; not a man of them shall stand before you."**
>
> **Joshua 10:8**

The Lovingkindness of God

Not only so, but He granted the greatest miracle recorded in Scripture outside of the resurrection: The sun stood still, giving Joshua the necessary time to defend the Gibeonites!

> Then Joshua spoke to the Lord in the day when the Lord delivered up the Amorites before the children of Israel, and he said in the sight of Israel: "Sun, stand still over Gibeon; and Moon, in the Valley of Aijalon." So the sun stood still, and the moon stopped, till the people had revenge upon their enemies. ...So the sun stood still in the midst of heaven, and did not hasten to go down for about a whole day. And there has been no day like that, before it or after it, that the Lord heeded the voice of a man; for the Lord fought for Israel.
>
> Joshua 10:12-14

There is never a time when God will not honor His *hesed*, even if made under false pretenses! How much more will God honor the covenant formed in the eternal mind of God, executed by His Son, and brought to us by the Holy Spirit?

This brings a new meaning to Hebrews 13:5: **For He Himself has said, "I will never leave you nor forsake you."** Wonderful as these words are, the original language conveys a description of covenant commitment that is very difficult to put into English. *The Amplified Bible* catches the sense of it:

> For He [God] Himself has said, I will not in any way fail you nor give you up nor leave you without support. [I will] not, [I will] not, [I will] not in any degree leave you helpless nor forsake you nor let [you] down (relax My hold on you)! [Assuredly not!]
>
> Hebrews 13:5

It takes five negatives in English to give the assurance that is conveyed in this verse that He will never leave us under any conditions! This is the covenant lovingkindness of God.

HESED AS MERCY

But why do the older translations consistently translate this word into the English "mercy"?

We noted in our last chapter that the covenants that God makes with us, finalizing in the ultimate new covenant, are unequal covenants.

We have many examples of unequal covenants from secular history. A conquering king would offer to enter into covenant with the conquered king and people both as an act of generosity and as a means of governing his new province. An example in Scripture is of Nebuchadnezzar, the conquering king of Babylon, entering into covenant with the conquered king of Judah, Zedekiah. At other times, the weaker person or tribe would seek the protection and patronage of a stronger person or tribe by asking for covenant.

The inequality of the covenants of God brings the mind to silence and worship. It is not a great, generous human king who offers covenant relationship; for, although unequal in their position in life, they are equal as being two human beings. But God the Creator enters into covenant with His creature men and women! This is not an equal partnership that is brought about by both parties' making their contribution. It is God's giving His all to men and women, who neither deserve it nor have anything to offer.

The Gospel of the covenant is presented by God to man not as a point to begin negotiations, but for humans to accept or reject. Love has accomplished the incredible, and all humans can do is either receive with thanks or establish themselves in their rebellion forever by refusing.

God's act of initiating covenant and then His fulfilling of every promise made in the covenant is an act of grace and mercy renewed every day. It is with this in mind that the translators chose the word "mercy" for the Hebrew *hesed*. The very thought of covenant love from God could only be translated in terms of mercy (which means that we do not get from God what we deserve) and grace (which means that we get from Him what we do not deserve)!

There was no pressure on God to seek after humans when they had freely chosen to sever themselves from Him. We must never forget that God freely chose to save us. There was no demand placed upon Him to do so from outside of Him, nor was there an incompleteness within Him that He needed humans to fill. Complete in Himself, He chose to save us out of sheer love. His covenant is a unilateral covenant originated in the mind of God before time, initiated and achieved by God alone. The only reason behind His desire to make such a covenant, to bring sinful humans into a relationship at infinite cost to Himself, is His unconditional love for us.

This is the Gospel, or as it was defined in the seventeenth century, "the good, glad, merry news that makes a man fairly leap for joy!" It is the news about God, who He is and what He has done for us. The word *hallelujah* literally means to brag and rave to others about God![2] When we realize that He is *hesed*, we will know why He is worthy to be raved about.

It is in the revelation of Himself that God has given us that we part company with all the other religions in the world. Up to a point, we can agree with other world religions when speaking of a supreme deity. Such a diety, we all agree, must be sovereign, omnipotent, and omniscient; but no other religion has the beginning of the concept that God is love, and He loves each man and woman with a passionate and unconditional love.

The human mind could never arrive at such a conclusion. We only know that He is love because He has revealed Himself to us through the Hebrew patriarchs and prophets and finally in His Son, the Lord Jesus.

With that in mind, *hesed* as mercy should never be far from our understanding. We are the weaker party of this covenant, seeking the protection and blessing of the God of infinite love. We do not dictate the terms, nor do we tell Him how and when He must fulfill His promises. There are many believers today who should deeply understand that the covenant and the ensuing acts of lovingkindness are pure mercy, and they should stop their ungodly demanding of God that He act according to their dictates.

However, there are millions of believers who have lived their lives around the cry to God, "Lord, have mercy," and they need to see the vast scope of *hesed* in terms of the strong love of God committed to being there for us at all times and under all conditions. If we do not see that mercy springs forth from the molten core of the infinite passion of holy love for us, we very quickly assume the posture of a beggar whining at the temple gates and shocked if told that the Lord has answered! As you invoke His covenant mercy, do so with a heart filled with praise. The mercy is in Jesus Christ, and we come not as beggars but as sons, heirs of God and joint heirs with Jesus.

THE GOAL OF *HESED*

Hesed is the goal of salvation covenant history, in that Jesus is the ultimate lovingkindness and He is the keeping, doing, and showing of His covenant oath. The Virgin Mary sings of the birth of her child as the remembrance of the *hesed* of God: **"He has helped His servant Israel, in remembrance of His mercy,** *(hesed)* **as He spoke to our fathers, to Abraham and to his seed forever"** (Luke 1:54,55).

Zacharias, the father of John the Baptist, also saw the birth of his son as the beginning of the fulfillment of all the promises of covenant love through the centuries:

The Lovingkindness of God

> **To perform the mercy** *(hesed)* **promised to our fathers and to remember His holy covenant, the oath which He swore to our father Abraham: to grant us that we, being delivered from the hand of our enemies, might serve Him without fear, in holiness and righteousness before Him all the days of our life.**
>
> **Through the tender mercy** *(hesed)* **of our God, with which the Dayspring from on high has visited us; to give light to those who sit in darkness and the shadow of death, to guide our feet into the way of peace.**
>
> Luke 1:72-75,78,79

Jesus is the *hesed* of God, the steadfast, unchangeable, and strong love of God in flesh. He by His blood-shedding brings to us every promise of God and is the personal guarantor.

> **For all the promises of God in Him are Yes, and in Him Amen, to the glory of God through us.**
>
> 2 Corinthians 1:20

As we move into our study of the covenant, know that God cannot let you down. He is the God who cannot lie.

Chapter 5

THE CORE OF THE COVENANT

As we pointed out in the last chapter, among humans a covenant is made in order to bring about the state of living in lovingkindness; the oath accompanied with blood-shedding is in order to give strength to such a high ideal. But God makes covenant not to make lovingkindness but to reveal that He is all that it means.

Behind the covenant that He makes is the core of His heart, which is infinite love, best understood among men as *hesed*. As we would not have the rays of the sun if there were no sun, so there would be no covenant if God were not the molten core of infinite and unconditional love! This is the heart of the revelation of God that comes to us in Christ and the Gospel.

Without this revelation of who He is, the thought of God produces great anxiety. And no wonder! Can we imagine life with a God who does not love us? What if God, who is almighty in power, who knows every thought and motive of our hearts, who is always present with us, who in His sovereignty rules our world, did not like us and plotted our destruction? Such a God could only be conceived as a terrifying, infinite Judge directing His wrath toward us, condemning and damning us for our many sins.

In conversations with thousands of church members, I am amazed that their thoughts about God are much like such a picture of Him. With such a concept of God, men and women live in a pagan anxiety at the thought of Him; they have an uneasy fear of Him, furtively looking over their shoulder to see if He is coming to hurt and make havoc of their lives.

THE GOOD NEWS OF LOVE

The first years of my Christian life and ministry tended in this direction. My first sermons smelled of brimstone and crackled with damnation. I called people to a salvation that essentially was running from the wrath of God the Father to the semi-safety of Jesus' protection.

My entire life changed one spring morning in Portland, Oregon, in 1965. I was the visiting speaker in a church there, and the previous night I had presented the Gospel as I understood it, portraying God as thoroughly irritated and annoyed with lazy lukewarm believers, making my message the basis for calling the congregation to rededicate their lives to Him.

The next morning, the pastor invited me to join him for breakfast. As we sat over our eggs and bacon, he began to tell me of how he had witnessed to a nonbeliever who was dying. He lingered over the details of the Gospel and how he had presented it to the dying man. As he did so, I saw the Gospel as I had never seen it before. He spoke of God's love that initiated and carried through the plan of salvation and the love of the Lord Jesus, God the Son in His death and resurrection, and the compassion of the Holy Spirit drawing us into that love.

I had never seen or even thought of the Triune God in terms of passionate, seeking love relentlessly pursuing us. He had always been a judge that was placated by the death of Jesus, to whom we fled from His wrath. I began to weep and finally pushed aside the breakfast and laid my head on the table and sobbed. I went back to the hotel and destroyed all of my sermons.

I saw for the first time in my life why the body of truth that Christians proclaim is called *Gospel*, which means "Good News."

Preaching the Gospel, we are announcing the news of the revelation of who God is and how He feels about us. We stand on the street corners of the world shouting the news that God is not the way we thought He was—He loves us! The love of God bursting into a world of lost and hopeless people is the greatest news that has ever been announced.

> **Beloved, let us love one another, for love is of God.... God is love. In this the love of God was manifested toward us, that God has sent His only begotten Son into the world, that we might live through Him. In this is love, not that we loved God, but that He loved us and sent His Son to be the propitiation for our sins.**
>
> **1 John 4:7-10**

"God is love." The Father in His infinite and unconditional love for us sent His Son, the Lord Jesus, to announce to us who He is and to make the new covenant on our behalf. The Holy Spirit is God pursuing us in passionate love, calling us to respond to His covenant and be united to His love. This is the greatest news in the world, and it brings peace and joy to those who will respond.

Notice what this passage tells us of God and His love: "...love is of God." This means that He is the original source of love, that He did not get love from elsewhere but is the spontaneous fount from which love flows.

"God is love"; He does not have love, as something added to Him, something that may or may not be present, that is capable of change, increase, or decrease. He is love; it is the way He is in His essential nature.

I may tell you that I have a glass of water or a reservoir of water, but it is in an entirely different category to say that I am water! To have water means that my possession of it is subject to change whether by increase or decrease, but to be water means I am never subject to change because it is what I am! He is the definition of love; love is the way He is.

AGAPE OR EROS

The word for love that is used in the original language is vital to our understanding of God. In the Greek of the New Testament, the word is *agape*.[1] It was a word that meant love but was a very general word and lacked a clear definition. It was hardly used and is not to be found in the Greek literature of the first century.

The word that was used for love in the days of Jesus and during the time the New Testament was written was *eros*[2], a word that answers almost exactly to our English word "love". It meant the love of the lovely and the beautiful; it reached up straining to possess the highest and the best and, therefore, was incapable of loving the ugly or that which was out of harmony with itself. *Eros* love is repulsed by what it perceives as ugly or, in fact, anything that is lower than its standard.

The source of *eros* is in the beauty of the person that is loved. *Eros* love is awakened and called forth by the beauty of the beloved. This is a very shaky foundation; it is a built-in weakness and is liable to fade with the fading beauty of the beloved. It is also liable to become distracted by the arrival of a more beautiful object to replace the now-boring beloved.

Human love works on the principle that the person who is loved has created and earned the love of the lover by his or her beauty, and the person must continue to earn that love by maintaining that beauty.

The Core of the Covenant

Eros is driven to fulfill its own needs and pleasures. It is characterized by a driving and urgent need to conquer and to exclusively own the object of its desires, so reducing the beloved to a thing or object to be used.

At the beginning of the twenty-first century whenever inhabitants of the Western world think of love, we tend to think of it through the lens of *eros*. It is certainly the definition of love that is fed our culture daily in advertising, movies, television, and trash fiction.

Teenagers, flushed with excitement, announce that they have fallen in love. They mean that they have met the person who, at least for the moment, is the highest, best, and most beautiful person in the universe and they must possess him or her and make that person their own.

It is significant that the word eros does not appear in the New Testament. In proclaiming and defining the Gospel, the Holy Spirit obviously forbade the use of *eros*, the word for human love, gave us what was essentially a new word for love, *agape*, and used the New Testament to fill it with His own meaning and definition.

Agape is not wakened or created by the beauty of its object, but arises spontaneously from the heart of God. It is therefore a love that cannot be earned or deserved, for it springs from the heart of God upon all persons. It reaches out to the spiritually ugly and those who are out of harmony with Him; it even reaches out to the enemy that would seek to destroy Him. It is not our spiritual beauty that awakens Him to love us; it is not our acts of goodness or track record of righteousness that arouses His loving attention toward us. His love for us originates in who He is, not in our being lovable. He is the source of His love, its reason and energy. He loves us because it is His nature to love.

It is a fact that millions of believers who would heartily agree that God is love, understand His love as human love taken to a higher degree—an ultimate *eros* love. They believe that God loves them as a human loves a human. This results in a relationship with God that is on very shaky ground. If God loves us to the degree that we please Him, then we are forever in doubt concerning His love toward us. And the flip side is that if we believe that we have attracted His love by our behavior, we are filled with pride and congratulate ourselves that we (unlike others) have achieved the kind of life that makes us His beloved.

We look at our relationship with God as based on our behavior; it is if we do thus and so, then God will accept and bless. He loves us if we are holy (or promise to try), if we spend an hour in prayer and Bible reading, if we are enthusiastically busy for Him, and so on. If we fail in any of these areas or fall into sin, then we believe His love fades, He becomes bored with us and turns His attention to others who are worthy of His love.

The Gospel declares the incredible news that our relationship to God is not based on "if" and "then" but rather on "because" and "therefore." The Gospel announces that because He loves us, therefore He is the source of our salvation and blessing in life, the One upon whom our faith and hope rest. This understanding governs our coming to Christ and every step of walking out our Christian life.

This is set forth in the parable of the tax collector and the Pharisee:

> **Also He spoke this parable to some who trusted in themselves that they were righteous, and despised others: "Two men went up to the temple to pray, one a Pharisee and the other a tax collector. The Pharisee stood and prayed thus with himself, 'God, I thank You that I am not like other men—extortioners, unjust, adulterers, or even as this tax collector. I fast twice a week; I give tithes of all that I possess.'**

The Core of the Covenant

And the tax collector, standing afar off, would not so much as raise his eyes to heaven, but beat his breast, saying, 'God, be merciful to me a sinner!'

Luke 18:9-13

The religious Pharisee understood God as having *eros* love—there must be spiritual beauty in the person He bestows His acceptance and blessing upon. There is the feeling that if certain religious duties are performed, then God will respond favorably. The Pharisee passed God's love through the grid of human love, *eros*. He could not imagine a God who would want, let alone love, a person who was less than perfect. He compared himself with others, especially the irreligious, while basking in the affirmation of his fellow Pharisees, and believed that he had attained the position of being good enough for God.

The tax collector accepted the God-given revelation that he was loved in spite of his track record as a lowlife tax collector and traitor to his people. He had the key to life in believing that because God was love and mercy, therefore he could call upon Him and be heard. The word he used as he called upon God, translated here as "mercy," is the covenant word *hesed*, which we have seen is also translated lovingkindness. The man called upon a covenant that was made on his behalf by the God who is love.

In an *eros* world, the Gospel is a scandal! It declares to all men and women that they are loved by God not because of who they are or what they have or have not done, but because of who He is!

As you read this, know that you are loved because you are alive and breathing. Stop reading, and let this sink in. Now, in this moment, you are the focus of the passionate and unconditional love of God. He loves you with His entire Being. You have all of His love as if you were the only human in existence. And He loves you because you exist without reference to your behavior. Understand and live in that reality, and behavior will change in response to such infinite love that leaves us in worshipping wonder. As John says, **We love, because He first loved us** (1 John 4:19 NASB).

This revelation of the heart of God is the foundation of the covenant and the truth upon which we build our entire Christian life. The love of God initiates the covenant and is the ultimate expression of His love. It is the magnetic north of truth by which we fix our position as we stumble lost in the wilderness of the world. It is from this North Star that we find all subsequent direction. To know that His love for us depends on Him and not on us is the beginning of the way out of our futile, meaningless lives and religious despair.

EVERLASTING LOVE

His love is spoken of as everlasting:

> **The Lord has appeared of old to me, saying: "Yes, I have loved you with an everlasting love; therefore with lovingkindness I have drawn you."**
>
> **Jeremiah 31:3**

This means that His love for us has poured forth spontaneously from His heart without beginning, before and outside of time space history. He set His love upon us before we were born, and therefore with no reference to our behavior or works, whether they were good or evil. When speaking of such love, we cannot think in terms of deserving or earning because it originates in His heart and is not based on our actions; an everlasting love is an unconditional love.

"I will heal their backsliding, I will love them freely..." (Hosea 14:4). He loves us freely even though we are wayward and rebellious. His love is unilateral, not drawn out by anything we have done. His love is not like a heat-guided missile, drawn to us by the heat of our holiness. His love springs spontaneously from who He is—He is the motivation for His love; He takes the initiative in seeking us out.

Everlasting love is a before love—there before we were born. None of us is an accident of life, alive by chance. Every man and woman has been the focus of God's love since he or she was a thought in His mind. Each one of us was called forth into existence by the love of God.

> **O Lord, You have searched me and known me...for You formed my inward parts; You covered me in my mother's womb. I will praise You, for I am fearfully and wonderfully made; marvelous are Your works, and that my soul knows very well. My frame was not hidden from You, when I was made in secret, and skillfully wrought in the lowest parts of the earth. Your eyes saw my substance, being yet unformed. And in Your book they all were written, the days fashioned for me, when as yet there were none of them.**
>
> **Psalm 139:1,13-16**

The psalmist is standing in wonder of the fact that he was known before he was born. The word in verse 1 of this Psalm "know" in the Hebrew is *yada*,[2] which is a word that means knowing intimately by observation. It is used to describe the knowing between lovers, and is the word used for the most intimate union of husband and wife.

He contemplates the fingers of God caressing and fashioning him and us in our mothers' wombs. He delights in the microscopic baby that God's love has called into being: "When I was made in secret, and skillfully wrought in the lowest parts of the earth."

The Amplified Bible renders these words:

> **...when I was being formed in secret [and] intricately and curiously wrought [as if embroidered with various colors] in the depths of the earth [a region of darkness and mystery].**
>
> **Psalm 139:15**

God was there at the delivery to welcome each one of us into the world. It is His love for us that draws us to Him even in the years when we do not recognize His voice. He puts the questions in our hearts concerning the emptiness of our existence; He creates the longings for a love we could not find on earth. He put within us the discontentment with our search for happiness and stirred up the longings for endless joy. He inspired all our yearnings after Him.

You were conceived into the love of God in the womb. You were birthed into the arms of His love. You are the object of His love here and now, simply because you exist.

LIMITLESS LOVE

When we think of His love, we must remember that in all that He is, He is limitless—or the theological word is *infinite*. It means that there is no limit or boundary to Him. We humans are limited in all that we are, and in terms of love we can only give ourselves away in total love commitment to one person. But God being unlimited is present to each one of us in the fullness of His love. Each one of us is the focus of His love as if he or she were the only person in creation.

In the parables of Luke 15 Jesus tells the story of one lost sheep that goes astray, even though any shepherd will tell you that sheep follow sheep, getting lost in groups! He speaks of one coin that rolls into the dirt to become the object of the woman's search. The last parable of the chapter is the story of a father who has two sons but deals with each of them as individuals. He runs out to meet the one son returning from his wasted life in the far country, ambushing him with his love. Jesus then portrays him as leaving the feast that welcomes the wayward son to go out to tenderly call the other self-righteous one into the feast.

The Core of the Covenant

He is portraying the sheep as being treated as the only sheep and having all there was of the shepherd to have. One coin is treated as the solitary desired object of a woman's search. Each of the sons is treated as if he were the only one, being the sole object of the father's love.

Paul could look at the love of God in Jesus Christ and His death and resurrection and speak of it as being for himself in the most personal application: **...who loved me and gave Himself for me** (Galatians 2:20).

We cannot find an illustration of this love among humans; the nearest we come to it is the love of a mother for the newborn child. She pours her love upon the baby, providing every need, feeding and protecting not because the child has done something to merit her attention and love but simply because the baby is there. The infant does not deserve all that is poured out; it would be obscene to speak in terms of earning and deserving in matters of maternal love. If we were to speak of deserving, then we would have to admit that the baby is selfish, demanding, and smelly! Even if she has other children, she gives her entire self to the baby. The love initiated and bestowed is freely given because of who the mother is—the baby contributes nothing except its existence.

Realize that you are the babe in the arms of God's love, loved because of who He is, loved as the one who has His sole attention and delight.

The love of God is ultimately revealed in the sending of the Son of God, Jesus Christ, into the world. In Christ, God joined us where we are in our sin-blasted world and futile existence, taking our humanity and living among us a true human life. It was finally demonstrated in His joining us in our death, dying for us and as us on the cross, and manifested love triumphant in resurrection. It is in this that His love achieves its ultimate goal and makes the covenant between God and humankind.

The believer is described as one who has come to know and believe the love of God and has entered into a union with Him. God becomes the believer's habitat even as the believer becomes the dwelling of God.

> **And we have known and believed the love that God has for us. God is love, and he who abides in love abides in God, and God in him.**
>
> **1 John 4:16**

DISCOVERING UNCONDITIONAL LOVE

To come to know and believe the love that God has for us must not be thought of as an interesting religious curiosity! The knowledge of God's love toward us constitutes a major revolution in our lives as the story that a young woman recently told me. Her name is Pam, and it would be hard to describe the state of her Christian life before she came to know and believe his love. She had made a commitment to Christ at a summer camp when she was ten. She never doubted that she meant it when, to signify her commitment to Christ, she deliberately threw a stick onto the fire in front of all her friends. The counselor prayed with her as she simply invited Jesus into her heart. She felt no great emotion but knew that God had accepted her, and with that she was content.

When she came back from camp and told her parents, they were very happy and the pastor said that it was the greatest decision she would ever make. And that was it. Through her teenage years, she was a member of the church youth group, who had all made the same decision to follow Jesus. They formed a kind of subculture in the Midwestern town she called home. They did not smoke, drink, take drugs, or smoke pot, and they went to church every Sunday twice a day and to the youth group on Wednesdays.

The Core of the Covenant

Through her teens and twenties, she tried to be a good Christian, read her Bible, and pray every day, and tried to witness to her neighbors about Jesus, which basically meant that she invited them to her church. Her Christian life came in spurts that usually began after she had answered a call to rededicate her life to Christ. At times, she would find herself wondering if she would be a Christian if she moved to another city. How much of her faith was bound up in her family tradition and their respectable little town? At other times, a longing rose up within her to know God in the way some of the speakers passing through her church seemed to know Him. At such times, she would tell herself that she knew no more of God now than she did when she was ten years old. If there was anything else to this Christianity, she would like to know it.

She married in her early twenties, and her husband, Jeff, had a faith that was much the same as hers. They sat in church every Sunday, the model couple, and would have remained that way for the rest of their lives, but a weekend changed their lives. A friend invited Pam to a retreat I was leading in Oklahoma. I will let her continue in her own words:

"I went along because Dorothy had paid for me, and I did not want to offend her. I expected the usual camp meeting kind of preaching, telling us how lukewarm we all were and calling us to rededicate our lives to God. It was about that time when my last dedication had worn off and I needed a verbal spanking and a renewal of my dedication to God, and so I figured the weekend would not be wasted. I always believed that one day I would make the dedication of my life that would bring me to really knowing God. Who knows? This retreat might do it.

"That retreat turned my whole life upside down. In the first hour, I heard that God loved me unconditionally. He loved me because He was love, not because I was good. I had been in church all my life, but I had never heard that before. I did not realize how desperately I needed to hear it until I heard it, and then I knew I was like a woman dying of thirst in a desert and someone had just given me a long drink of cold water.

"Whatever our pastor believed, I had always heard that I had to reach a certain level of behavior, a certain determined dedication, before God would love me. In fact, I had the strong impression that God was tired of us half-hearted backsliders and was always on the verge of giving us a good thrashing. That He loved us with no reference to our behavior was a totally new thought to me.

"I could not sleep that Friday night. My mind was racing, or maybe I should say dancing, with this new concept. Now I know that the Holy Spirit was working overtime, having finally got through to me! I lay in the bed listening to the crickets outside as I made a survey of my life. Why did I go to church, read my Bible, and pray? Why did I abstain from the things that others of my age were doing? Why did I attempt to witness to my neighbors? I realized that my true motive was to make sure He wouldn't be really mad at me! My whole Christian life was a halfhearted attempt to earn His love.

"And now this new concept changed everything. If He loved me because He is love and not because of my good behavior, then I did not have to earn His love because I was already loved! As I lay there, I found myself weeping with relief and joy as I drank in the water I had not known I was looking for. I said, 'Thank You, Jesus!' over and over, and the words felt strange on my tongue. I had not said or felt anything like that before. I found myself saying, 'I love You, Jesus!' I had certainly never said anything like that before!

"I knew my life could never be the same again. This wasn't a rededication; it was a changing of my understanding of life. It wasn't something I was doing to try to be a better Christian but my response of love to His loving me. That night, my life of

The Core of the Covenant

trying to earn His love and please Him (or maybe I should say, keep Him happy) was over. It died and was buried that night in Oklahoma. The entire weekend, I found myself quietly praising God, laughing, my eyes overflowing with tears of joy. I repeated the words over and over to myself, 'I am loved; I could not be more loved by God, because He is love!'

"If He loved me, what was I doing spending my whole life trying to convince Him that He should love me? In those few hours, a burning desire rose within me to read my Bible and discover this God I had never known. I wanted to pray and talk to Him. I was not afraid of Him anymore. I had the greatest news in the world to tell my neighbors and couldn't wait for the first opportunity.

"When I got home and tried to explain everything to Jeff, he thought I was nuts. Since then he has come to see God's love for him, but it took time and there were difficult days. I was amazed that many of my church friends did not want to hear what I had come to see; they preferred the drudgery of trying to earn God's favor, and I lost some friends. It has not been easy. I have had many personal trials since that day ten years ago, and I have not been all I long to be; but I have had a compass to guide me through it all—the magnetic north of His love for me."

Like Pam, there are countless believers who go through life with no concept of the unconditional love that He has for us. Part of our being lost from God is that we are born into a world that has turned away from His love. We have been raised in a society of sin; selfish, failing, human love; abuse; and dysfunction. As children, we were shamed and taught in hundreds of ways that we were not worthy of being loved. We were taught to despise our poor efforts to perform in a way that would make us worthy of love. Our contact with the church has often projected the shame that we knew from our family into our understanding of God. He was presented to us as shaming us and demanding the keeping of impossible standards before He would love us.

Let us be honest: Many believers reading this chapter will have the reaction that such love is for someone else; God could not love them being the kind of people they are. When confronted with His unconditional love, they feel disgusted and ashamed, designating themselves as the exception to the rule of His limitless love.

Among the words I hear the most from believers when I teach and confront them with the unconditional love of God are "I cannot believe that God loves me like that." There are others who despise themselves and bitterly say that it would be impossible for God to love ones as sinful and worthless as they believe themselves to be. And there are always the pious "humble" who, with downcast eyes, tell me that they are not worthy of His love. They are shocked when I tell them that what they believe to be their extreme humility is, in fact, their extreme bloated pride!

If any of these statements of disbelief in the totality of God's love is taken seriously, then we are denying some of the most basic tenets of the Gospel. All these statements have in common the total misconception of the Gospel. All of the above people who cannot find it in them to believe that God so loves them, find it difficult because they believe themselves to not be good enough for Him.

I have some very serious questions for such persons that will help determine whether they have truly heard in their hearts this Gospel:

- If God is infinite, unconditional love, then are we not slandering His character to say that He does not love us, or could not love us? By making ourselves the exception,

we are denying both that His love is infinite and that it is unconditional.
- What has being worthy to do with the good news contained in the new covenant?
- Do we think that God loves us because we have done something good?
- Do we think that the love of God is the warm feeling we get after we have evaluated our lives and decided that we are good enough, at least for the present, to be loved by Him?
- Are we not trying to control God, telling Him that we are not ready to be loved by Him and when we are ready, we will give Him permission to extend His love to us?

"I do not feel worthy" is a feeling of religious flesh. It must be crucified and named as a lie that comes from the one who first said, "Has God said...?" I do not doubt that you do not feel worthy, but what has that to do with faith, which in the face of such feelings declares the truth and stands in speechless awe before such a God? To believe in those feelings and exclude oneself from His love is to build a twisted, distorted idol and call it the God revealed in Jesus.

When we first hear of His unconditional love, our response is delight; they are the most wonderful words that we have heard. But it is not long before the words become a scandal to us—how could He love me? It would be true to say that we do not truly know His love until we have deliberately submitted to it against all the better judgment of our moral, religious flesh. Submitting to His love means that we take a stand against the raging feelings of our phony flesh that despises itself, and against the sneering voice of the accuser of the brethren.

While our feelings hypnotize us with the lie, and self-loathing demands that it be believed, we must open our mouths and declare aloud His love for us. Faith is not a feeling; it is a choice against our feelings, sometimes against every feeling in our being, to believe the revelation of God in Jesus Christ.

One thing is sure—all of our whining that He could not love us does not stop Him from loving us! His love is almighty and does reach us wherever we are. He set His love upon us before we were born, without asking our permission; it is eternally too late to argue with Him on this issue. He is the God who, so Jesus tells us, delights to throw wild parties for the undeserving failures in life, to celebrate them and declare them His own.

You are not working toward His love; you are now, in this moment, loved. We begin our journey into understanding the new covenant by knowing that we are loved and highly valued by God. The only explanation to His making the covenant is His love for us. We receive His love with thanks; we surrender to that love and rest secure in it.

Chapter 6

THE REPRESENTATIVE MAN

God has a radical agenda of love! He reaches to every man and woman to reconcile us to Himself, to include us in the circle of His intimate friends, and to return each one of us to the reason for our creation. How does He achieve this goal of totally transforming the man or woman who is dead in sin?

He achieves it with no help from us. He makes the new covenant: a unilateral covenant, originating solely with Him and freely offered to man as His gift; a covenant based on the oath of God, who swears by Himself because He can swear by none greater.

But a covenant is between two parties, and each party has its representative. How shall such a covenant take place when the human side of the covenant is sinful, unfaithful, and loving their darkness rather than the light of God? There is no one on earth to represent humankind. Job cried for such a one who could explain God to him and speak for him to God.

> For He is not a man, as I am, that I may answer Him, and that we should go to court together. Nor is there any mediator between us, who may lay his hand on us both.
> **Job 9:32,33**

For such a covenant to take place, we need a human being to represent every man and woman to God. We need a second man to restart the human race, another Adam who can set right what the first Adam brought to destruction and then take humankind to the intimacy with God that he had been created to enjoy. We need one who can represent us to God saying the yes to Him that the first Adam failed to say, and in that yes lead us all to the destiny for which we were created.

THE DIVINE REPRESENTATIVE

The Gospel is the announcement that God has provided this Man in a way that no one could dream of in one's wildest imagination. Before time, everlasting love and infinite wisdom produced the plan. God the Father in His great love for us determined to send His Son who, without ceasing to be God, would take to Himself our humanity and become flesh. The Son in love for us agreed to come and as a true human live out our human life, face our hardships and temptations, and finally offer Himself to die as and for us. He would rise from the dead, having put away sin and achieved the reconciling of the world to God, and bring about the new covenant. The Holy Spirit agreed to come and make the covenant a reality in the lives of those who believe.

As our representative, He is the *Mediator* of the new covenant. The word in the Greek literally means "a go-between,"[1] one who goes between two parties to bring peace. He possesses the nature and attributes of God and so represents Him to humankind; He has taken the nature of humankind (without sin) and so fully knows the needs of each one of us and can represent us to God. This is the same word that Job used—his cry for one who could lay hands on God and man is answered in Jesus.

> For there is one God and one Mediator between God and men, the Man Christ Jesus.
>
> 1 Timothy 2:5
>
> My little children, these things I write to you, so that you may not sin. And if anyone sins, we have an Advocate with the Father, Jesus Christ the righteous.
>
> 1 John 2:1

Another word that belongs to this family of words is "intercessor," which means to go or pass between; to act between parties with a view to reconciliation; to mediate.[2] He was our intercessor and ever lives to make intercession, or to be our representative.

The word also means "one who acts as a guarantee" so as to secure something which otherwise could not be obtained. Jesus is our guarantor of the better covenant, guaranteeing its terms for His people.

> But now He has obtained a more excellent ministry, inasmuch as He is also Mediator of a better covenant, which was established on better promises.
>
> Hebrews 8:6
>
> And for this reason He is the Mediator of the new covenant, by means of death, for the redemption of the transgressions under the first covenant, that those who are called may receive the promise of the eternal inheritance.
>
> Hebrews 9:15
>
> To Jesus the Mediator of the new covenant, and to the blood of sprinkling that speaks better things than that of Abel.
>
> Hebrews 12:24

Jesus, the Son of God, is the covenant in Himself. The representative of God and the representative of the human race meet in this one person, Jesus Christ.

The first and most basic thing we have to understand is that the new covenant is not made with us as individuals. It is a covenant made by God the Father with God the Son. The Father guarantees the divine side of the covenant, and the Son guarantees the human side having taken our humanity as us and for us. It becomes ours individually as we believe on the Lord Jesus and are joined to Him. The new covenant is out of our hands and beyond our ability to break; it is guaranteed by the Triune God and, therefore, is unconditional and unbreakable.

Jesus Christ is the representative Man of the new covenant. As the Son of God, He stands in an eternal, infinite love relationship with the Father; and as the sinless Man, He is worthy to enter into covenant with Him. He makes the covenant solely as and for us. As the eternal object of the Father's love and delight, He does not need to enter into covenant with Him; He has no need of any of the promises and blessings of the covenant. In limitless love for us, He has joined Himself to us, never to leave us. We are inseparable from Him; He achieves the covenant and earns all of its blessings not for Himself but for us. When the Spirit joins us to Him, all the promises of the covenant made to Him become ours.

The prophet Isaiah, in a series of prophecies, spoke of Jesus as the Servant of the Lord. One of these prophecies defines Him as the covenant:

> **Thus says the Lord: "In an acceptable time I have heard You, and in the day of salvation I have helped You; I will preserve You and give You as a covenant to the people, to restore the earth...."**
>
> **Isaiah 49:8-13**

Jesus is the Man who is God: He is the covenant, the joining of God and Man in Him. He represents God to humankind and is the final revelation of God to man. In Old Testament days prophets brought the message of God's self-revelation, but He is the message in flesh.

> **No man has seen God at any time; the only begotten God who is in the bosom of the Father, He has explained Him.**
>
> **John 1:18 NASB**

The word "explained" literally means to exegete or interpret;[3] Jesus is God explaining God to the human race.

> **Therefore, holy brethren, partakers of the heavenly calling, consider the Apostle and High Priest of our confession, Christ Jesus.**
>
> Hebrews 3:1

He is the Apostle from God to humankind, and the Priest carrying humankind to God. He is the ultimate Man. We must not think of Him simply as an individual man who lived in Israel. He was an individual, but as the Mediator of the covenant He must be thought of as Humankind. When Pilate brought Jesus, having been cruelly beaten and mocked and adorned with a crown of thorns and a purple robe, to the religious leaders and people of Jerusalem, he said, "Behold the Man." He spoke in Latin, and the sentence would have been "Ecce Homo."[4] The Latin lacked the definite article and, literally translated, he said, "Behold Man." He said more than he realized, for that brutalized One who stood before him was indeed more than a man, He was Humankind. Jesus is not just a man but the Man saying the yes of unqualified obedience to the Father, and at the same time He is God achieving all the terms and promises of the covenant.

Even as Adam was an individual but also literally contained humankind within him, so Jesus contains the New Creation in Himself; He is the New Man. He takes our place, representing us to God in covenant. He enters into and walks our history into the death where sin had put us, and in resurrection joins us to His history carrying us into union with the Father.

QUALIFICATIONS OF THE REPRESENTATIVE

For Him to be our representative in the covenant He must be infinitely more valuable than any one human, for He is taking the place of every man and woman of Adam's race. Even one perfect man could not represent everyone, for one human life even if perfect could only take the place of one human. Only the sacrifice of God would be enough to take the place of the entire race and the fallen creation. In Him, the Lord Jesus, we have the Man who is of infinite worth to God and man; for He is God the Son, infinitely beloved of the Father. Such a Man who is God can take the place of and represent every man and woman born of Adam. He can embrace us all in His history and live and die and rise again as us, making His history ours.

But the one who would represent us in covenant must be our relative, a human who is one of us, one whom we can call our kin. If he came as a new kind of created being, then he would start his own race of which we would have no part. This one must be fully human, a brother to us all. He could then truly represent us and speak for and as all humankind in saying the yes to God and the no to Satan that the first Adam failed to say.

But God is not a human relative. He is our Creator and we are creatures. He is pure unembodied spirit, and He is not one of us. He cannot experience our temptations, nor can he experience our death. If God is to be our representative Man, He must take to Himself our humanity and become our brother with a body in which He may experience the limitations and privations of human life. He must face the temptations that can only be experienced with a human body and human passions.

He needed a body to take the sin, grief, and sorrow of humankind to Himself and suffer and die on our behalf. God needed tear ducts to weep over humankind that He had joined Himself to. He needed hands and feet that He might be nailed to the cross as the criminal that we were. He needed the flesh of man that He might be whipped and scourged for our healing. Above all, He needed blood, the blood that was the blood of the God Man, that it might be poured out for our sin. He was born to be the sacrificial Lamb that would take away the sin of the world.

The Representative Man

Psalm 40:6-8 is described in Hebrews 10:5-7 as being the voice of Jesus:

> **Therefore, when He came into the world, He said: "Sacrifice and offering You did not desire, but a body You have prepared for Me. In burnt offerings and sacrifices for sin You had no pleasure. Then I said, 'Behold, I have come—In the volume of the book it is written of Me—To do Your will, O God.'"**

In the womb of the Virgin Mary God became flesh, taking to Himself our humanity, His body prepared for Him by the Holy Spirit from the humanity of the Virgin.

In order to represent us, He must be totally free from the virus of sin that Adam infected the race with, also having faced temptation in His own experience and overcome it. A representative who had his own sin to deal with could not take the place of anyone else, for he would be in the same plight that we are in.

He experienced all of life as us and for us. He was God as a human babe in the womb of the Virgin, God in the human birth process, God as a human toddler and young boy, God as a teenager and young businessman. He fully experienced all that it meant to be a developing human being. He was tempted with the temptations unique to childhood, the temptations that only teenagers experience, and the temptations of the adult—and all without sin. He as us said the yes to God, His Father.

Without a body, God cannot know the hunger pains that are so strong that a man will steal to have food in his stomach. He cannot know the torture of thirst that would make a man kill for a drop of water. He cannot know the exhaustion of the body that is unable to put the next foot before the other. He cannot know the fear of death, the separation from the body, that is a dark shadow over humans throughout their entire existence. He cannot know what it is like to have a body that shakes under the sobs of grief at the loss of a dear friend. God cannot be the sport of leering, evil men. He cannot know the horror of a fist smashing His face, nor can He have His body tortured until He screams with pain. He cannot know the humiliation of nakedness and the mocking laughter of perverted men. In all of this He cannot know the questions, the confusion of the persons so treated, the feelings of abandonment by friends and by God Himself.

If God is to represent us He must know all of this, entering into the hell of human suffering and the agonizing temptations that are found there, and to come through it without sin.

TEMPTATION, GRIEF, AND SORROW

At thirty years old, He was driven by the Spirit into the wilderness to meet with Satan. The first Adam met with Satan in a luxurious Garden with every physical need supplied. This One, the Last Adam, having been without food for forty days, met with Satan in a desolate wilderness.

In each step of the temptation presented to Him, He said the resounding yes to His Father and no to Satan. For the first time in the history of creation, a human said no to Satan. And He did it as a human. We in Him said yes to the Father.

He knew intense hunger in the wilderness after forty days without food. (Matthew 4:2.) He knew a craving thirst on the cross and begged for water. (John 19:28.) He sat tired and thirsty at noon beside Jacob's well asking for a cup of water, and on another occasion was so exhausted that He slept on the deck of a fishing boat through a raging storm that threatened to drown everyone.

He not only would bear our sin, but in the hours of suffering before He went to the cross He went to the bottom of all the hurt and suffering and anguish that sin brought to human experience. Isaiah 53:4 says, **Surely He has borne our griefs and carried our sorrows.** The words "grief" and "sorrow" carry the idea of mental, emotional, and physical pain that has been caused by others; the agonizing pain of living in a sinful world bearing not only one's own guilt but being hurt by the sins of others.

He knew the anguish of betrayal by His dearest friend; He knew abandonment as His other disciples forsook Him and His closest friend denied that he knew Him. He experienced it as us and for us that He might come under our burdens in similar situations and be our strength. He was physically abused in vicious beatings and mocking. He was verbally abused in cruel, jeering words. Crucifixion included the victim being stripped and hung naked on the cross. The leering Roman soldiers laughed and shouted their bawdy jokes at the sight of the naked Man on public show. In such treatment, Jesus the Son of God knew the horror and terror that only the sexually abused know. He came under the whole spectrum of human suffering caused by sin and took it to Himself.

The final yes of obedience to the Father was in the Garden of Gethsemane on the night of His suffering and death. He was the Man facing the unspeakable horror of being nailed to a cross as a criminal, for crimes He had not committed, the wickedest death by torture ever invented by man.

God the Father did not force Him. As Man, He freely chose to do the will of the Father and willingly take the place of each one of us. The yes did not come easily. His blood began to be shed as His sweat turned red with the blood oozing through the pores of His skin, so great was the agony of the choice. But He said the final yes:

> **"Father, if it is Your will, take this cup away from Me; nevertheless not My will, but Yours, be done."**
> **Luke 22:42**

Having submitted freely to the will of His Father, He gave Himself to those who came to arrest Him.

LAYING DOWN HIS LIFE

Freedom from sin would mean that He was unaffected by the penalty of death that we are under. If He were going to die one day like the rest of us, His death on the cross would merely be premature death and not an offering for sin. The representative would have to be able to take His sinless and immortal life and freely lay it down in death.

> **As the Father knows Me, even so I know the Father; and I lay down My life for the sheep.**
>
> **Therefore My Father loves Me, because I lay down My life that I may take it again. No one takes it from Me, but I lay it down of Myself. I have power to lay it down, and I have power to take it again. This command I have received from My Father.**
>
> **John 10:15,17,18**

The religious leaders were insistent that He be crucified. One would think they would have hired an assassin to quietly kill Him in far-off Galilee. Why have Him publicly crucified in Jerusalem at the Passover when to do so would bring the city to the verge of riot? Under the law, capital punishment was by stoning or strangling; but in some cases after the victim was dead he would be crucified, hung on a tree until sunset, declaring him cursed by God.

> **If a man has committed a sin deserving of death, and he is put to death, and you hang him on a tree, his body shall not remain overnight on the tree, but you shall surely bury him that day, so that you do not defile the land which the Lord your God is giving you as an inheritance; for he who is hanged is accursed of God.**
>
> **Deuteronomy 21:22,23**

The leaders wanted Jesus crucified so that He would be declared the cursed of God in the eyes of the people and all His claims to being Messiah invalidated. They did not know that in so doing the curse that was upon the law-breaker was being transferred from us to Him and the blessing of God that He had walked in all of His life given to us.

> **For as many as are of the works of the law are under the curse; for it is written, "Cursed is everyone who does not continue in all things which are written in the book of the law, to do them."**
>
> **Christ has redeemed us from the curse of the law, having become a curse for us (for it is written, "Cursed is everyone who hangs on a tree"), that the blessing of Abraham might come upon the Gentiles in Christ Jesus, that we might receive the promise of the Spirit through faith.**
>
> **Galatians 3:10,13,14**

He took the sin, the insolent no of humankind that had been hurled at God throughout all of time, and accepted the death that came with it.

On the cross, the sin of the world met in Him. He experienced being made sin for us. (2 Corinthians 5:21.) The guilt of every man and woman's sin from the beginning till the end of time met in Him. Every sin of humankind became His responsibility, all the afflictions of humankind due to sin were laid at His door and He was afflicted with our afflictions.

> **Who Himself bore our sins in His own body on the tree, that we, having died to sins, might live for righteousness—by whose stripes you were healed.**
>
> **1 Peter 2:24**

We are sinners by choice; He faced the prospect with abhorrence and was made sin against His will, taking it only because it was the will of the Father that He should do so. It was the cup He had anticipated in Gethsemane. The prophet describes Him on the cross as being submitted and passive in all that took place—it was done to Him:

> **Surely He has borne our griefs and carried our sorrows; yet we esteemed Him stricken, smitten by God, and afflicted. But He was wounded for our transgressions, He was bruised**

for our iniquities; the chastisement for our peace was upon Him, and by His stripes we are healed. All we like sheep have gone astray; we have turned, every one, to his own way; and the Lord has laid on Him the iniquity of us all. He was oppressed and He was afflicted, yet He opened not His mouth; He was led as a lamb to the slaughter, and as a sheep before its shearers is silent, so He opened not His mouth. He was taken from prison and from judgment, and who will declare His generation? For He was cut off from the land of the living; for the transgressions of My people He was stricken.

Isaiah 53:4-8

He experienced all that is meant by Isaiah 59:2:

But your iniquities have separated you from your God; and your sins have hidden His face from you, so that He will not hear.

From the midst of bearing our sins and being treated as the sinner who had committed them, He cried, "My God, My God, why have You forsaken Me?"

We can never know what this means. We are so used to sin that we do not notice it, and we have neutralized most of the shame. For the sinless Son of God, who had never known or felt sin or guilt, to be suddenly identified with all the sins of human history, knowing Himself personally responsible for them, consciously guilty and feeling the full shame of them, was a horror beyond words to describe.

He was God with us, and He had joined us in taking our humanity and becoming brother to each of us. He had lived our life and faced our temptations, but this was the heart of making the covenant: Then, in those hours of darkness, He joined us in our sin.

For He made Him who knew no sin to be sin for us, that we might become the righteousness of God in Him.

2 Corinthians 5:21

The Representative Man

Each one of us was there in the hours that spanned time. Each of us was there, each with his or her sins, condemned by the law and under the penalty of death. We brought our every act of disobedience, our myriad futile searches for meaning in our flesh as we reject the love of God; He identified with us and took them to Himself. We brought our pride that had despised others and raised us above and ahead of them; He took it and made it His own. We brought our acts of selfishness against our fellow humans, expressed in the lies, our control and manipulation of others, the lust, the pornography that has selfishly used others as impersonal objects, denying that they are made in the image of God. We brought to Him all our foul language of gossip that we delighted in, even though it destroyed others. We brought corrupt hearts seething with bitterness, malice, and hatred, that took pleasure in others' destruction even as they corroded and destroyed us; our proud hearts that refused to forgive; our envies that smoldered within us against those more successful. We brought them to Him, and He took them as His own. Our rage and ill temper, our abuses of others—even to violent sins of rape and murder—all of the black river of the sewage of human sin against God and fellow man met in Him. Every man and woman can look at the Son of God who joined us and took our sins to Himself. With Paul, each of us can say that Jesus is **...the Son of God, who loved me and gave Himself for me** (Galatians 2:20).

The horror is multiplied when we remember that He is the Holy One and knew sin as we have never known it. We have become so used to sin and the presence of its corruption that we are hardly aware of it until it hurts us. On the cross was the first time He knew the filth and contamination of sin, knowing its pain and anguish as we have never experienced it.

IT IS FINISHED

The cry before He died **"It is finished!"** (John 19:30) is not the last gasp of a defeated man. Matthew 27:50, Mark 15:37, and Luke 23:46 do not record what He said but join as one to say that He cried out with a loud voice, which was a miracle considering His sufferings and the crushing of the lungs caused by crucifixion.

The phrase "It is finished" was used in at least two ways in the days of the New Testament. In Roman warfare, the general would be positioned on a high elevation so that he could watch the battle taking place below him. From where he stood he could see when the battle had been won, while a foot soldier in the thick of the battle would not know it. When he could see that the enemy had been routed, he would shout the same phrase Jesus cried—"It is finished"—and every foot soldier would know that the battle had been won.

But the phrase has also been found written across the bottom of statements of account in ancient Greece answering to our "paid in full." Jesus emerged from the spiritual death He died as us and shouted through the smoke of battle that the battle had been won and the sin of man had been canceled, paid in full.

He had been through the hell of bearing our sins in His body on the cross and out of that darkness had cried, "My God, My God why have You forsaken Me?" but then it was accomplished and in full, conscious fellowship with His Father He said, "Father, 'into Your hands I commit My spirit.' Having said this, He breathed His last" (Luke 23:46).

Crucifixion was the cruelest torture ever invented by man. It was an agonizing death that took sometimes days to accomplish, during which time the victim was slowly suffocated as his lungs were constricted as he hung on the nails. Many times the birds of prey would come and peck out the victims' eyes as they hung helpless between life and death. Certainly it was many hours before the victim died.

We must understand that Jesus did not die by crucifixion. The Roman centurion who had witnessed hundreds of crucifixions and knew the length of time needed for death to occur was astounded when he saw that He was dead by three in the afternoon. Pilate could not believe the report.

> So when the centurion, who stood opposite Him, saw that He cried out like this and breathed His last, he said, "Truly this Man was the Son of God!" Pilate marveled that He was already dead; and summoning the centurion, he asked him if He had been dead for some time.
>
> Mark 15:39,44

Jesus did not die at anyone's hand. He deliberately chose to die, the willing sacrifice for sin, freely choosing to join us in our death. This is brought out in the phrase that is used to describe His death:

> ...And bowing His head, He gave up His spirit.
>
> John 19:30

The phrase "gave up His spirit" means to dismiss or hand over something, which is not the word that is used to describe the act of dying.[5] He did not die by the hands of the Jews or the Romans. Crucifixion did not kill Him. He had power over His life; and choosing to die, He dismissed His spirit.

Paul consistently uses this same phrase to describe the death of the Lord Jesus:

> ...who loved me and gave Himself for me.
>
> Galatians 2:20

> ...Christ also has loved us and given Himself for us, an offering and a sacrifice to God....
>
> Ephesians 5:2

> ...Christ also loved the church and gave Himself for her....
>
> Ephesians 5:25

In so doing, He deliberately joined us in our death. In Eden, the first couple were warned that to eat of the fruit would result in death: "In the day you eat you shall surely die." They ate and heard the words "Dust you are and unto dust you shall return." Made in the image of God with bodies never intended to die, humans now live with the horror of death, the fear of which overshadows all of life.

There is no such thing as death by natural causes! Death is the most unnatural ending to the life of the one created to be immortal. We cannot imagine the horror for God to experience the rending apart of spirit and body and to enter into human death.

> **But we see Jesus, who was made a little lower than the angels, for the suffering of death...that He, by the grace of God, might taste death for everyone. Inasmuch then as the children have partaken of flesh and blood, He Himself likewise shared in the same, that through death He might destroy him who had the power of death, that is, the devil, and release those who through fear of death were all their lifetime subject to bondage.**
>
> **Hebrews 2:9,14,15**

He not only was able to choose when He would dismiss His life but also had the power to take it again and come out of death to take us with Him into the new covenant. And so, on the third day, He rose from the dead. That made His death not a tragedy but a triumph.

The resurrection of Jesus, the representative Man, signaled the end of the age of death and the beginning of the new humankind, the new creation that is no longer subject to death but shares the very life of God, everlasting life. The stone rolling away from the tomb announced the beginning of the eternal age that knows no end.

Enoch and Elijah had cheated death, and numerous others had been resuscitated from the dead to die again later. But Jesus had freely entered into death, destroyed it, and risen out of it never to die again. In His resurrection, the reign of death was declared over and finished and every man and woman carried in Him out of its grasp.

Henceforth, the race of Adam outside of Him would be termed the "old man(kind)." All who believe upon Him and are part of the new creation founded on the new covenant would be the new man(kind) who partake of eternal life, the life of eternity, the powers of the age to come, the life of God Himself. For such believers, the end of the world has come; in His resurrection, the new creation has dawned.

The New Testament never speaks of believers dying; we "fall asleep in Jesus." The pain of death is in those who live having lost for a short while their loved ones. For the believer, death is a "life-ing" into the presence of Jesus. Death has lost its sting and is the old servant to escort us to Jesus until his retirement at the resurrection at the Second Coming.

> **Jesus said to her, "I am the resurrection and the life. He who believes in Me, though he may die, he shall live. And whoever lives and believes in Me shall never die. Do you believe this?"**
>
> **John 11:25,26**
>
> **For to me, to live is Christ, and to die is gain. ...to depart and be with Christ, which is far better.**
>
> **Philippians 1:21,23**

We who are in the new creation live between the ages. A new age has begun in the midst of the death throes of the old age. At this time, the two ages exist side by side. We are partaking of everlasting life, the life of the age to come, while living alongside of the old creation that is in the process of passing away. We wait for the Second Coming of the Lord Jesus, who will consummate the new creation, and all those in it will be seen for who they really are, the sons and daughters of God. We will be delivered from the pain and sorrow of living in the world while not being of it.

> Behold what manner of love the Father has bestowed on us, that we should be called children of God! Therefore the world does not know us, because it did not know Him. Beloved, now we are children of God; and it has not yet been revealed what we shall be, but we know that when He is revealed, we shall be like Him, for we shall see Him as He is.
>
> 1 John 3:1,2
>
> For you died, and your life is hidden with Christ in God. When Christ who is our life appears, then you also will appear with Him in glory.
>
> Colossians 3:3,4

We must begin to think in these terms. We are the people who have, in the resurrection of our representative, exited the old creation; we are in the new creation. All that belonged to that old creation of death through Adam is ended, and we are now living in the powers of the age to come. We are living in the power of the life of eternal heaven, the life of God Himself.

As the representative Man, He ascended to the Father, carrying us into the divine presence, and there receives as us and for us the gift of the Holy Spirit. He has received the Spirit without measure; the gift is for those He represents.

> **Therefore being exalted to the right hand of God, and having received from the Father the promise of the Holy Spirit, He poured out this which you now see and hear.**
>
> Acts 2:33

The making of the new covenant in the blood of the Lord Jesus that took place in time space history on Golgotha outside of Jerusalem 2000 years ago is made real in this moment in our lives and carried to its fullest potential by the Holy Spirit. The Holy Spirit now brings into this present moment, into the lives of men and women, all that was achieved by Him out there in history. The new covenant is the covenant of the Spirit; and apart from Him vitally and dynamically with us today, the new covenant is only an impossible dream that we read of in the Scripture.

Chapter 7

THE STORY OF MEPHIBOSHETH

The making of the new covenant is foreshadowed in many of the Old Testament stories. We must remember that they are records of actual events that took place in the lives of real people in Israel. They are helpful signposts that anticipate and point the way to what Jesus would do. They are not meant to explain His work of covenant-making, nor do they fit every detail of what He did; but they help us to understand how the one act of Jesus 2000 years ago transforms our lives today.

One such story is found scattered through 1 and 2 Samuel. It is the story of a covenant that took place between Jonathan, the son of King Saul and the crown prince of Israel, and David, who at that time was a general in Saul's army and previously a peasant from Bethlehem.

Saul was a tragic person who, though called to a high destiny, chose the path of disobedience to God. He ended up a broken man seeking the counsel of a witch. His family was weak and walked after the pathway of their father.

However, the crown prince, Jonathan, stood out as utterly different. He was of the family of Saul but completely other than his father, having a dynamic faith in God and a desire to do His will and please Him. When David was introduced to the court,

Jonathan was immediately drawn to him, recognizing a like faith. Their friendship deepened to the point of making a covenant.

> **Then Jonathan and David made a covenant, because he loved him as his own soul. And Jonathan took off the robe that was on him and gave it to David, with his armor, even to his sword and his bow and his belt.**
>
> **1 Samuel 18:3,4**

This describes the elementary steps of covenant-making, in which gifts from the covenant maker are given to the covenant partner. Even though they were two teenage boys, the effects of their sacred covenant would be felt down through generations to come. Each one of the young men stood as the representative of his family yet unborn. Their children's children would stand by the oath and swear responsibilities by which the covenant would be worked out.

A short time later they reaffirmed the covenant, filling in the details:

> (David said to Jonathan,) **"Therefore you shall deal kindly with your servant, for you have brought your servant into a covenant of the Lord with you. Nevertheless, if there is iniquity in me, kill me yourself, for why should you bring me to your father?**
>
> **"And you shall not only show me the kindness of the Lord while I still live, that I may not die; but you shall not cut off your kindness from my house forever, no, not when the Lord has cut off every one of the enemies of David from the face of the earth." So Jonathan made a covenant with the house of David, saying, "Let the Lord require it at the hand of David's enemies."**
>
> **Now Jonathan again caused David to vow, because he loved him; for he loved him as he loved his own soul.**
>
> **Then Jonathan said to David, "Go in peace, since we have both sworn in the name of the Lord, saying, 'May the Lord be between you and me, and between your descendants**

The Story of Mephibosheth

and my descendants, forever.'" So he arose and departed, and Jonathan went into the city.

1 Samuel 20:8,14-17,42

The word that the boys used "kindly" and "kindness" is our word *hesed*, the lovingkindness of covenant. It speaks here of how the covenant would be worked out in the lives of their children and children's children. The entire covenant was really for the descendants of the two young men, as a careful reading will show. The holy love between David and Jonathan did not need a covenant to hold it together, but by the time their children were grown a covenant would be needed to ensure that the love would continue through generations. Jonathan's words assumed that both he and David stood as the representatives of their unborn children and the promises and blessings of the covenant they were making would extend to immediate heirs and beyond.

Saul was afraid of the popularity of David, fearful that he would snatch the throne from him; and his fear turned to hate and hate to an obsession to murder him. He tried to take David's life on more than one occasion and finally made it his life's passion to kill him.

But the plots of Saul against David only served to bring Jonathan to face the reality that God had chosen David to be king after Saul. Jonathan was the crown prince, having the right of succession, and was to rule after Saul died. If he wanted to make his throne secure, he should have sided with his father in removing David. In making the covenant, he made a life-changing decision and in this final statement of the covenant between them died to his right to be the next king and swore allegiance to David.

> And he said to him, "Do not fear, for the hand of Saul my father shall not find you. You shall be king over Israel, and I shall be next to you. Even my father Saul knows that." So the

> two of them made a covenant before the Lord. And David stayed in the woods, and Jonathan went to his own house.
> 1 Samuel 23:17,18

This is the heart of their covenant. Not only as Prince Jonathan, but also as and for his unborn children, Jonathan laid down his throne and proclaimed David his king. To enjoy this covenant, his family had to say the amen to the decision of their covenant representative. He was the voice of his family declaring David as the rightful king of Israel, and in him his family pledged allegiance to him.

Time passed, and the two young teenagers grew up into manhood and married and Jonathan had children. The old enemies of Israel, the Philistines, once again attacked Israel; King Saul, with Jonathan by his side, led the armies into battle. It was a day of great defeat for Israel, and both King Saul and Crown Prince Jonathan were killed in the battle.

The Near Middle East in 1000 BC was a violent place. The first act of a conqueror was to assemble the family of the conquered king and kill all of his heirs to the throne. They eliminated immediately all potential problems in ruling the newly conquered people that might come from the recognized leaders of the people.

It was not surprising, therefore, that when the news that the king and the prince were dead and Israel was defeated reached the palace, there was panic; everyone fled in a mad rush to escape the threat of death by Philistine hands. The royal nurses rushed to the nursery to take and hide the young sons of Prince Jonathan. A nurse picked up one of the princes, a little boy called Mephibosheth, and fled from the palace with him in her arms. She slipped and fell, and the baby was flung from her arms and smashed on the pavement; his legs were crushed, and he never walked again. He was taken secretly across the Jordan River to the wilderness, where he was raised in an insignificant desert town called Lo Debar.

The Story of Mephibosheth

A period of unrest followed the death of King Saul, after which David became king of all Israel. The years passed by, but David never forgot the covenant made with Jonathan. When he had established his kingdom, he began searching for any of Jonathan's sons that he might fulfill his oath and show covenant kindness to them.

Now David said, "Is there still anyone who is left of the house of Saul, that I may show him kindness for Jonathan's sake?"

2 Samuel 9:1

It was a difficult task to find someone who would tell him where any of the family of Jonathan was to be found; no one would believe that David intended good. All the relatives of Saul believed David to be an impostor sitting on the throne that rightly belonged to an heir of Saul. In those barbaric days, the expected action would be for David to kill all the house of Saul before they killed him and claimed back what they perceived to be their throne. If he was looking for them, it must be to do them harm; no one could understand a covenant love that extended even to potential contenders for the throne.

The story is told in 2 Samuel 9 of how David finally found the location of the crippled Mephibosheth and sent men to bring him from Lo Debar to his royal palace. Imagine how the young man must have felt as, leaning on his crutches, he watched the soldiers of David come to his house. He hated David, even though he had never seen him and had no knowledge whatsoever of the covenant between David and his father. He had been taught by the family of Saul to believe that David was the enemy who had stolen everything that rightly belonged to him, the rightful heir to the fortunes of his father, Jonathan, and his grandfather, Saul. He would most certainly share the common belief that the only reason David would want him in Jerusalem was to kill him.

Taken before the king, he threw aside his crutches, fell on his face, and waited to hear the order for his execution. What he heard must have left him speechless.

> **So David said to him, "Do not fear, for I will surely show you kindness for Jonathan your father's sake, and will restore to you all the land of Saul your grandfather; and you shall eat bread at my table continually."**
>
> **2 Samuel 9:7**

He was not treated on the basis of his track record of loyalty to David but on the basis of a covenant entered into before he was born, made by his father, who had stood as the covenant representative for his children's children. David delighted in him as if he were Jonathan. He was accepted in the oath and yes of his father. The covenant, made years before in the blood-shedding of Jonathan, still held as fresh as the day it had been made. Although he was confronted personally with the covenant and its promises, there was no need of a further individual covenant between David and Mephibosheth; David accepted him solely on the basis of his having been in Jonathan at the making of the original covenant.

But now confronted with the gift of covenant, he had a decision to make. To accept the covenant, he had to enter into the pledge of allegiance Jonathan had made to David, which would separate him from all the other members of the family of Saul, to never share in the hatred they bore to David. To enter into the covenant would be a death to all that he called life—its goals, hopes, and ambitions, and all the friends who shared them with him—and to rise again from that death to being a prince in the royal house of David.

Lying on the floor before David, he accepted the yes of his father, swore allegiance to David, and allowed the covenant to change his life forever. He was taken into David's house and treated as a prince, eating with David every day as a kind of continual meal of covenant.

The Story of Mephibosheth

...**"As for Mephibosheth,"** said the king, **"he shall eat at my table like one of the king's sons."**

So Mephibosheth dwelt in Jerusalem, for he ate continually at the king's table. And he was lame in both his feet.

2 Samuel 9:11,13

The human race, born of the family of Adam, bears all the traits of the family of Saul. Each one of us walked in disobedience to God and lived under the authority of the domain of darkness. Then there came into the family of Adam one who was of us but utterly different.

Christ's story is similar to Jonathan's. Christ was bonded in love to the One hated by the family of Adam, the true God and King of all humankind. As Jonathan in the story, Jesus summed us up in Himself, stood as us and for us and entered into covenant with the Father on our behalf. The covenant was made solely with us in view.

As our covenant representative, He declared and lived the pledge of love and obedience to His Father that was realized to its fullest in His blood-shedding on the cross. His obedience was summed up in His prayer in Gethsemane: **"Father, if it is Your will, take this cup away from Me; nevertheless not My will, but Yours, be done"** (Luke 22:42).

We were born two thousand years after that covenant was made. We were born into the family of Adam, crippled by the lie and ignorant of the covenant. We lived in the darkness with a distorted image of God, never knowing of His love or of His designs of love toward us. We lived in our wilderness, lost and dead to God, in our hideout of Lo Debar.

But He never gave up His pursuit of us, and finally we were summoned by the Holy Spirit to hear the Gospel. We believed we would hear the words of an angry God; instead we were stunned by the words of His love and forgiveness. Our track record of rebellion and disobedience had been forgiven, dismissed in the covenant made before we were born in our representative head, the Lord Jesus. And all the riches earned by the Lord Jesus were turned over to us; we have become heirs of God and joint heirs with Jesus.

We are not treated as individuals in isolation; we do not have a private covenant with God. The covenant was made, its terms and promises made sure in Christ 2000 years ago; in all that He did, He acted for us and as us. The Gospel called us to personally enter the covenant because we were in Christ when the covenant was made.

Our decision was our response to the covenant that divine love had made: to say yes to the yes of Jesus the covenant head, to die in His death to independence and disobedience, confessing Him as Lord and in Him submitting to the Father. It meant nothing short of a death and resurrection, actually changing families. We died to being part of the family of Adam, the old man, to being included into the royal household of the new Man. Such a response meant incurring the wrath of the family of sin and darkness that we were once a part of. They would, in fact, treat us as they treated Jesus.

This takes place by the powerful work of the Holy Spirit. We, who live two millennia from the making of the covenant, are united to Jesus, our covenant head, and made part of His history, partaking of His life. We take our place at the royal table along with the royal princes and, basking in the love of our Father, we eat the meal of covenant.

Chapter 8

THE BLOOD OF GOD

We have seen that a covenant in Bible times was a matter of life and death. This was underscored throughout the ritual by the death of the covenant animal, the oath taken by the two parties, and the shedding of their own blood, which flowed down their arms as they swore to keep the covenant even to the shedding of their own blood.

For God to make the new covenant, the representative—the God Man, Jesus—had to shed His blood in death and, rising out of death, bring us the blessings of the new covenant in the authority of His shed blood.

> **Now may the God of peace who brought up our Lord Jesus from the dead, that great Shepherd of the sheep, through the blood of the everlasting covenant.**
> **Hebrews 13:20**

But what is this obsession with death that must involve the shedding of blood? Why the death of millions of animals by the shedding of their blood? Why did the love of God finally focus in the shedding of the blood of Jesus Christ?

From the beginning to the end of the Bible, we have the shedding of blood. In the Old Testament, a river of blood flows from the animals that were slain daily as sacrifices in the tabernacle and the temple. In the New Testament, the central celebration is in giving glory to the blood of Jesus that fulfilled all of the Old Testament sacrifices.

> **And they sang a new song, saying: "You are worthy to take the scroll, and to open its seals; for You were slain, and have redeemed us to God by Your blood out of every tribe and tongue and people and nation, and have made us kings and priests to our God; and we shall reign on the earth."**
> **Revelation 5:9,10**

It is not only within the pages of the Bible that we find the shedding of blood. Around the world, I have witnessed the sacrificial shedding of blood among peoples far removed from each other, with diverse forms of religion. Records of the ancients universally contain the shedding of blood in sacrifice to the gods, both animal and human sacrifice. Where did such a universal idea come from? Because it is to be found among all people and throughout history, one would have to believe that it arose in the babyhood of the human race and spread along with the spread of humankind across the earth.

Secular anthropologists tell us that it originated in the fear of the supernatural, the belief that an angry God demanded to be placated with blood. But the Bible gives us a very different picture.

Leviticus 17:11-14 is the key Scripture to understanding what lies behind the shedding of blood. The blood contains the life of the creature, **"For the life of the flesh is in the blood"** (verse 11). God, the Creator and source of all life, owns all life and the blood in which it is contained. Therefore, throughout the Bible all blood, animal as well as human, was regarded as sacred. It was never to be eaten, and when an animal was killed, its blood had to be reverently buried.

> **"No one among you shall eat blood.... Whatever man of the children of Israel, or of the strangers who dwell among you, who hunts and catches any animal or bird that may be eaten, he shall pour out its blood and cover it with dust; for**

The Blood of God

> it is the life of all flesh.... 'You shall not eat the blood of any flesh, for the life of all flesh is its blood....'"
>
> **Leviticus 17:12,13**

The first response of God to the sin of man was to give them the gift of animal sacrifice, in which the sacred lifeblood of the animal was shed in death, being poured out on behalf of the sinner under the penalty of death. The animal literally took the place of the sinner. The man or woman's sins, one's entire condition of separation from God, was placed upon the animal; then as the sinner's substitute, its lifeblood was poured out in death. The life of the substitute animal was yielded up in death by the shedding of blood to the One against whom sin had been committed.

The principle of substitutionary sacrifice was not revealed in detail to the human race until it was spelled out in minute detail in the Law of Moses:

> **"For the life of the flesh is in the blood, and I have given it to you upon the altar to make atonement for your souls; for it is the blood that makes atonement for the soul."**
>
> **Leviticus 17:11**

Although this was thousands of years after the first couple fell, the principle was true in the eyes of God from the beginning of time.

But how could the blood of an animal have any effect upon sin? There was absolutely no virtue in the blood of animals to cover the sin of humankind. Where, then, do we look for the effectiveness of animal blood through the centuries before Jesus came?

To fully understand the sacrifices, we must look backward into the secret purposes of the Trinity. We have already seen that before time and space were created, the Triune God determined in covenant love to create humankind to eternally share His life. That was decided even though God knew that man would sin and wreak havoc upon creation. It was purposed that the Father would send the Son, who would join humanity in their sinful condition, taking their place and bearing their sin in His body, pouring out His life blood for them and as them. Before time and space were created, the ultimate gift of the sacrifice of the Son had already been given in the heart and determination of God.

> ...the precious blood of Christ, as of a lamb without blemish and without spot. He indeed was foreordained before the foundation of the world, but was manifest in these last times for you.
>
> 1 Peter 1:19,20

> ...the Book of Life of the Lamb slain from the foundation of the world.
>
> Revelation 13:8

The ultimate gift of the sacrifice of God the Son, who had already been given before time, was pictured and anticipated in the gift of the blood of animals in sacrifice. Apart from the determination in the heart of God to give His Son, animal sacrifices meant less than zero. The blood of animals could not take away sin, and God was affronted by sacrifices that were presented merely as a religious ritual.

> "To what purpose is the multitude of your sacrifices to Me?" says the Lord. "I have had enough of burnt offerings of rams and the fat of fed cattle. I do not delight in the blood of bulls, or of lambs or goats."
>
> Isaiah 1:11

In itself, the pouring out of animal blood could contribute nothing to bringing a person to God. The animal sacrifices had significance and meaning only because they shadowed in time and space the sacrifice already accomplished in the heart of God from before creation, awaiting its accomplishment in earth's history. The benefits of the blood of Jesus were present to the worshippers in the Old Testament by virtue of the fact that He was slain in the heart of God from the beginning of time and shadowed in the animal sacrifices. Every animal sacrifice prepared the people for the actualization in time space history of the secret determination of God to become the substitute for His creature human.

The Bible is the only book that gives the account of when God gave the original blood sacrifice to sinful humans. When man and woman fell from their lofty position by the great disobedience and set the course of the race according to the satanic lie, they came under the penalty of death. In love, God came to the couple and initiated the unfolding of His gift of salvation, which would come to its full expression in the cross and resurrection of Jesus. At that time God gave the first promise of this salvation, announcing that there would be a seed or descendant who would crush the head of the serpent, Satan. (Genesis 3:15.)

At the same time, there is the record of what appears to be a strange act of God: He replaced the tunics of fig leaves the guilty couple had made to cover their shame and gave them instead coats of animal skin.

> **Also for Adam and his wife the Lord God made tunics of skin, and clothed them.**
>
> **Genesis 3:21**

It is obvious that for them to wear clothes made of the skin of an animal, an animal had to die. Some commentators see this as an act of God's generosity in providing them with adequate clothing, but the context points to something far more significant. If it was only a matter of clothes, what was wrong with the fiber of clothes made of fig leaves that they already had? Does God prefer fur coats? Obviously something of far greater importance is taking place here.

The key to what God was doing is in the fact that the skin coats were given to replace the fig leaves that the couple had made to cover the shame that engulfed them upon their disobedience. The fig leaves were directly connected to sin and their attempt to hide its results in their life. By giving them another covering, the Lord was saying that the fig leaves were inadequate to deal with the situation they found themselves in. Sin had left them in the state of death, of which the guilt and shame were but the immediate sensations. Something more drastic was needed that would deal with that death.

Fig leaf fiber temporarily covered the shame they experienced in each other's presence. It made them respectable. But it did not and could not deal with the guilt or the cause of it. They were in the state of death, and it was that condition that needed to be dealt with. God gave them a vivid picture that prefigured what the woman's seed, who was yet to come, would accomplish.

The first gift of God, outside of the gift of life itself, was His gift to the first man and woman of a sacrificial animal that would shed its blood in death and give to them its skin to provide for them coats to cover their nakedness. It must have been an unforgettable moment of horror in the life of the first couple. They had never seen death before, let alone death accompanied by the shedding of blood, and to know that the Creator was doing this in order that their guilt and shame might be covered would leave an indelible mark on their senses.

They could never forget that God rejected their own, rather creative idea of a covering of fig leaves and first venture into needlework as an inadequate covering. He demanded the shedding of blood to cover the result of their sin, and He acted as the Priest on behalf of the sinful couple and made the first sacrifice to Himself from among the human race.

Humankind would never forget that when approaching God they had to come as those under the penalty of death, bringing with them the gift of a substitute animal, which God had provided. Even when the nations had become lost in deep spiritual darkness and had replaced the true God with idols of every kind, still they knew by a vague memory imprinted in the race that they had to have the shedding of blood in connecting with the spirit world. Its meaning was distorted and used by demons; sometimes it took the most degraded form of human sacrifice; but the shedding of blood was always there and is so to this very day.

This explains the story of Cain and Abel found in Genesis 4:2-7. The story takes place some years after Adam and Eve were expelled from Eden. Their first two sons had become farmers. Cain grew vegetables, and Abel raised sheep. It would appear that there was a specific time when individuals came to worship God, bringing with them their offering. The phrase in the Genesis account "in the process of time" literally reads, "at the end of days," suggesting a specific time that came around after so many days had passed. It also tells us that they brought their offering "to the Lord," which suggests a specific place, probably the gates of the Garden of Eden, the dwelling of God.

Genesis 4:4 tells us, **Abel also brought of the firstborn of his flock and of their fat.** His offering was accepted. Why? Hebrews 11:4 tells us it was because of his faith:

> **By faith Abel offered to God a more excellent sacrifice than Cain, through which he obtained witness that he was righteous, God testifying of his gifts; and through it he being dead still speaks.**

Biblical faith never initiates an action; it is a responsive act of trust in a word from God. What was Abel responding to? He was responding to what he had been taught by his father, Adam, concerning that first gift of sacrifice that God had given to them in the Garden. He was coming with the blood of a lamb, which would suggest that the animal God had slain was a lamb. It is ridiculous to think that Abel happened on the right sacrifice by chance and the acceptance and witness that God gave him that he was righteous was a whim on God's part. Something was working out here that all parties knew about.

Cain, on the other hand, chose to be innovative, to reject the plain word and gift of God.

> ...**it came to pass that Cain brought an offering of the fruit of the ground.**
>
> **Genesis 4:3**

Not only was Cain deliberately refusing God's gift of the appointed way to cover sin and be accepted by Him, but he was going back to that which God had already plainly rejected. Adam and Eve had covered their guilt and shame with the fruit of the ground in the fig leaves, and God had refused it as an adequate covering.

Abel brought the lamb appointed by God that its life may be poured out for Abel's sin. Cain brought the vegetables and fruit that he had grown with his own hands and the sweat of his labor. He was bringing the best he could.

Cain brought the harvest, as if to give thanks to the Creator for His provision. He appeared to deliberately ignore the fact that there was more at stake here than saying a thank you to the Creator and provider: Sin has to be faced and dealt with, and the results of sin cannot be covered by a harvest of the best that human hands can produce. Along with the rest of the race, Cain stood under the sentence of death; and the only way out of that was for another to take his place, a life offered up and blood poured out on his behalf.

We cannot feel sorry for Cain, for he knew what God demanded. "If you do well, will you not be accepted? And if you do not do well, sin lies at the door" (verse 7). God gently reminded Cain that he knew what he had to do to be accepted, and if he didn't do what he knew to do then sin like a wild animal was crouching ready to take him.

The New Testament makes a strong statement about his offering:

The Blood of God

> **Not as Cain who was of the wicked one and murdered his brother. And why did he murder him? Because his works were evil and his brother's righteous.**
>
> 1 John 3:12

The works that the verse talks about are the fruits he brought as an offering, and they are designated evil works. Cain was not misguided but the first to go further in sin than his parents, for he rejected God's gift of salvation and substituted what he deemed to be better. It is one thing to sin; the greater evil is to refuse the God-appointed way of salvation.

His evil was the evil of a manmade religion that seeks the way of salvation by the sweat of our brow and the works of our hands, by which we would presume to please God. Such must then reject the divinely revealed and only way, which is through the sacrificial blood of Jesus, the Lamb of God, being poured out.

These stories from the dawn of man's history are the seeds from which the full understanding of the meaning of sacrifice would finally come. The Law of Moses developed these first offerings into a sacrificial system that gave a much clearer picture of Him who was to come. Every day, bloody sacrifices were made in the tabernacle and later the temple to cover the sins of the people. Each sacrifice looked forward with hope to the day when God would deal with sin in a final, all-sufficient offering.

The hope and straining toward a final offering that would take away sin and bring man and woman out of their state of death was brought into focus on one solemn day each year called the Day of Atonement.

At the center of the way of ritual and sacrifices that made up the old covenant was the high priest. He was the representative, the mediator, of the covenant on behalf of the people of Israel. When wearing his full ritual dress, he symbolically carried each tribe of Israel on his breastplate and on his shoulders by means of precious stones with the names of the tribes engraved in them. It was a vivid picture that declared to every Israelite that he or she was in the high priest, carried on his shoulders in his strength, and was ever upon his heart. Where the high priest went, there Israel went.

This all came into focus on the Day of Atonement. On this day, all the offerings that had been offered daily throughout the last year were to be summed up into one offering: a goat which was sacrificed by the high priest on behalf of all the people.

It pointed forward to the coming day when one offering would end all offerings, for He would encompass the sin of the world and fulfill the hopes of all offerings because He would deal with sin once and forever.

On that day the high priest laid aside his symbolic, richly embroidered garments and came to the people dressed in the simple white robe of a priest. Two goats that had been examined and found physically without blemish were brought, and one of them was chosen for death. The high priest, standing on behalf of the people as their representative, laid his hands on the head of the goat and confessed the sins of the people, symbolically transferring the condition of the people to the animal that would stand in their place.

If you were there in the crowd on that day, as you heard the sins being confessed you would recognize that your sins were laid on the substitute animal. It would not be an empty ritual but God's gift to you to bear away your sin. You would watch as with a quick flash of the knife the jugular vein of the goat was cut and the animal was slain and its blood caught in a basin. The sacrificed goat died as the substitute for the people, and its life-blood was poured out.

The high priest then carried the blood into the sacred precincts of the temple to its holy center, a room where no person could venture except the high priest and he only on this

The Blood of God

day. The room was separated from the rest of the temple by a veil; the sacred room was the place within the temple where the glory of God was visibly made manifest. It was a symbol of heaven, the dwelling place of God.

It takes us back to Eden, which was the first dwelling of God in His creation. Sin cast the man and the woman out of Eden, the way being barred by a sword of fire and the guard of the cherubim. The veil that cordoned off the Holy of Holies was embroidered by figures of cherubim reminiscent of the guardians of Eden. Humans could not enter the glorious presence, not because God did not love them but because their sin placed them in a relationship to God that would cause their destruction.

Inside that room, the Holy of Holies, was the ark of the covenant, a box overlaid with gold and covered by a lid of solid gold called the mercy seat, with cherubim fashioned from the gold at each end. Between the cherubim and above the mercy seat the uncreated light of the glory of God, the presence of the God of covenant, was visible.

The high priest took the blood of the goat and sprinkled it on the mercy seat. The slab of gold was already encrusted with the blood that had been sprinkled there each year for generations. The blood was the symbolic registry before God that one more time the sin of the people had been covered. The blood that stained the mercy seat was the promise of the blood of the final offering that one day would not merely cover sin but take it away forever. Every sprinkling of blood on that golden slab was a promise and an IOU given by God to God that awaited payment in the blood of Jesus.

The sacrifice on the Day of Atonement was unlike other sacrifices that took place throughout the year; there was a second part to it. At this time, the living goat that had not been chosen for sacrifice was taken; again the high priest laid his hands on it and the sins of the people were confessed over it. It was then taken and led into the wilderness and sent away, never to return.

The sending away of the second goat in full view of all the people declared in vivid imagery what had happened to their sin when the blood had been sprinkled out of sight behind the veil. Their sin was covered and lost from the eyes of God, and they could go to their homes rejoicing.

However, as dramatically as the ritual on the Day of Atonement gave them the assurance that their sin had been covered, it did not deal with sin but in fact only brought it to remembrance.

Although the animal taking the place of sinful men and women was the gift of God given to cover sin, the system had many weaknesses. To begin with, the blood of an animal carrying animal life could never be the substitute for human blood carrying the life of the one made in the image of God.

The animal victims were not willing substitutes, giving themselves in love for those for whom they died. They had been chosen and volunteered for sacrifice without their willing participation. Nor were they obeying God in being led to the altar of sacrifice. They were non-rational creatures who made no decision to die and, therefore, offered themselves neither to God nor man.

Such could never take the place of the one made in God's image who had chosen willfully to disobey the command of God. The blood of animals never dealt with sin or took it away but covered it until the sacrifice to which they pointed was made that would take away sin.

The continual sacrifices were a promise of the future day when the blood of infinite value would be shed by One who had fully obeyed God in life and in infinite love freely chose to offer Himself in death, shedding His blood on behalf of humankind. Such a sacrifice was the goal to which all animal sacrifices pointed; the shedding of His blood would bring an end to sacrifices. The need for sacrifices would be eliminated, for this offering would finally deal with sin and resurrect sinners out of their state of death. Reconciliation would be celebrated and enjoyed rather than continually reached for in the continual sacrifices of substitute animals.

For these reasons, the sacrifices of the Day of Atonement were never finished. They could not be finished until the One they pointed to came and accomplished His work. There was no chair in the Holy of Holies; the high priest never sat down after he had sprinkled the blood. He did not sit down, because sin had not been put away—only covered, only promised. The Day of Atonement finished with his work still unfinished. Along with the people, he would be back the next year to sprinkle the blood again in hope of the final offering.

> For the law, having a shadow of the good things to come, and not the very image of the things, can never with these same sacrifices, which they offer continually year by year, make those who approach perfect. For then would they not have ceased to be offered? For the worshipers, once purified, would have had no more consciousness of sins. But in those sacrifices there is a reminder of sins every year. For it is not possible that the blood of bulls and goats could take away sins.
>
> And every priest stands ministering daily and offering repeatedly the same sacrifices, which can never take away sins.
>
> Hebrews 10:1-4,11

Imagine the shock and the thrill that would go through the hearts of those who first heard the prophets announce what the new covenant would accomplish:

> "But this is the covenant that I will make with the house of Israel after those days, says the Lord. ...For I will forgive their iniquity, and their sin I will remember no more.
>
> Jeremiah 31:33,34

> Then I will sprinkle clean water on you, and you shall be clean; I will cleanse you from all your filthiness and from all your idols. I will give you a new heart and put a new spirit within you; I will take the heart of stone out of your flesh and give you a heart of flesh. I will put My Spirit within you and cause you to walk in My statutes, and you will keep My judgments and do them.
>
> Ezekiel 36:25-27

Daniel speaks of a day that would

> Finish the transgression, to make an end of sins, to make reconciliation for iniquity, to bring in everlasting righteousness, to seal up vision and prophecy ...Messiah shall be cut off, but not for Himself...Then he shall confirm a covenant with many for one week; but in the middle of the week He shall bring an end to sacrifice and offering.
>
> Daniel 9:24,26,27

God the Son would take to Himself our humanity, live out our human life, suffer and die as us, and shed the blood of God. Only then could sin be remembered no more. A blood had to be shed that transcended human blood as the Creator transcends the creature.

Jesus, the God-Man, appointed to be the High Priest of the new covenant, laid aside the glory that belonged to Him as the Son of God and came among us as a carpenter in Nazareth. He was both the High Priest and the sacrifice. On the cross He, as Priest, offered Himself as the final sacrifice that all sacrifices since the first blood shed in Eden had pointed to.

Is it not a wonder that in Eden the man and the woman actually desired the death of God so that they might take His place, but in pursuing this desire they died. God responded to their rebellion with infinite love; He placed Himself in the hands of the creature human and died with the result that the human is made alive, is forgiven and reconciled.

The Blood of God

The blood began to be shed in Gethsemane when He anticipated the horrors that awaited Him. He sweat great drops of blood through the pores of His skin. When guards came to arrest Him, His tunic was stained crimson with the blood of the covenant. It continued to be shed in the vicious torture that was inflicted upon His body, the scourging and the crown of thorns' being jammed into His forehead. It was completed on the cross with the nails through His hands and feet and finally with the spear thrust of the soldier into His side, releasing a flow of blood and water.

God the Son in our humanity, as us, was making covenant with God the Father. **The life is in the blood** (Leviticus 17:11), and in this case the blood that was shed was the physical blood of God that flowed through the veins of the God-Man Jesus Christ. It was both the blood shed from His humanity, the blood of our race, and also it was the blood of God as He swore by Himself to the terms of the covenant that He had determined to bring to pass.

We have seen that when He cried "It is finished," it was not the gasp of a man who was defeated and exhausted but the triumphant cry of the Man who had finished and accomplished what He had come to do. What began before time in the heart of God's love was accomplished in His ravaged body, shed blood, and opened wounds on the hill outside of Jerusalem.

The shedding of the blood of God in covenant brought the representative out of death and brought us with Him.

> **Now may the God of peace who brought up our Lord Jesus from the dead, that great Shepherd of the sheep, through the blood of the everlasting covenant.**
> **Hebrews 13:20**

In rising from the dead, He became the declaration that the sin that had carried Him into death had been dealt with forever and the death the sin had brought had been swallowed up. He was the announcement that now the terms of the covenant could be fulfilled in us.

Every covenant is sealed, or ratified, by blood; and the new covenant, being sealed in the blood of the Lord Jesus, is no exception. The old Gospel hymn assures us that there is "power in the blood." Although I am not going to crusade to change that, it is actually not true. The power of the new covenant is in the Holy Spirit; the authority of the covenant, which declares that it is in full effect, is the blood. The fact that the eternal blood of God has been sprinkled in the heavens is the authority that releases us from sin and ushers us into all the blessings of the new covenant.

Jesus made reference to this at the first covenant meal, which we will deal with in detail in a later chapter:

> **For this is My blood of the new covenant, which is shed for many for the remission of sins.**
> **Matthew 26:28**

The Amplified Bible captures the meaning of the phrase "My blood of the new covenant" with the extended translation: **"My blood of the new covenant, which ratifies the agreement...."**

The same event recorded by St. Luke, again in *The Amplified Bible,* gives us the meaning in its extended translation:

> **And in like manner, He took the cup after supper, saying, This cup is the new testament or covenant [ratified] in My blood, which is shed (poured out) for you.**
> **Luke 22:20**

The word *ratify* literally means to make something fixed; to give formal approval to and thereby validate or make legally valid with official sanction.[1] The blood Jesus shed is that which makes the new covenant legally valid with the official sanction of the Triune God, a reality recognized in heaven, earth, and hell.

The Blood of God

He then carried His own blood into the true Holy of Holies, the center of existence, of which the Holy of Holies in the temple was an earthly symbol. The blood of God in heaven declared that sin had been put away, never to be remembered again, that the reconciliation of humankind to God had been achieved and the new covenant ushered in.

Then He sat down, declaring that it was finally and forever done; there would never be need of another offering. The one offering of Him was the last sacrifice humankind would ever need. The covenant was made and God and humankind could sit down together in joyful union.

The epistle to the Hebrews spells out this end of all sacrifices in Jesus:

> **For Christ has not entered the holy places made with hands, which are copies of the true, but into heaven itself, now to appear in the presence of God for us; not that He should offer Himself often, as the high priest enters the Most Holy Place every year with blood of another—He then would have had to suffer often since the foundation of the world; but now, once at the end of the ages, He has appeared to put away sin by the sacrifice of Himself.**
>
> Hebrews 9:24-26
>
> **But this Man, after He had offered one sacrifice for sins forever, sat down at the right hand of God, from that time waiting till His enemies are made His footstool. For by one offering He has perfected forever those who are being sanctified. But the Holy Spirit also witnesses to us; for after He had said before, "This is the covenant that I will make with them after those days, says the Lord: I will put My laws into their hearts, and in their minds I will write them," then He adds, "Their sins and their lawless deeds I will remember no more." Now where there is remission of these, there is no longer an offering for sin.**

> Therefore, brethren, having boldness to enter the Holiest by the blood of Jesus, by a new and living way which He consecrated for us, through the veil, that is, His flesh.
>
> **Hebrews 10:12-20**

Chapter 9

THE OATH OF GOD

We have taken note that covenants in Bible times were sealed with an oath taken by both of the parties to the covenant. Their taking oaths and calling on God to be their witness was the guarantee of the covenant. In the new covenant that God makes with us, He swears by Himself; He is the guarantee both of the human and divine side that the covenant shall be made and kept. This is the absolute certainty that we have of the covenant: It is made and guaranteed by God. If the covenant had been made with us, then it would have depended upon our oath for its fulfillment and would have been broken within hours of being sworn to. But sworn to by God, it is as sure and unchangeable as God is.

> **For when God made a promise to Abraham, because He could swear by no one greater, He swore by Himself, saying, "Surely blessing I will bless you, and multiplying I will multiply you."**
>
> **Hebrews 6:13,14**

All of the announcements of the new covenant through the prophets came with the same solemn, unilateral commitment by God to do what He promised. The making of the covenant and the bringing to pass in history the promises depended solely upon God.

From the very beginning, the initiative for our salvation has come from God. Humankind has not asked Him for salvation, nor have we shown any desire to be saved. The newly fallen couple in the Garden of Eden did not show any signs of repentance; they were insolent and hiding from God, wishing that He would go away and leave them to work out their sin agenda in peace. When He spoke to them, they dodged His questions and showed no interest in confessing that they had sinned, only willing to talk about the feelings that sin had left them with.

The Holy Spirit's commentary on humankind is devastating:

> **And this is the condemnation, that the light has come into the world, and men loved darkness rather than light, because their deeds were evil.**
>
> **John 3:19**

IT ALL HANGS ON GOD

If humankind was to be saved and the eternal purpose of God to make us His sons and daughters and intimate friends realized, then God had to do it with no help from humanity. And this He swore by Himself to do.

In the Garden of Eden, a very short time after our first parents had sinned, God made a covenant with the entire human race in Adam. In it, He announced what He would do to save the race that was potential in the first couple. He announced the very first promise of their salvation and deliverance from bondage to Satan.

> **"And I will put enmity between you and the woman, and between your seed and her Seed; He shall bruise your head, and you shall bruise His heel."**
>
> **Genesis 3:15**

Notice that this promise contains no reference to humans' part in bringing it to pass; it refers only to the "I will" of God. He was the guarantee of the covenant salvation that He announced. He committed Himself to placing a supernatural enmity between humankind and the serpent that would culminate in the coming of a certain seed who would utterly defeat the serpent, crushing his head. There were no "ifs," no conditions that humans must fulfill if this wonder were to come to pass in their history, only the unconditional announcement that hung on the oath of God.

As the history of the race unfolded and humans plunged further and further from God, He announced His intention to bless humankind through the seed of Abraham. Again, He swore by Himself:

> "Blessing I will bless you, and multiplying I will multiply your descendants as the stars of the heaven and as the sand which is on the seashore; and your descendants shall possess the gate of their enemies. In your seed all the nations of the earth shall be blessed, because you have obeyed My voice."
>
> Genesis 22:17,18

As the promises and prophecies of the Old Testament unfolded, the details of the salvation that would be contained in the new covenant were made known. They were made with a series of "I will's," declarations made by God of what He would unilaterally do:

> "But this is the covenant that I will make with the house of Israel after those days, says the Lord: I will put My law in their minds, and write it on their hearts; and I will be their God, and they shall be My people. No more shall every man teach his neighbor, and every man his brother, saying, 'Know the Lord,' for they all shall know Me, from the least of them to the greatest of them, says the Lord. For I will forgive their iniquity, and their sin I will remember no more."
>
> Jeremiah 31:33,34

> "Then I will sprinkle clean water on you, and you shall be clean; I will cleanse you from all your filthiness and from all your idols. I will give you a new heart and put a new spirit

within you; I will take the heart of stone out of your flesh and give you a heart of flesh. I will put My Spirit within you and cause you to walk in My statutes, and you will keep My judgments and do them."

Ezekiel 36:25-27

In Daniel's prophecy, He announced that He had determined or carved out a period of time in which He would accomplish a certain work.

> "Seventy weeks are determined for your people and for your holy city, to finish the transgression, to make an end of sins, to make reconciliation for iniquity, to bring in everlasting righteousness, to seal up vision and prophecy, and to anoint the Most Holy."

Daniel 9:24

For God to swear by Himself to accomplish the promises of the covenant is shocking; it means that if He did not perform the terms of the covenant, then He would cease to be and all creation would fall into nothingness. His spoken word would be enough, for He is the God who cannot lie; but in order that we would have an understanding of His absolute, unchangeable purpose, He added to His word a covenant oath. We are given a covenant oath by which we may never doubt that He will fulfill every word of the covenant promises to all who call upon Him.

> For men indeed swear by the greater, and an oath for confirmation is for them an end of all dispute. Thus God, determining to show more abundantly to the heirs of promise the immutability of His counsel, confirmed it by an oath, that by two immutable things, in which it is impossible for God to lie, we might have strong consolation, who have fled for refuge to lay hold of the hope set before us.

Hebrews 6:16-18

These promises, bound to fulfillment by the oath of God, cover every cry of the hearts of human beings in their state of sin and spiritual darkness. They guarantee that God will:

- Remove their guilt and shame, freeing them from the authority of sin and death.
- Give them the motive, desire, and enabling power to live in love for God and their neighbors.
- Cause them to belong to Him, bringing them into the covenant family of God.
- Free them from bondage to Satan and all the power of darkness.
- Grant them the knowledge that God is with them, blessing them and all they do.
- Bring them into union with Himself, placing His Spirit within them.

THE FAITHFULNESS OF GOD

Another word that drew me into discovering the covenant as the foundation upon which the faith of the men and women of God in Scripture stood was the word "faithfulness." His faithfulness is the outworking of His covenant oath. He did not need, as humans do, to swear an oath in order to bind Himself to keep the covenant. The covenant does not make Him what He would not otherwise be but is the means of revealing to us who He eternally is.

The root Hebrew word for "faithfulness" is *aman*,[1] which means "to be certain, enduring, to trust or believe." From this root, we have three words. The first word is *amen,* which we translate into English as "amen" or "so it is." The second word is *emet,* which is translated as "truth" or "true." And the third word is *emunah,*[2] which simply means "faithfulness." Put all of these together and we have a God who is infinitely reliable, to be counted on at all times, constant, and unchangeable.

> **If we are faithless, He remains faithful; He cannot deny Himself.**
>
> 2 Timothy 2:13
>
> **"For I am the Lord, I do not change...."**
>
> Malachi 3:6

All that God is, He always is; He never contradicts Himself or acts in a way that is inconsistent with Himself. He cannot improve any more than He can degenerate. Who He is, is who He was and forever will be.

> **Every good gift and every perfect gift is from above, and comes down from the Father of lights, with whom there is no variation or shadow of turning.**
>
> James 1:17

James undoubtedly had the sun, moon, and planets at least in mind when he wrote this verse. The sun is the light of our solar system, and the word "turning" was used to describe the rotating of the planets, which always left one side in the dark. God has no dark side; He is the Father of uncreated radiant light, and in Him there is no shadow, no darkness. There is no change or variation in Him; all that He was, He is and ever shall be.

I stand in my garden, and it is in a state of constant change as the sun moves across the sky; the shadows change, come, and go, until finally all is in the shadow of twilight.

I do not come to God wondering what will have changed in Him today; He does not turn and change. We can be utterly sure that He will be unchangeably the same forever.

The Message captures this with its paraphrase: **The gifts are rivers of light cascading down from the Father of Light. There is nothing deceitful in God, nothing two-faced, nothing fickle.**

His faithfulness is often described as His being the Rock:

The Oath of God

He is the Rock, His work is perfect; for all His ways are justice, a God of truth and without injustice; righteous and upright is He.
Deuteronomy 32:4

The Lord is my rock and my fortress and my deliverer; my God, my strength, in whom I will trust; my shield and the horn of my salvation, my stronghold.
Psalm 18:2

He is incapable of making a promise that He cannot perform, for every word He says is the perfect expression of who He is. His Word is in complete accord with reality; His Word and deed are one. For Him to speak His Word is for it to be done, even though it may take centuries to be made manifest in history. He knows the end from the beginning; therefore, there is no contingency that could arise that would not have been taken into consideration and worked into His purpose.

"So shall My word be that goes forth from My mouth; it shall not return to Me void, but it shall accomplish what I please, and it shall prosper in the thing for which I sent it."
Isaiah 55:11

Blessed be the Lord, who has given rest to His people Israel, according to all that He promised. There has not failed one word of all His good promise, which He promised through His servant Moses.
1 Kings 8:56

O Lord, You are my God. I will exalt You, I will praise Your name, for You have done wonderful things; Your counsels of old are faithfulness and truth.
Isaiah 25:1

The covenant faithfulness and lovingkindness meet in Him. He is the faithfulness and lovingkindness of God walking among us in flesh. He does not have the truth; He is the truth:

Jesus said to him, "I am the way, the truth, and the life. No one comes to the Father except through Me."
John 14:6

> Now I saw heaven opened, and behold, a white horse. And He who sat on him was called Faithful and True, and in righteousness He judges and makes war.
>
> **Revelation 19:11**
>
> Therefore, in all things He had to be made like His brethren, that He might be a merciful and faithful High Priest in things pertaining to God, to make propitiation for the sins of the people.
>
> **Hebrews 2:17**

THE NATURE OF FAITH

Biblical faith looks outside of itself to the God who made the promises. It rests solely on the character of God and the covenant oath that He has sworn. Faith is the committing of one's whole person—past, present, and future—to the faithfulness of God, knowing that He cannot deny Himself. Faith is totally absorbed with its object, the God of covenant; the believer's faith is as sure as the faithfulness of the One he or she rests in.

We live in a world filled with definitions of faith given to us by advocates of self-help, positive thinking, New Age, and witchcraft. Many of these definitions have found their way into the Christian media and greatly affect the way Christians understand what faith is. Sincere believers caught in this deception seek to bring to pass the promise of God with a pseudo faith born of the flesh that is both futile and wreaks havoc in the believer's walk with God.

Let us quickly look at what biblical faith is not.

Faith is not an energy that resides within the believer. It is not a power that, when built up and focused, the believer has the ability to use to make things happen, even to the point of forcing God's hand. Faith is not a work, a struggle to arrive at a state of mind where the hoped-for blessing can be seen or felt as being possessed.

The Oath of God

There are thousands of believers who look upon the acquisition of faith as a mental struggle, the intense focusing of thoughts on a desired object or promise in order to bring it into being. This is a work of the flesh arising from the creature mind and has nothing to do with the faith the Bible speaks of, which is a rest in God.

Others understand faith as being in the words of a promise found in Scripture. The words of the promise are repeated, as if their continual repetition will draw the desired blessing into physical existence. This reduces the holy words of Scripture to the level of a magic spell in which God is being manipulated into doing what He has said.

The Christian understanding of faith radically parts company with witchcraft, New Age, positive thinking, and self-help. All of these have in common the using of words as a formula for gaining a desired end. The faith of the Christian has nothing to do with formulas or spells but is rooted in the relationship with God that has been established by covenant. Faith is not directed at the words of a promise but rests in the One who made the promise.

Biblical faith is not found within us, either as a natural energy or as a labor, but in beholding and responding to His faithfulness to His covenant oath. We trust in His character that what He has spoken, He will do.

Faith is to be likened to the eye of the spirit. The physical eye is not aware of itself unless there is something wrong. The eye functions by seeing and recording an object. If it becomes self-conscious and is ever looking at itself to see how good an eye it is, then it ceases to function as an eye. Likewise, faith is not self-conscious, morbidly checking on itself to gauge its strength, but is continually looking at its object, God revealed in the Lord Jesus.

Faith comes from a revelation of the love and faithfulness of God specifically revealed in Jesus, who is the covenant. He is the author and finisher of our faith. (Hebrews 12:2.)

> **So then faith comes by hearing, and hearing by the word of God.**
>
> **Romans 10:17**

The Word of God is more than the words written on the pages of our Bible. The Word of God ultimately is Jesus, the Son of God who became flesh and lived among us. (John 1:1-14.) He is the final out-speaking of God to us.

Faith is a relationship with Him, a submission and obedience to Him, and so we read of "the obedience of faith." Faith is not a mental marathon with the goal of bringing to pass our agenda using a formula fashioned out of the words of Scripture. Faith never forces the hand of God but submits to Him, responding to His covenant words knowing that He who promised is faithful to perform them. Faith is trust in God, who He is, and what He has done. From that trust arises our belief that He will be faithful and do as He has said.

When God made covenant with Abraham it is said that **And he believed in the Lord, and He accounted it to him for righteousness** (Genesis 15:6). First of all, he believed the Lord, and then he believed the words of the promise made by the One he counted faithful.

We speak much of Abraham's faith in the birth of Isaac, but what about Sarah? It was her ancient body that was renewed to bear a child! This was not by gritting her teeth to make it happen but by faith in His faithfulness:

> **By faith Sarah herself also received strength to conceive seed, and she bore a child when she was past the age, because she judged Him faithful who had promised.**
>
> **Hebrews 11:11**

The Oath of God

The fact that the Gospel contained in the covenant is based solely on the oath of God separates Christianity from every other religion on earth. Until we see this, our Gospel will not in fact be Good News but a distortion of the truth, jagged rocks on which the believer sooner or later wrecks his or her life.

The Christian life is not approached with gritted teeth, summoning determination and willpower to obey God and show Him our love for Him. The sincere folk who try to do so are found dedicating their lives to God on a regular basis in an effort to summon the ultimate strength from their flesh to live the life of Jesus. They make promises they can never keep and sooner or later burn out, walking away from the church in despair of ever being good enough. They see the Christian life based on their oath, instead of resting in the oath of God.

Nor is the Christian life a shared effort between God and the believer. Thousands set out to live the Christian life with promises and dedications, while calling on God to help them. God does not lend a hand to help our efforts to achieve the impossible. We are utterly helpless, and the life described in the covenant is brought to pass by God alone on the basis of His oath.

There are others who plainly do not expect to live the Christian life! Such persons would actually describe the Christian life in terms of wallowing in their guilt and shame and their impotency to live it! They call to God for mercy like a beggar asking for a quarter. They continually cry to God for His help and salvation without any genuine expectancy of receiving it, for they know nothing of the oath of God in which He has committed Himself to answer our cry. Some of them would be shocked and offended if God did answer, for they would feel deprived of the miserable cry for mercy that they call their Christian life!

It is in the oath of God that we discover the uniqueness of the Gospel. The key words of the Gospel are not "struggle," "try," and "try harder" but "surrender to," "yield to," "rest in," and "believe on the Lord Jesus," who is the covenant. All these words indicate that we have come to the end of our struggles and failing attempts to live a godly life and have come to stake our hope on who He is, what He has promised and achieved.

MY DISCOVERY OF THE FAITHFULNESS OF GOD

From the beginning of my Christian life, I lived in a continual struggle to be a victorious Christian. As a young man, I had knelt in my kitchen and asked Jesus to come into my life and save me and do with me as He wanted. Soon after that, I became part of a local church. They knew the power of the Spirit but knew little or nothing of the grace of God or His initiative of love in being the prime mover in salvation. Certainly, they knew nothing of His covenant oath to save us. A life of holiness, as they understood it, was a matter of keeping God's rules and the rules of the church and a strict regime of Bible reading, prayer, and witnessing to those outside the church.

Our salvation seemed to hinge on the Sunday evening service; we all knew what was coming and braced ourselves. With amazing insight, the pastor would expose all the sins of the congregation committed during the previous week and assure us of the impending judgment of God. At the end of the service, we fearfully trooped forward to ask God to forgive us, trying to explain to Him that we had not meant to act so sinfully in the past week. The tone of our voices was somewhere between a whine and a wail as becomes those trying to convince deity that they are sorry. We would then promise that we would read our Bible, pray, and win the lost in this new week. By the time we would go back to our seats for the closing hymn, our mood was optimistic and we were enthused, ready to become saints by the next Sunday.

The Oath of God

Monday was always a day of victory. With my dedication of the previous evening clear in my mind, I would be awake by five and out of bed to read my Bible, pray, and set my schedule to win my school to Christ. I went to school ready to attack any unsuspecting soul with a question concerning their eternal salvation. On Tuesday, it was harder to get out of bed; the Bible reading was through half-closed eyes, and the prayer rambling and fuzzy. The plan to win the class to Christ was seen as a half-wits dream. Invariably by Wednesday I would sleep late and rush from the house without prayer, Bible reading, or plans to witness. I remember the feelings of shame that swept over me throughout the day. I had stood God up on a date! I could not face Him and did my best to avoid thinking about Him, certain that He was mad at me. All my resolutions to overcome temptation came crashing down, and by Thursday there was no attempt to pray and the Bible sat on the shelf. I managed by Friday to forget what I had promised the last Sunday! What was the point? I was certain that God was disgusted with me, and the best I could do was to forget about Him. Saturday came with the nagging reminder that Sunday was only hours away. With Sunday would come the inevitable Sunday night. Once more, I would join the other teens that slunk shamefully to the front of the church auditorium to explain to God that we didn't mean to live as we had done in the last week but this week would be different.

Week after week we would rededicate our rededications! No one seemed perturbed by this continual restarting of our Christian life. In fact, the pastor seemed pleased that so many responded to his message indicating that they wanted to live for God. He seemed to have forgotten it was the same people every week that populated the front of the church. The older members of the congregation did not join us but beamed at us from their pews as if something wonderful was happening in our lives. I often wondered why they didn't join us—now I wonder if it was because they had given up on the whole thing as a lost cause and were indulging the enthusiasm of the youth.

One day I was reading my Bible—it must have been early in the week! I was in Jeremiah 31 reading the terms of the new covenant. Now, believe me, I did not know what a covenant was or that the Gospel was the announcement of the new covenant. I didn't even know that there was an old one!

I found myself reading the words with interest even though they were in the *King James Version,* which was an awkward read for me at the time. They reached out to me and drew me into them.

> **"But this is the covenant that I will make with the house of Israel after those days, says the Lord: I will put My law in their minds, and write it on their hearts; and I will be their God, and they shall be My people. No more shall every man teach his neighbor, and every man his brother, saying, 'Know the Lord,' for they all shall know Me, from the least of them to the greatest of them, says the Lord. For I will forgive their iniquity, and their sin I will remember no more."**
>
> **Jeremiah 31:33,34**

I read the words over and over. **"I will put My law in their minds, and write it on their hearts."** I realized that my concept of the law of God was something outside of me, an imposition that interfered with my way of life. The very idea that this verse promised that the law would no longer be outside of me, demanding of me a life I could not live and condemning me when I inevitably failed, excited me as nothing in the Bible ever had before.

I read on: **"I will be their God, and they shall be My people."** To be able to know Him as *my* God and for Him to include me as being part of the company who uniquely belonged to Him brought an unspeakable yearning in my heart. I realized I had never thought of Him as *my* God and certainly never thought of myself as belonging in a special way to Him.

The Oath of God

> "No more shall every man teach his neighbor, and every man his brother, saying, 'Know the Lord,' for they all shall know Me, from the least of them to the greatest of them, says the Lord...."
>
> Jeremiah 31:34

As I read these words, it dawned on me that in the short time I had been a Christian I had not really known Him; I had known about Him and the behaviors I was supposed to adopt as a believer. There rose in me a longing to have a firsthand relationship with Him instead of the rules to live by that I had come to associate with being a Christian.

It was the last phrase that arrested my attention: **"For I will forgive their iniquity, and their sin I will remember no more."** I could hardly believe what I read. God would not remember my sins anymore! My experience of Christianity in weekly church attendance meant that we continually remembered and mourned over our sins. Every week we were reminded in great detail of our sins—that is what going to church seemed to be about. We were preached upon week after week about the standard we must uphold in order for God to accept us. Consequently, many of us wallowed in our sense of shame and guilt, thus making us feel as if God was constantly angry at us because of our sin.

What life was this Scripture talking about? A life where there was no sense of guilt and shame before the God who knew every thought that passed through my mind, every word on my tongue, and every act I did.

These were incredible words. I had never heard of such a life, and in that early dawn kneeling in my bedroom I wanted it more than anything I had ever wanted before.

How did one get it? What did I have to do? I had been drilled since becoming a Christian that there was a price to pay, a dedication to make, in order to get something from God. What was the price tag here? What did I have to do receive such a life? I read the passage over and over again, searching for what I was convinced must be an enormous price tag.

Nothing! Instead, what stood out to me was the reiteration of "I will" throughout the passage. The two verses plainly stated that it was God's intention to do these things and there was no price tag for me to pay. In that moment, I saw for the first time the nature of faith. Faith did not originate in my making promises with ever-increasing intensity and determination, promises that I had no hope of keeping. Nor was it my vowed intentions to be a better Christian for Him. Rather, it was in my simply saying thank You for the promises He had made, submitting to His intention for me.

This was radical, turning everything I had understood of the Gospel on its head. My starting point was no longer me but Him, and my part was not to say "I promise to try harder" but to respond to Him and say "Yes! Do in me even as You have said."

A great joy swept through my being. For the first time I was excited about the Gospel, and I went to school as if I were walking on air. All week long I reveled in my newfound God, who had made the promises and was responsible for keeping them. I knew life in Christ that I had never dreamed possible. No longer did I get up to pray to somehow win God's favor, but to know this incredible God who made promises to a teenager like me!

Sunday night rolled around, and I sat smiling through the pastor's tirade. I joined the regular trek to the front and fell on my knees with the others. Instead of my usual burying my face in my hands, I lifted my face and prayed, "I promise You that I will never make another promise to You! You made the promises, You keep them, and I thank You for it! Amen." I stood to my feet, leaving my brothers and sisters wailing on the floor, and went back to my seat, smiling with the joy of God in my heart.

After that week, I had many ups and downs, falls, and failures in my walk with God, but what I had seen never left me. Sometimes I would wander confused, but I remembered what I had seen and knew that was the key to life. Like a strike of lightning on a pitch-black night, for a moment everything had been clearly seen and could not be forgotten. It was many years later that I realized I had been led by the Spirit to rest my life on the covenant oath of God.

LIVING IN RELIANCE UPON HIS OATH

This is the first step in living the Christian life. It is also the energy behind every step; we never graduate from that state of helpless dependence upon Him. We will never be able (and God never intended that we would be able) to achieve the promises of the covenant in our own strength or willpower. We are utterly helpless to bring them to pass, to make them happen by resolve, dedication, or twelve-step programs. We invoke the God who has made covenant, swearing by Himself, to achieve all of this in our lives. We thank Him for His mercy in giving us the covenant but now call upon His faithfulness to keep it.

So we do not attempt to cleanse ourselves but lay before Him the case of our sins and weaknesses, our idols and filthiness, and call on Him to do what we never can achieve by our promises: wash us and cleanse us from it all.

> **If we confess our sins, He is faithful and just to forgive us our sins and to cleanse us from all unrighteousness.**
> **1 John 1:9**

I remember when this verse first made its impact on me. I was puzzled by the word "faithful"; I did not associate it with someone forgiving another. I thought of other words that would fit much better, such as "kind," "compassionate," or "loving"; but "faithful" did not fit. To whom or what was He being faithful when He forgave us? When I discovered that faithfulness is one of the great covenant words of Scripture, it made perfect sense. In forgiving us, He is being faithful to the covenant, to Jesus the covenant representative, to whom He swore He would remember our sins and iniquities no more.

It is He who must write the law upon our hearts and minds, place His Spirit within us, and cause us to walk in His ways. We lay our weakness and the pull of the flesh before Him and say plainly, "This is Your work to draw me into Your ways." The entire Christian life is lived out on the sure foundation of His faithfulness to His covenant word that He will do in us what He set out to do.

> **Being confident of this very thing, that He who has begun a good work in you will complete it until the day of Jesus Christ.**
>
> **Philippians 1:6**
>
> **God is faithful, by whom you were called into the fellowship of His Son, Jesus Christ our Lord.**
>
> **1 Corinthians 1:9**
>
> **Let us hold fast the confession of our hope without wavering, for He who promised is faithful.**
>
> **Hebrews 10:23**

In covenant oath, God has taken it upon Himself to conform our entire persons to the image of the Lord Jesus, to write His law upon our hearts. Most of us at least act as if it were entirely on our shoulders: We have to attempt to achieve our sanctification, while God is the judge who grades our poor efforts.

> **Now may the God of peace Himself sanctify you completely; and may your whole spirit, soul, and body be preserved blameless at the coming of our Lord Jesus Christ. He who calls you is faithful, who also will do it.**
>
> **1 Thessalonians 5:23,24**

The Oath of God

Our feelings about our salvation ride a roller coaster as temptations and trials whirl about us. The anchor that holds us steady is not faith in our willpower or the constancy of our feelings but His faithfulness, by which He has promised to save us.

No temptation has overtaken you except such as is common to man; but God is faithful, who will not allow you to be tempted beyond what you are able, but with the temptation will also make the way of escape, that you may be able to bear it.

1 Corinthians 10:13

Our shield in the day we battle with the powers of darkness is utter reliance upon His faithfulness. We are shielded by His resolve to save and keep us. If we were shielded by our resolves, our shield would be made of cardboard! However, we have invincible armor when we are sheltered behind the oath of God.

He shall cover you with His feathers, and under His wings you shall take refuge; His faithfulness will be your shield and buckler.

Psalm 91:4

His faithfulness stands guard over us whether we are awake or asleep, keeping us from the powers of darkness. We walk without fear, knowing that He has sworn with covenant oath to keep us.

But the Lord is faithful, who will establish you and guard you from the evil one.

2 Thessalonians 3:3

Understanding the oath of God takes all of the pressure and tension out of life and introduces us into the rest of God. The whole burden of bringing the promises of the covenant to pass in our lives is upon God. Instead of laboring to exhaustion trying to please God, we live in the rest of faith in His faithfulness.

Chapter 10

ENTERING THE COVENANT

The covenant, above everything else, means union, the coming together of two parties to make a functional one. In the making of the old human covenants, the parties took each other's name to indicate that they were united as one. But in the new covenant we do not merely take His name, but His Spirit actually joins us to Him and we are made truly one. **But he who is joined to the Lord is one spirit with Him** (1 Corinthians 6:17). The miracle of the new birth, by which we pass from the death of sin into the eternal life of the new covenant, is to be understood as our being actually joined to Christ.

Union with Christ is not to be thought of as an advanced mystical experience, a higher life reserved for the elite, but the common experience of the whole body of believers. To become a Christian is to enter into Christ and partake of His life and be His vehicle of living on earth.

This is seen clearly in Jesus' parable of the lost sheep recorded in Luke 15. In order to find the lost sheep, the shepherd went into the wilderness treading the same path as the sheep had trodden in its journey away from the shepherd. He entered into the wilderness where the sheep was and participated in its lost condition without his being lost. He came to where the sheep was and united the sheep to himself, wrapping it around his neck so that it might participate in his life and strength. The union of the shepherd with the sheep and the union of the sheep with the shepherd were the sheep's salvation, the way out of the wilderness.

So Jesus is God coming to where we are, joining us in our lost condition without being lost Himself, taking to Himself our death and carrying us out in His resurrection. We now must be united to Him, partake of His life and strength, and be taken into intimate fellowship with Him and be where He is.

He merited the covenant as and for us; we must now be united to Him, and in Him inherit all that He gained for us. God does not give us the blessings of new covenant as isolated individuals selected for our worthiness or something that we have done. Nowhere does the Scripture say that any blessing or promise of the covenant is given to Malcolm based on his merits. Jesus, our representative Man, merited all the blessings of the covenant by His obedience. He was not earning them for Himself—He did not need them; He was earning them as and for each one of us. Therefore, every blessing is given to Him, and we receive them because we are "in" Him. We have been made "joint-heirs" with Him and so receive all the benefits of covenant as Him: **If children, then heirs—heirs of God and joint heirs with Christ...** (Romans 8:17).

How do we enter the covenant? All has been done as and for us in Christ, our representative Man. How do we become involved in the covenant commitment and the covenant promises that He has earned for us?

Peter quoted from the prophet Joel instruction on entering the covenant:

> **And it shall come to pass that whoever calls on the name of the Lord shall be saved....**
>
> **Joel 2:32**

Entering the Covenant

In Bible times, the name of a person was understood to be a window to one's true person, who one was, and one's accomplishments. The name of the Lord is an expression that means the revelation God has given to us of who He is and what He has done. The Gospel is the Good News concerning who God is and what He has done in Christ.

To call on the name of the Lord means to invoke that revelation, asking Him to be to us who He has declared He is. He has revealed Himself in the Lord Jesus as the God of love, the covenant-making One. All that we can do is call on that revelation. God achieved the covenant, and our only action is to receive it in grateful faith. All we can do is to respond to the initiative of God's love and believe on His covenant oath.

But the revelation of God comes with the inevitable revelation of who we are. Our response to the Good News of the covenant is in itself a response to our realizing our condition before God. We call on His name because we have come to see that we are in need of the covenant and are dead without Him.

Jesus said that He came to seek and to save the lost. If we have no sense of being lost, then we have no excitement that Jesus is the way out of our trackless wilderness. He also said that He did not come to call the righteous but sinners to repentance. If we do not see ourselves as sinners, we have no interest in the mission of Jesus and do not see ourselves as part of it. His promises of total forgiveness are only of interest to those who know that they have sinned and are in need of divine forgiveness. Promises of forgiveness are of no interest to the person who has no consciousness of sin. That He would write His law on our hearts is of no interest to people who are unacquainted with their own helplessness to love God and walk in love with all people. The heart of the covenant calls us to union with Him; unless we desire such a relationship, at least to some degree, we will find the prospect boring and dismiss the offered covenant relationship with a yawn.

But it is unnatural for humankind to want God. Men love the darkness of the lie rather than the exposing light that is in God, and we would stay in the darkness hiding from the burning light of truth until we perished if left to ourselves. The awareness of our need and the first flickering desire to know God is awakened in our hearts by the call of God reaching into our darkness.

He comes to us in the dead ends of life as we face the chaos of our lives apart from Him. He comes to us in the futility of our false religion that leaves us empty and lifeless. He calls to us when death seems very near. His voice is interpreted to us as longings, yearnings after the nameless God, or even longings after that which we cannot define with words.

It is God who initiates the covenant, and it is He who as the Shepherd calls into our wilderness, as He did to Adam, "Where are you?" Our first awareness of a need of God is actually our awakened desire to respond to God, who calls us to Himself. If we follow that light, we will be led to Him who is the Way, the Truth, the Life, and the covenant.

The Gospel is not only information about the life, death, and resurrection of Jesus. In the proclaiming of the Gospel, Jesus, alive and glorified, actually comes to us and confronts us with His love by the Holy Spirit. The news of who He is and what He has done is also the presence of that One by the Spirit. In that announcement, He opens our eyes: We have a confrontation, a meeting, with the living Jesus. The preachers of the New Testament did not see themselves as talking about Jesus but proclaiming Him, the living One, actually present with them and in their words:

> Then Philip went down to the city of Samaria and preached Christ to them. Then Philip opened his mouth, and beginning at this Scripture, preached Jesus to him.
>
> Acts 8:5,35
>
> For I will not dare to speak of any of those things which Christ has not accomplished through me, in word and deed, to make the Gentiles obedient—in mighty signs and wonders, by the power of the Spirit of God, so that from Jerusalem and round about to Illyricum I have fully preached the gospel of Christ.
>
> Romans 15:18,19
>
> For since, in the wisdom of God, the world through wisdom did not know God, it pleased God through the foolishness of the message preached to save those who believe.
>
> But we preach Christ crucified, to the Jews a stumbling block and to the Greeks foolishness, but to those who are called, both Jews and Greeks, Christ the power of God and the wisdom of God.
>
> And I, brethren, when I came to you, did not come with excellence of speech or of wisdom declaring to you the testimony of God. For I determined not to know anything among you except Jesus Christ and Him crucified.
>
> 1 Corinthians 1:21,23,24; 2:1,2

In response to the proclaiming of the Gospel, whether in church, in an auditorium, or in a one-to-one conversation, the listener actually meets with Jesus, the love of God incarnate, resurrected and ascended, who has accomplished our salvation. In the proclaiming of the Gospel, the power of God is dynamically present, bringing salvation:

> For I am not ashamed of the gospel of Christ, for it is the power of God to salvation for everyone who believes, for the Jew first and also for the Greek.
>
> Romans 1:16

It is this power resident in the living Jesus, who comes to the lost in the preaching of the Gospel, that terrifies Satan, the god of this world. He works continually to blind the minds of unbelievers lest in Jesus, the Word of God, they should know the light of God's glory and the calling forth to be united to His death and resurrection:

> **Whose minds the god of this age has blinded, who do not believe, lest the light of the gospel of the glory of Christ, who is the image of God, should shine on them. For we do not preach ourselves, but Christ Jesus the Lord.... For it is the God who commanded light to shine out of darkness, who has shone in our hearts to give the light of the knowledge of the glory of God in the face of Jesus Christ.**
>
> 2 Corinthians 4:4-6

In Jesus' coming to us in the words of the Gospel, we meet with the love of God reaching out to embrace us, the light of God revealing what He has done for us. In the Gospel, He brings to us the news that we have been included into Him, that He is the way out of the state of death, out from under the condemnation of the law. In Him, we meet with the oath and faithfulness of God, the covenant now accomplished.

We are not signing up to submit to a list of rules, but entering in to relationship with the Triune God in Christ Jesus. To accept the Gospel is to accept Him, submitting to Him as the only truth. In so doing, we renounce all of our attempts to find meaning to life, recognizing them to have been pathetic, shabby counterfeits to be turned from for what they truly are—sinful rebellion that sought to find the meaning of life independently of God.

Throughout the rest of our Christian life we will grow in the knowledge of the divine love, of who Jesus is and what He has done. When we first meet Him and submit to Him, we know very little of what we are doing. We are giving all we know of ourselves (which is very little) to all we know of Him (which is even less).

Entering the Covenant

Faith does not believe about Jesus; it does not simply believe something is true—the devils believe in that fashion. Faith is trust, believing *on* rather than a believing *in* or *about*. It is the commitment to obey and bring our lives into conformity to the newly discovered truth.

To submit to Jesus in the Gospel demands that we turn away from all that we falsely believed to be the meaning and way to life. The word that describes this aspect of the Gospel is *repentance,* which means a radical change of mind.[1] It is the realization that all of one's life has been wrong because it has been lived from the wrong center. It is not repenting of a certain sin, but a change of mind about oneself, realizing that he or she is lost and does not know the way to life. It is a definite act in which one turns from what he or she thought was life, now recognizing it as death.

The real issue now, in fact, is not sin. The Jesus who comes to us in the Gospel has dealt with sin. The issue now is whether we will accept the divine amnesty, let Him send away our sins from us, and be reconciled to God. Will we turn from our self-sufficiency and submit to love? We are confronted with the love of God and the action of His love in Jesus, and the whole issue now is whether we will turn from our independence, our faith in the lie, and submit to the love of God and His gift of covenant in Jesus.

Many years ago before airports were ruled by the fear of terrorists and airlines were computerized, there were none of the checkpoints we have to go through today. It was a lot easier to get on a plane. I was flying from Los Angeles to New York, and some minutes after we had taken off, the captain welcomed us aboard and proceeded to tell us that the flight was headed to Phoenix, and we would be landing shortly. I was on the wrong flight! That meant everything was wrong. I had the wrong stewardess, the wrong seat, the wrong person in the seat next to me, the wrong snack—everything that I should have had was on another flight. I could not repent of being in the wrong seat, or of sitting next to the wrong passenger; they were part of a bigger package of wrong I had gotten myself into.

Repentance is the sickening realization that we are wrong because we are going in the wrong direction, with a wrong definition of life, with a wrong image of who we are and a distorted image of God, not knowing Him as love. The Gospel is the announcement that we can change planes in midair! We can abandon the way of the lie and receive forgiveness, be reconciled to God, and be made His child—or we can commit the ultimate sin, which is to refuse the covenant and entrench ourselves in our sin.

So the emphasis of repentance is not so much our turning from sin, though that is obviously there, but rather our turning to Jesus, the Son of God, in whom are the covenant and our salvation. To refuse Him is to perish.

He who believes in the Son has everlasting life; and he who does not believe the Son shall not see life, but the wrath of God abides on him.

John 3:36

That one act will be established and confirmed for the rest of our lives as we continually discover the futility of life lived independently of God. As we behold the love of God, we see with increasing clarity the horror and corruption of sin and live a life of turning from it.

When I first came to America from England, I came across the Atlantic on the SS France. It took a week, and about the third day out from Southampton, the captain announced that we were running directly into Hurricane Donna and we would have to change our course. It took more than an hour to turn that great ship to its new course. I realized as I stood on the deck watching the turnaround take place that repentance, the changing of our life course, is the decision of a moment that will take a long time to work out.

Repentance is always joined to faith. Faith is the helpless submission of my total self to the news of the action of God's love in Christ Jesus. To the extent of my understanding I say yes to the news that He has included us in the covenant through the journey of Jesus through death and resurrection as and for us.

Faith that helplessly submits to and rests in Jesus, who He is and what He has done, is alien to the man or woman who believes one must be independent and self-sufficient. We who have been part of the world system, married to the lie, find it so hard to say the yes of faith to the oath of God. The only response to life that we have ever known is to the inviolable rule that a person gets what he or she deserves. But the covenant confronts us with the God who loves us unconditionally and rewards us not according to what we have done but according to what Jesus has done. To believe this is the first radical change of mind that believing the Gospel demands of us.

In the New Testament, this act of repentance and faith in the person and work of Christ always came to focus in baptism, the dipping of a person into water, or pouring it on them, invoking the name of the Trinity. Many object to this, but I ask you to bear with me and see that baptism was unquestionably part of the salvation process in the New Testament.

Jesus included it into His instructions to the disciples regarding the content of their message when He sent them into the entire world:

> **And Jesus came and spoke to them, saying, "All authority has been given to Me in heaven and on earth. Go therefore and make disciples of all the nations, baptizing them in the name of the Father and of the Son and of the Holy Spirit, teaching them to observe all things that I have commanded you; and lo, I am with you always, even to the end of the age."**
> **Matthew 28:18-20**

> And He said to them, "Go into all the world and preach the gospel to every creature. He who believes and is baptized will be saved; but he who does not believe will be condemned.
> Mark 16:15,16

Certainly the apostles understood that baptism was the act where repentance and faith came to focus. The command to be baptized is contained in the very first call to receive the Gospel; and being baptized designated as Christians those who received the message into their hearts.

> Then Peter said to them, "Repent, and let every one of you be baptized in the name of Jesus Christ for the remission of sins; and you shall receive the gift of the Holy Spirit. For the promise is to you and to your children, and to all who are afar off, as many as the Lord our God will call.
>
> Then those who gladly received his word were baptized; and that day about three thousand souls were added to them.
> Acts 2:38,39,41

Like the apostles in Jerusalem, Philip counted his converts as those who were baptized.

> But when they believed Philip as he preached the things concerning the kingdom of God and the name of Jesus Christ, both men and women were baptized.
> Acts 8:12

In Philip's presentation of the Gospel to the Ethiopian, he must have given a very similar appeal as Peter had on the day of Pentecost, for upon seeing water the man asked to be baptized.

> Now as they went down the road, they came to some water. And the eunuch said, "See, here is water. What hinders me from being baptized?"
>
> Then Philip said, "If you believe with all your heart, you may."
>
> And he answered and said, "I believe that Jesus Christ is the Son of God."

> So he commanded the chariot to stand still. And both Philip and the eunuch went down into the water, and he baptized him.
>
> Acts 8:36-38

When Peter went to the house of Cornelius, the Holy Spirit fell upon the listeners as he was speaking. It would seem that Peter was somewhat thrown off balance; they had received the Spirit before being baptized! He quickly commanded baptism to have them properly initiated into Christ

> "Can anyone forbid water, that these should not be baptized who have received the Holy Spirit just as we have?" And he commanded them to be baptized in the name of the Lord. Then they asked him to stay a few days.
>
> Acts 10:47,48

This certainly would suggest that baptism was given a place of great importance in the infant church. With everyone in the house filled with the Spirit and praising God, one would think that the subject of baptism could be left for another day; but obviously it could not wait, and Peter commanded that it take place at once.

In Philippi, Paul and Silas were cruelly beaten, their limbs twisted and locked into the stocks; an earthquake brought about their release and was followed by preaching the Gospel to the entire household in the middle of the night, resulting in their conversion to Christ. One would think that would be enough for a night's work! But Paul did not call closure to the night until they had all been baptized.

> So they said, "Believe on the Lord Jesus Christ, and you will be saved, you and your household." Then they spoke the word of the Lord to him and to all who were in his house. And he took them the same hour of the night and washed their stripes. And immediately he and all his family were baptized.
>
> Acts 16:31-33

I have taken this amount of time to show that very obviously baptism was not an afterthought to the early church, not something that took place once or twice a year, but was the rite of initiation into the new covenant. Circumcision was the rite of initiation into the old covenant, and baptism answers to that in the new covenant.

> **In Him you were also circumcised with the circumcision made without hands, by putting off the body of the sins of the flesh, by the circumcision of Christ, buried with Him in baptism, in which you also were raised with Him through faith in the working of God, who raised Him from the dead. And you, being dead in your trespasses and the uncircumcision of your flesh, He has made alive together with Him, having forgiven you all trespasses.**
>
> Colossians 2:11-13

The Amplified Bible renders verse 12 to say, **[Thus you were circumcised when] you were buried with Him in [your] baptism....**

The Message paraphrase of this verse puts it very plainly:

> **If it's an initiation ritual you're after, you've already been through it by submitting to baptism. Going under the water was a burial of your old life; coming up out of it was a resurrection, God raising you from the dead as he did Christ.**

Faith cannot be merely a matter of the mind; there is much that we hold as true in our minds but never commit ourselves to. Each one of us is more than a mind, and faith must include the whole person. Faith may include intense feelings but is far more than feeling; it is possible to have overwhelming feelings while we are in an emotionally charged meeting but the next morning to live as if nothing ever happened.

Faith is the moving of one's whole person to rest in Christ and what He has accomplished for us, and that must be a movement of spirit, mind, emotion, and body. Our glory as humans made in His image is that we are spirits united to and functioning in and through the dust of the earth. We are more than invisible spirits; our faith and obedience need an expression that is more than mental or verbal. The first couple fell by a physical act of eating from the forbidden tree. Although the sin was an act of the spirit, it was not complete until the whole human was involved in a physical act. Faith must have a physical expression, or the mental transaction or the feelings of the moment become ethereal and remote.

The modern Christian recognizes this but strangely has avoided baptism and substituted other physical actions to express faith in Christ. To accept Christ, people are told to raise their hand, walk down to the front of the church, or even to look up into the face of the evangelist. Children and teens at summer camps are often challenged to throw a stick into the fire.

All these actions are the attempt to involve our physical bodies in our faith. Why not simply do as Jesus commanded? Why invent new and strange ways? But these various substitutes for baptism emphasize the human acceptance of salvation. Raising the hand and like responses place the whole emphasis on the human decision to accept what God has done, a kind of giving a vote of confidence in Jesus and His salvation. It becomes a rather strange means of saying to God and my fellow believers, "Me too—I have accepted Him as well."

But in baptism, we are passive; it is something we submit to; it is a rite that is done to us by another. It is the dynamic action of the faith by which we helplessly present ourselves to the Holy Spirit for God's acceptance through the cross and resurrection of the Lord Jesus.

Even a cursory reading of the New Testament shows that to the early church, baptism was a lot more than the symbol by which one announced to God and humans that he or she had accepted Christ. Something happens in baptism. It is a symbol, but a symbol by which the Spirit actually conveys to us what the rite symbolizes. Baptism is where the Spirit lays hold upon us and declares that we are included into the covenant and joined to Christ; He is saying, "This one is Mine!"

The New Testament speaks of baptism both as an act performed in water and also as the work of the Spirit connecting the believer to the work of Christ. We come to baptism as to the doorway into the death of Christ, that by the action of the Spirit we may rise joined to the living Christ.

Notice the wording of the verse we discussed above:

> **...by putting off the body of the sins of the flesh, by the circumcision of Christ, buried with Him in baptism, in which you also were raised with Him through faith in the working of God, who raised Him from the dead.**
>
> **Colossians 2:11,12**

Baptism was the event in which the convert released faith in the working of God and experienced resurrection with Christ. This is further stated in Romans 6.

> **Or do you not know that as many of us as were baptized into Christ Jesus were baptized into His death? Therefore we were buried with Him through baptism into death, that just as Christ was raised from the dead by the glory of the Father, even so we also should walk in newness of life.**
>
> **Romans 6:3,4**

Paul testified of how Ananias ministered to him after his meeting with Jesus on the Damascus road with the words **"And now why are you waiting? Arise and be baptized, and wash away your sins, calling on the name of the Lord"** (Acts 22:16).

We know that water cannot wash away sins! Then what did Ananias mean by the phrase "be baptized and wash away your sins"? There is nothing magic in water! Without faith and the work of the Spirit, nothing is accomplished—except maybe an unnecessary bath. But for faith, baptism is the physical doorway to the covenant through which we walk in the power of the Spirit. All that is happening physically in baptism is also happening through the Spirit at the deepest level of our beings.

Many years ago, I was the pastor of a church in New York. One day a person named Joey slipped into the back pew. I later found out that Joey was a drug addict and lived the lifestyle that included petty thieving, selling drugs, and living in a drug-induced high. His world was a network of young men and women whose world from dawn until late into the night was the pursuit of getting high. He continued to come back week after week, eagerly listening to the preaching of the Gospel.

We had a baptismal service almost every Sunday; and after hearing the Gospel and being awakened by the Spirit to faith in Christ, Joey asked for baptism. He sent out invitations to his family and the network of persons who made up his world that read simply, "You are invited to Joey's funeral and resurrection on Sunday night." They came, curious and confused. Joey stood by the baptismal water and addressed his stunned family and friends with the words, "Goodbye, I am leaving the world that all of us know for real life in Jesus. You will see me around, and we will talk, and I hope I will continue to be your friend. But the Joey you have known has died and in a few minutes will be buried; the man you will be talking to is somebody who has risen from the dead and for the first time in his life is really alive! And seeing as he is dead, Joey will not be selling drugs anymore and will not be joining you to shoot up or be at the parties."

He walked the streets in Brooklyn, seeing the old haunts and friends, but although in the world he was not of it. He was a man who had been joined to Christ; he had returned home from his own funeral to see the world and all of life through resurrected eyes.

As we come out of the waters of baptism, the Father announces to us as surely as He did to Jesus, "This is My beloved son in whom I am well pleased." The Spirit, who came upon Him, came upon Him for us; and as we enter the family of God, the Spirit comes and enfolds us in the arms of God's love.

We become partakers of God's life, His everlasting life. The divine life is added by grace to our humanity; we are reborn, and our lives begin again on a totally different plain. We are moved out of the domain of the lie and the darkness to be at home in the new creation founded on the new covenant in Jesus.

> **Giving thanks to the Father who has qualified us to be partakers of the inheritance of the saints in the light. He has delivered us from the power of darkness and conveyed us into the kingdom of the Son of His love, in whom we have redemption through His blood, the forgiveness of sins. He is the image of the invisible God, the firstborn over all creation.**
> **Colossians 1:12-15**

What of the person who has not been baptized? I believe the Scripture is plain that the Spirit-energized rite stands at the beginning of our salvation. Often those who trek to "get saved" every time an evangelist comes through town are trying to nail down an ethereal faith that exists in vague thoughts and fleeting feelings. Baptism integrates the whole person in the act of faith that abandons to God and His work for us in Christ while the Spirit initiates us into Christ and the new covenant. And so to those not baptized, as Ananias said to Paul, "Arise and be baptized!"

Is a person saved if he or she is not baptized? Questions like this turn the grace of God into law. It is a pointless question that any Pharisee would have loved! God commands it; so do it, and stop discussing how many angels can stand on a pinhead.

When I began to teach the covenant in the church in Brooklyn, a number of the older members came and asked, "When I was baptized, I did not understand all of this! Do I have to get baptized again?" My answer was "No, because baptism is the Holy Spirit's working out the mystery of joining you to Christ; it is not your making an adequate act of faith that will make something happen. Do you fully understand today the mystery of the covenant, that you are in Christ and that He is in you? Then give thanks to God that He took you and said, 'This one is Mine!'"

We do not get *re*-baptized every time we see more clearly the nature of our salvation, but we humbly thank God for what He did even though we did not understand. Our whole salvation depends on Him, not on our clear understanding; otherwise, none of us would be saved! We do not pass exams in the laws of electricity to enjoy switching on the light, and we do not need to know how He does it to know that we are in Christ and He is in us.

Chapter 11

THE COVENANT MEAL

In Jesus Christ the mystery of God, who is the love that is for others, has come and taken up residence with us. In so doing He has opened up a new world foreign to all that we have known, a world where selfishness, pride, greed, envy, violence, and hatred do not rule but are swallowed up by His almighty love that gives itself away for the other person.

In this God-love, meaning has been given to existence, and the addictions and private hells that men and women have made for themselves by seeking to find meaning in the creature and the created are dismissed. He has been to the bottom of death and hell and come out of it in resurrection, bringing us with Him; in Him is a new humankind, in whom all things are possible and potential.

To be joined to Him is to be reborn, part of that new race, and alive with that eternal life, a participant in that almighty love. The way we were still haunts us, and the world we were once a part of is all around us; but in Him, we have come to the ultimate reality. The reality that is in Him makes that old life and our old selves to be seen for what they were, a shadow of true life, the walking dead inhabiting the domain of darkness.

It was into a new company of people that the Spirit plunged us when we came into Christ, a company that is made up of men and women who all believe that He is the final reality. A company who believe that the world they were once part of is finished and in process of passing away, that His love is stronger than selfishness and indifference, that His life has swallowed up death and by us His love will fill the earth.

We gather with our people—this company of lost prodigals now found, forgiven, made new, and crazy with joy at the thought of His love—to worship and give Him thanks. In our gathering and encouraging one another, the Spirit is present, establishing us in the reality and causing the unreality to increasingly be seen for what it is.

At the center of this worship is the meal of the covenant, where we meet with the eternal God, partake of His death-conquering life, are embraced by His love, and participate in the covenant promises. It is known by many names: the Holy Communion, the Eucharist (or the great thanksgiving), the Lord's Supper, or the Mass.

Tragically, this meal has been the battleground of believers through the centuries; for many, it is the most misunderstood practice of the Christian faith. In many seeker-friendly churches, it has been marginalized and nearly forgotten. In conversations with many charismatic and evangelical pastors, I have realized that they do not know what to do with the meal. They intuitively know that it is important and cannot do away with it; but they do not know what it means or where it fits, so it becomes an awkward postscript to the programs of the church.

This meal is at the heart of the covenant; misunderstanding here has repercussions throughout the Christian life. Please stay with me and view this meal through the lens of the covenant.

Even a surface reading of the writings of the apostolic and church fathers of the first centuries of the church make it plain that they gave a place of prime importance to the meal. The martyrs and heroes of the first three centuries considered the

The Covenant Meal

Holy Communion as central to their worship and life of the Christian community.

COVENANT MEALS IN SCRIPTURE

Every covenant ended with a meal that declared that the covenant was valid and now functional in the lives of the parties to it. The meal showed the covenant as the two representatives would eat of the same bread and drink of the same wine, telling the world that they were one. (Genesis 26:28-31; 31:44-46.)

The covenant that God made with Abraham came into effect with a covenant meal, at which time Abraham killed the calf and Sarah baked her cakes; the Lord, in the form of a Man, and two angels ate and drank the meal Abraham and Sarah had prepared. (Genesis 18:6-8.) The meal was the signal, for the covenant promise made long ago was about to be fulfilled and ancient Sarah would have her miracle son.

The Israelites were delivered from Egypt and slavery in fulfillment of one of the promises of the covenant with Abraham, but the deliverance was in fact a little covenant that centered in the Passover meal. (Exodus 12.) The door of each home had been smeared with the blood of the lamb that they were about to eat. As they walked through the bloody door, they were declaring their covenant status with God, sheltered by Him from the judgment that was to fall on Egypt; by eating the lamb, they became one with the covenant sacrifice. Their being taken from Egypt and formed into the people of God took place in a covenant meal.

The covenant made at Sinai, which we now call the old covenant, recorded in Exodus 24, came into effect when the covenant meal was eaten with God. The amazing sight is recorded in verses 9-11 of that chapter, which tell us, **Then Moses went up, also Aaron, Nadab, and Abihu, and seventy of** the elders of Israel, and they saw the God of Israel....So they saw God, and they ate and drank.

God and man sat down and ate together! This was the making of the old covenant, and we must anticipate something even far more wonderful in the new and better covenant.

On the eve of His death—or, if we use the Jewish method of counting days, on the same day as His suffering and death—Jesus instituted the covenant meal of the new covenant.

> **And He took bread, gave thanks and broke it, and gave it to them, saying, "This is My body which is given for you; do this in remembrance of Me." Likewise He also took the cup after supper, saying, "This cup is the new covenant in My blood, which is shed for you."**
>
> **Luke 22:19,20**

As we have seen, the expression "new covenant in My blood" is better understood as "new covenant *ratified*, or *validated*, in My blood" It was a meal that declared the coming into being of the new covenant with all of its promises.

THE MEAL OF FELLOWSHIP

Upon first hearing, it sounds strange to our ears to be commanded to eat bread and wine in order to remember Him. It does not sound like a spiritual activity; it is too physical and disconnected from our ideas of what one should do to remember and draw close to Him. To remember Him is understood by many as a spiritual or mental pursuit and therefore would be best pursued by a Bible study, a convention that expounds the deeper Christian life, or at least a prayer meeting. Where do a table with a white cloth, a chalice of wine, and a piece of bread fit in?

Yet Jesus said that in the eating and the drinking of bread and wine, we would remember Him; in the experience of the

The Covenant Meal

disciples in the Emmaus meal, He would make Himself known to them in the breaking of bread.

Meals have tremendous significance in all cultures, less so in the cultures of the West, but still there. We mark each of the significant events in our lives with a meal. Celebrating our anniversaries, weddings, and birthdays—all involve eating together. More business deals are closed and contracts signed over a meal than in any office. In all probability, many of your dates with your spouse involved some form of eating.

I remember living in Brooklyn alongside the Italians, who would never allow a job to be finished without sharing with the carpenter, electrician, or painter a small glass of wine and food of some kind. It was the way they declared a job was finished and all parties satisfied.

In Africa, I have sat with paramount chiefs and eaten with them, knowing that as I shared a piece of the bread from a common loaf we were bound in a strong brotherhood. He would use all his powers to protect me and give me safe passage in his tribal territories. To hurt me in any way would be to declare war on the chief!

Jesus, God incarnate, is known for His eating and drinking: the wedding of Cana; the feeding of the multitudes; and of course His eating with tax collectors and sinners, horrifying the Pharisees—many such examples fill the pages of the Gospels. When He met the woman of Samaria, He asked for a drink of water; and His method of evangelism with Zaccheus was to announce that they would have dinner together. Risen from the dead, He first spoke to the gathered disciples to ask if they had something to eat; He proceeded to eat bread and fish before their wondering eyes. He met them in Galilee and cooked a breakfast of fish for them over an open fire.

Peter pointed to eating and drinking together with Him as one of the proofs of the resurrection: **...witnesses chosen before** by God, even to us who ate and drank with Him after He arose from the dead (Acts 10:41).

The parables of Jesus are full of references to eating and banquets—especially the parables of Luke 15. Each parable of that chapter speaks of ecstatic rejoicing at the lost being found; but when Jesus tells of the lost son being found, the rejoicing takes the form of killing and eating the fatted calf, as well as the music and dancing.

> **"'And bring the fatted calf here and kill it, and let us eat and be merry; for this my son was dead and is alive again; he was lost and is found.' And they began to be merry.**
>
> **"'It was right that we should make merry and be glad, for your brother was dead and is alive again, and was lost and is found.'"**
>
> Luke 15:23,24,32

The father told the elder brother that "it was right" that they should have such a feast with music and dancing at the homecoming of his brother. The Greek word can also be defined to mean "it is necessary in the nature of the case": The inclusion of the son into the family demanded a covenant meal; he could not be welcomed home merely with a smile, a handshake, and a cheese sandwich!

Such hints of the covenant meal are also found in Old Testament Scriptures. Psalm 90:14, apart from a covenant meal in which the participant partakes of God Himself, makes little sense: **Oh, satisfy us early with Your mercy, that we may rejoice and be glad all our days!** The word "satisfy" is a word that describes eating to the full, being filled with food, satisfied with a meal, even to the point of overeating. The word "mercy" is the translation of the covenant word *hesed*, which we have seen is the word of covenant love, lovingkindness or steadfast love. The psalmist longed to feast at a banquet where the food was the covenant love of God. Though shrouded in the Old Testament twilight, this certainly anticipated a day when the covenant people would do exactly that in the Holy Communion.

Psalm 23 is quoted the world over, but few realize that there is a brief reference to the covenant meal hidden in it.

> **You prepare a table before me in the presence of my enemies; You anoint my head with oil; My cup runs over. Surely goodness and mercy shall follow me all the days of my life; and I will dwell in the house of the Lord forever.**
>
> **Psalm 23:5,6**

Has it never struck you as a little odd that the climax of the psalm is in David's eating with his divine Shepherd? The psalm reaches its climax with God and man eating a holy meal of victory, for his enemies look on but are defeated and afraid to attack in the presence of the Shepherd. His head is anointed with oil, which is always a symbol of the Holy Spirit's coming upon us; and his cup of covenant blessing overflows. The last verse describes him being pursued by mercy, and again the word is *hesed,* the steadfast love of the covenant.

What sounds awkward at first hearing actually fits the human/divine fellowship perfectly. The covenant demands more than a private inner faith; we celebrate our union with God with our entire person and that includes a meal, as did every other covenant. The meal is fitting to our makeup as humans. The bread and wine is a door between two worlds, a point of contact with the world of the spirit. We are not pure spirits but spirits that exist in and through a physical body; the meal is the point where not only our spirits but also our physical beings meet with Spirit even as Spirit comes to us through physical bread and wine.

IN REMEMBRANCE OF ME

To understand the meal, we have to understand the word "remember." The question I wrestled with as a young believer was how we could "do this in remembrance of Me" when we had not been there two thousand years ago. Remembering surely means thinking about and reconstructing an event in the past. I did not see how we could think about and reconstruct the events of His death and resurrection when we had not been there! It would be like someone saying, "Do you remember that vacation we had in Hong Kong?" when I had not been with this person when he'd gone to Hong Kong years before my birth! His question would make me ask if he was senile.

The only way that I could make sense of it was to take out the word "remember" and substitute it with "imagine"! Surely, remembering being impossible, I was left to imagine what His suffering and death must have been like. But I knew that was not the answer, and I was left confused and frustrated.

The word "remember" had a totally different meaning to the people of both the Old and the New Testament than it has to us in the Western world in the twenty-first century. In one sense, the word meant the same to them as it does to us; it meant and means "remember." The vast difference in meaning is in how that remembering is achieved, the kind of activity that is understood to be going on when the word is used.

"Remember" in the West describes a mental activity, a recall of an event with the mind, to think about a past event. It describes the mental exercise of digging around the cobwebs of memory to put together again that vacation in Hong Kong, assuming you were there. If that is what the word meant to Jesus and those disciples around the table with Him, then, at best, the meal was meant to be a (rather strange) aid to their devotional imagination. But His words could only truly be obeyed by those men gathered around the table, for they were the only ones there who could at a future time cast their minds back and remember.

The Covenant Meal

But to the Greek and Hebrew mind of the first century, "remember" described something totally different. First, it was not only a mental activity, a "thinking about" a past event, but an activity of the whole person—spirit, mind, emotion, and body. Second, it meant to do the past event, not merely to think about it. To remember meant to re-create the past event, bringing it into the present moment by reenacting it, employing rituals and symbols to do so. Third, to remember meant that the persons remembering totally identified with and participated in all the powers and effects of the original event.[1] Every year the people of God in the Old Testament "remembered" their deliverance from Egypt in exactly this fashion, reenacting it in the Passover meal.

Remembering could be understood as a bridge in time that effectively brought the past into the present, almost a kind of time warp. It was a dramatically played-out "you are there," so that even if you had not been at the original event you immediately encountered it and participated in it. The emphasis was on the doing again the past event, not merely thinking about it, which explains the words of Jesus "Do this in remembrance of Me"—not merely "think this about Me."

Let me try to sum that up in a working definition: Remembering is never to be understood as thinking about the past. It is always an active participation in the historical reality of the past by reenacting it, and in so doing realizing the powers released in that past in such a way as to shape the present moment.

This definition of "remember" means that at the celebration of the holy meal we do not look back to the cross and empty tomb. In this remembrance His finished work is brought forward into the present moment, even as He in His glory is uniquely here, present with us in the rite. We receive in the present moment all the effects of the covenant; in this now moment we rejoice in our redemption achieved, that the burden of sin and guilt has been sent away from us, and we are now declared righteous in Christ. We glory in our deliverance from the domain of darkness and in the eternal life that we partake of. All the terms, promises, and blessings of the covenant are here now in this present moment and released to us by the Spirit in the meal of remembering.

It might help us to understand the two ways of thinking by using a wedding as an example. If I were to say to a Western couple, "Let's remember your wedding," the response would be a mental reconstruction of the event, groping through memories for the guest list, the minister who performed the ceremony, what happened at the celebration afterward, and so on. If I said the same thing to any couple of the New Testament days, the response would be "Let's do it!" It would be the only response they would be capable of making, for remembering to them was a matter of doing, not only thinking. They would go back to the synagogue where they had been married or one that was much the same, try to find the rabbi who had married them, and invite as many of the guests who had been there as possible. If the original guests were not available, the couple's present friends would be able to join right in because in this remembering one did not have to be at the original event; it would be re-created in rite and symbol. Of course, the couple would not get married a second time, but the original vows would be renewed with a new depth and mature love; all the powers of the original wedding would be present at this reenactment and renewal.

Thus, we see that Jesus was saying, "Reenact this meal; do it again. In whatever moment of time you are, this moment will be present to you; you will be here at the ratification of the new covenant and immediately present to Me, the Mediator of the new covenant."

The Covenant Meal

THE SPIRIT AND REMEMBERING

How can this be? All four gospel writers relate the events that took place on the night of His sufferings and death, including all that took place in the Upper Room, each with his own unique contribution. Matthew, Mark, and Luke relate the institution of the meal and His command to remember Him. John omits the meal but supplies us with everything He said that night as the twelve sat around Jesus with the meal before them. The first three Gospels tell us He said that in the meal we must remember Him, but it is John who tells us how such a miracle would take place:

> **But the Helper, the Holy Spirit, whom the Father will send in My name, He will teach you all things, and bring to your remembrance all things that I said to you.**
>
> **John 14:26**

The word "remembrance" is from the same word that Jesus used when He instituted the meal. It is the Holy Spirit who achieves the remembering of Jesus. This takes the whole matter out of the hands of the dreary and futile efforts of our minds to imagine His sufferings and death. This verse assures us that the Holy Spirit will achieve the "remembering"; we set the table with bread and wine, but it is He who brings the past into our now time and brings about our being immediately present to the Lord Jesus, the guarantor of the new covenant.

It should also be noted that the subject of our remembering is not only His sufferings and death. He said "…in remembrance of Me"—the oceans of glory wrapped up in "Me" from the Incarnation to His exaltation to the right hand of the Father, which of course includes His sufferings and death but from the perspective of the glory that followed.

I believe that Luke deliberately recorded two meals, the one in the Upper Room the night of His sufferings and death that Matthew and Mark and Luke record, and then the Emmaus meal that is unique to Luke's gospel. Compare the description Luke gives of the two meals; he uses exactly the same words to describe the action of Jesus.

> And He took bread, gave thanks and broke it, and gave it to them, saying, "This is My body which is given for you; do this in remembrance of Me. Likewise He also took the cup after supper, saying, "This cup is the new covenant in My blood, which is shed for you."
>
> Luke 22:19,20

Of the meal in Emmaus, he writes,

> Now it came to pass, as He sat at the table with them, that He took bread, blessed and broke it, and gave it to them.
>
> Luke 24:30

In both cases, Jesus took, gave thanks or blessed, broke, and gave the bread to them. The night of the institution of the meal was overshadowed by the enormous cost of ratifying the new covenant: sufferings, bloodshed, and death. The meal in Emmaus was the celebration of the triumphant Jesus, who had achieved the covenant; He was made known to them in the breaking of bread, and the disciples were filled with unspeakable joy and burning hearts.

> And they said to one another, "Did not our heart burn within us while He talked with us on the road, and while He opened the Scriptures to us?"
>
> And they told about the things that had happened on the road, and how He was known to them in the breaking of bread.
>
> Luke 24:32,35

When we remember Him at the celebration of the covenant meal, all these elements are present, for we are immediately present to Him who loved us, died for us, has risen, and is ascended to the place of ultimate glory.

The Covenant Meal

THIS IS MY BODY; THIS IS MY BLOOD

The early church never argued as to the nature of the bread and wine to which they gathered every week. All of the writings of the first century consistently refer to the meal as partaking of the body and blood of Christ. They did so as the great mystery of the faith, not to be explained but accepted by adoring faith. Trouble began when, centuries later, the theologians attempted to explain the mystery in terms of the science of the day. They took the dancing butterfly from the air and pinned it to a board and dissected it.

In considering the words of Jesus, "This is My body...this is My blood," I do not approach it as a scientist to dissect and explain but as a believer looking at the great mystery to be embraced by faith.

The word "symbol" comes from a Greek word meaning to throw together with.[2] It is taking something in the material world and throwing it together with abstract ideas that would take volumes to explain. When the invisible truth has been thrown together with the physical object, to see the object is to connect with the invisible associated ideas.

We have taken a piece of metal shaped as a circle with a precious stone set in it and thrown it together with love, commitment, and faithfulness. When the young man gives the engagement ring to his wife-to-be, she is overwhelmed with joy; when she wears it to work, the whole office knows without a word being said that a commitment has been given and received. Will anyone stand up and hush the excitement in the office and say, "Now please understand this is only a symbol; it means nothing; it is only a piece of metal twisted into a circle; please do not get excited..."? No! It meant nothing in the store along with a hundred other rings; but it was set aside to become an uncommon ring that conveyed the unique love and commitment of one man to one woman. In taking it and wearing it, the young lady received and responded to that love and commitment and forever changed her life. That kind of symbol does not only announce what it symbolizes but actually conveys what it symbolizes.

Another illustration that may help you understand is the dollar bill in your billfold. I often hold up a dollar bill and ask the congregation what is in my hand. Someone invariably will say, "A dollar," and my response is "How can that be? A dollar is a weight of precious metal. This is a piece of paper!" There is a little confusion, and I go on: "This is a piece of paper; but if a person says it is a piece of paper he is a fool, for it is a dollar!" I go on to explain that this is, indeed, a piece of paper that is the symbol of a dollar, a symbol that has been invested with the power to convey what it symbolizes. By due authority, it has been set aside from all other pieces of paper to become an uncommon piece of paper that actually becomes to us and conveys the value of precious metal.

My illustrations only point to what a symbol is, and they are far from what we are talking about. The man invests a ring with power to communicate and convey his love commitment to his wife-to-be, and the U.S. government authorizes a piece of paper to convey a dollar's value. But what we are speaking of here is infinitely more than that. We are speaking of the Lord Jesus' conveying Himself to us through the bread and the wine, at which point all illustrations fail to the point of becoming worthless. They can only point down the road that disappears into the mist of mystery, where the brain submits and the spirit worships.

Hear how the New Testament believers understood it:

> **The cup of blessing which we bless, is it not the communion of the blood of Christ? The bread which we break, is it not the communion of the body of Christ?**
> **1 Corinthians 10:16**

The Covenant Meal

The key word in the text is "communion," and it means fellowship, a participation in, a uniting together in partnership.[3] He is saying that in eating and drinking the believer participates in, unites with, and has a fellowship and communion in the blood of Christ. We take into ourselves the body and blood of Christ. The next verse points to their unity as the body of Christ, in that eating the bread they eat the Bread who is Christ.

Here is the great mystery of the new covenant. The bread and the wine are set aside from all other pieces of bread and cups of wine; the Spirit makes them uncommon elements by which He will actually convey to us what they symbolize—the body and blood of Christ. A believer eats of the bread and drinks of the wine and, in so doing, partakes of Christ; he or she participates in the greatest mystery of the ages—that in the new covenant He is in us and we are in Him.

Our problems arise when we try to say what happens and how it happens. To the early church the question did not arise and, therefore, neither did the answer. We eat and are fed with Him who is the covenant.

Jesus made reference to this in very strong language that caused many to walk away from Him, but in it all He never addressed how it could be.

> And Jesus said to them, "I am the bread of life. He who comes to Me shall never hunger, and he who believes in Me shall never thirst."
>
> "I am the living bread which came down from heaven. If anyone eats of this bread, he will live forever; and the bread that I shall give is My flesh, which I shall give for the life of the world.
>
> "Most assuredly, I say to you, unless you eat the flesh of the Son of Man and drink His blood, you have no life in you. Whoever eats My flesh and drinks My blood has eternal life, and I will raise him up at the last day. For My flesh is food indeed, and My blood is drink indeed. He who eats My flesh

and drinks My blood abides in Me, and I in him. As the living Father sent Me, and I live because of the Father, so he who feeds on Me will live because of Me."

John 6:35,51,53-57

The Greek word translated "eat" here is a very physical word; it means to chew the food in the mouth.[4] It could never be used to describe a mental or spiritual eating only; it is speaking of putting something in the mouth and chewing and swallowing it.

The bread and wine of the covenant meal, through the Spirit, are conveying symbols through which grace comes to us and are therefore called "the means of grace." That He is in us and we are in Him is made real not only to our minds but also to our physical bodies. The bread and wine are God's delivery system whereby all the blessings of the covenant come to us. Healing for our entire person is to be found here.

The glorified Lord calls us to the covenant feast; the food He serves us is His body and blood, conveying to us all that He has purchased for us in covenant. Faith reaches out and partakes of the mystery, saying amen, and is nourished with everlasting life.

MY BODY, GIVEN FOR YOU

In saying, "This is My body given for you," Jesus gave Himself to us with absolute finality. We may give others our best wishes and tell them that we are thinking of them, giving them our thoughts; we may give others service and deeply care; we may give great sums of money but in it all hold back the gift of our true self. But when we willingly present our bodies in total gift, a self-donation to another, we have come to the ultimate concept of covenant, the total gift of one's entire self to the other; then and only then is union complete.

The Covenant Meal

One's body is the last to be given over to another; it is not given without first one's will, thoughts, mind, and soul being totally given. Giving one's body means the surrender of one's intimacy, all of the private and most secret things about ourselves; He surrendered the secret of Himself when He gave us His body. He did this ungrudgingly, saying, "With desire I have desired to eat...." He longed for the moment when He would share Himself with us in the gift of His body. In the covenant meal, this surrender of the secret of Himself continues.

The Emmaus meal hints at this in the words **He was known to them in the breaking of bread** (Luke 24:35). The words "made known to them" are used throughout the Scripture to describe the intimate, personal knowing of husband and wife. They are never used to describe academic and impersonal knowing about a person.

This must never be thought of as being limited to His sufferings and death. All His life, He had given His body; for in the totality of His being, He is the Word of the Father's love. He is the incarnation of the joy and delight of God over His people; He is the Word of peace, the Word of life, and the Word of compassion. In giving His body, He thus gave all that He was; and in the covenant meal, He continues to give the totality of His self to us.

THIS IS MY BLOOD

"The new covenant in My blood" is the validating authority that the covenant union is achieved. To drink is to share in that covenant and all its terms. As we drink down the mystery of His blood, we are celebrating that He as us has accomplished the putting away of our sins and that they will never be remembered again. We declare that the law is written on our hearts and etched in our minds and that we intimately and personally know Him, that He is our God and we are joined to His people.

It means that we are partaking of and participating in the life of the ascended Christ. We drink of the life that has passed through death and overcome it, never to die again.

In Scotland some centuries ago, believers were bitterly persecuted by the English. The believers would meet in the mountain crags of the Scottish Highlands and, there, have their secret meetings, which included the Communion, the covenant meal. Many times, these secret gatherings would take place in the night or in the early dawn hours. On one occasion when they were meeting for the covenant meal, the English Redcoats had heard that a meeting was to take place but they did not know where. They watched for anyone moving in the predawn darkness to arrest and torture to find the names of the believers and the place where they met. A young teenage girl was slipping through the mist on her way to the Communion service when the soldiers surrounded her, demanding she tell them where she was going. Being well-educated in the new covenant and what she was about to do, she answered, "My elder Brother has died, and I am going to hear the reading of the will and claim my share in the inheritance!" The ignorant soldiers had no idea that she was referring to the Communion service and patted her head, gave her a quarter, and sent her on her way.

Chapter 12

SIN IS REMEMBERED NO MORE

We have seen that Jesus lived and died as our representative; therefore, the men and women who believe are participators and sharers in all that He suffered, endured, and earned. On the cross, He stood as us not in some monstrous pretend game but in awful, agonizing reality. We were truly there in Him and He as us received pardon, justification, and resurrection. These blessings of covenant were given to Him first as our representative and then to us as we are united with Him and participate with Him through the Spirit.

When God raised Him from the dead, He declared that the penalty for our sins, which Jesus had freely taken, had been paid in full; our sentence placed on Him was fulfilled. Jesus risen from the dead is Jesus no longer carrying our sins that took Him to death. He as our representative was forgiven of all our transgressions; our guilt no longer weighs Him down, and He has been freed from all necessity of further punishment for them. If Jesus is alive from the dead, we are forgiven of all our sin!

The instant a sinner is united to Christ, he or she becomes identified with Him in His representative forgiveness.

Forgiveness and all the blessings of covenant do not come to us merely *through* Christ but *in* Him. We do not receive them only because He earned them but by our being united together *with* Him and *in* Him, members of His body, made dynamically one with Him by the Spirit.

He as our representative returns to the Father with His blood of the new covenant, and the Father declares to Him and to us, the ones He represents, that the slate has been wiped clean: **"For I will forgive their iniquity, and their sin I will remember no more"** (Jeremiah 31:34). In Him, humanity for the first time is declared not guilty and free from punishment.

THE FIRST OF NEW COVENANT BLESSINGS

There is no other religion on earth that announces the forgiveness of all our sins. It is the complete forgiveness of our sin that is the foundation of everything else that is ours in the covenant. Before we could enter the new covenant, the judgment hanging over our heads since Eden had to be totally and forever removed, as well as the curse of the broken law. Free from sin and the curse, we are now in Christ the candidates for the blessings He delights to richly pour on us.

In instituting the covenant meal, Jesus spoke of the remission or forgiveness of sin; for when that is accomplished, the covenant blessings are released upon us in abundance.

> **Then He took the cup, and gave thanks, and gave it to them, saying, "Drink from it, all of you. For this is My blood of the new covenant, which is shed for many for the remission of sins."**
>
> **Matthew 26:27,28**

We have seen the blessings Jeremiah announced that would come in the new covenant, but let us read them again with the necessity of forgiveness in mind.

> "But this is the covenant that I will make with the house of Israel after those days, says the Lord: I will put My law in their minds, and write it on their hearts; and I will be their God, and they shall be My people. No more shall every man teach his neighbor, and every man his brother, saying, 'Know the Lord,' for they all shall know Me, from the least of them to the greatest of them, says the Lord...."
>
> Jeremiah 31:33,34

All this will take place, he says, because sin, the foundation problem, has been dealt with: **"...For I will forgive their iniquity, and their sin I will remember no more"** (Jeremiah 31:34).

Dealing with the sin question is basic to the covenant; it is the foundation upon which all the promises are based. Jesus has put away sin, and we now stand forgiven and only then are we **...blessed...with every spiritual blessing in the heavenly places in Christ** (Ephesians 1:3).

Our assurance that our sins have been forgiven and we have been accepted by God is the first of covenant blessings and the most important in our experience. Without this, we cannot imagine any of the other blessings. This is the kindergarten of the new covenant, yet for multitudes of church members such a joy has not been even sighted.

Knowing this truth is the beginning of the victory in spiritual warfare, for while we are under the condemnation of our sin we are paralyzed before the powers of darkness by our own sense of unworthiness. Until we know the oath of God that He removes sin from us through the covenant blood of Jesus, when we are confronted by our sin, we cannot believe that we are welcome in the presence of God; we may even believe that He has cast us aside. Believing we are unworthy, we are unable to pray, we have no expectancy of being heard, we cannot believe that the promises of God are for us. We cringe under the sense of guilt, and our hands are paralyzed to take the blessings that are ours under covenant. If we begin to feel any sense of acceptance, we are hurled to the ground by Satan, "the accuser of the brethren"; and instead of resisting him with the truth, we agree with him!

I was raised in a poor family in England. I was born at the end of the Depression, and my introduction to life on the planet was the Second World War. In those days, we knew real poverty.

The English were very aware of class and where everyone belonged in society. The right family, the right school, and wearing the right school tie after graduation, joining the right club, made way for a person not only in the position one held in a job but also the restaurants one could eat in and the pursuits one could follow. There was no sign outside the door of a restaurant to say we couldn't enter; it was simply understood that every Englishman had his place according to his wealth and position, and only gentlemen of the higher class could enter.

All of my aunts were servants in the mansions of the rich and were congratulated for having found such good employment. There was no thought of advancement; being servants was their place in society.

When I said that I wanted to drive a car when I was older, my mother looked horrified: "No, mate. That's not for the likes of us, you'll 'ave a bicycle just like your father." It seemed to me growing up that the places I wanted to go, the things I wanted to do, and the restaurants I wanted to eat in were "not for the likes of us." I was reared in an atmosphere of shame, of the belief that our status in life made us unworthy of anything but the leftovers.

I wrestled with the voice of my mother inside my head for a number of years after I left home and was in ministry. I found that in my mind the English class system spilled over into my walk with God. The favor of God, the rich gifts of the Spirit, and answers to prayer fell in my mind into the category of "not for the likes of us." The "likes of me" was not worthy to be so blessed. The basic problem was that I did not truly see with the eyes of my spirit that my sin had been taken away and I was no longer doomed to dwell in the slums of heaven! It took a major revelation of the Spirit that swept my mind clean, followed by much renewing and renovation of my thought patterns, that brought me to see myself as totally forgiven, accepted, and, in Christ, a member of the aristocracy of heaven. All covenant blessings were for the likes of me, for I was in Christ.

I see multitudes of believers who live believing that they are unworthy of the covenant blessings, that they are not really separated from sin—such blessings are not for the likes of them. If we are unsure of our forgiveness and acceptance, we have a barrier in our minds forbidding us to consider taking all He has purchased for us. We have a self-image of unworthiness that holds us in chains and forbids us to take of all the blessings of the covenant.

Faith dares to accept such an unlimited and unconditional acceptance even though to the natural mind it seems illegal and ungodly! When Satan accuses us of past sin, we must hurl the promises of the new covenant, validated by the blood and the oath of God, in his face and deliberately rejoice in the unlimited forgiveness of God.

WHAT IS FORGIVENESS?

But now we have a problem with the English word "forgiveness"; the word translated "forgiveness" in Scripture does not mean forgiveness as the word is defined today.

This is Webster's definition of forgiveness: "to excuse for a fault or offense; to renounce anger or resentment against; to absolve from payment of a debt."[1] What Jesus accomplished in the blood of the new covenant is infinitely more than what the English word "forgiveness" means. We have been more than excused for our sins; He accomplished infinitely more than giving up anger and resentment toward us, and we have more than the payment for our sins. We will have to drop the word "forgiveness," for it in no way describes what He did and what we have in Him.

The word translated "forgiveness" is *aphiemi*[2] in the original Greek of the New Testament and means to send away, to dismiss, to forsake, to leave; it is the word used for divorce or to put away a wife. Jesus "sent away" *(aphiemi)* the crowd, and it would be nonsense to say that in so doing He forgave them! It is the word used in Matthew 27:50 to describe how the spirit of Jesus left His body: **And Jesus cried out again with a loud voice, and yielded up** *(aphiemi)* **His spirit.** He sent away His spirit, dismissed it away from Him, with the result that His body was dead. It was a total sending away, not just a weakening. There is no way that we could fit the English word "forgiveness" in there!

Another word in the same family and derived from *aphiemi* is *aphesis*[2]. It is translated as "liberty" in the Greek Old Testament, when in the Year of Jubilee all slaves were set free and sent home to their families:

> "And you shall consecrate the fiftieth year, and proclaim liberty throughout all the land to all its inhabitants. It shall be a Jubilee for you; and each of you shall return to his possession, and each of you shall return to his family."
>
> **Leviticus 25:10**

Jesus, quoting the prophet Isaiah, announced that in Him a Jubilee without end had begun:

> "The Spirit of the Lord is upon Me, because He has anointed Me to preach the gospel to the poor; He has sent Me to heal the brokenhearted, to proclaim liberty *(aphesis)* to the captives and recovery of sight to the blind, to set at liberty *(aphesis)* those who are oppressed."
>
> **Luke 4:18**

The new covenant declares that our sin has been sent away from us, banished from our presence; we have been divorced and set free from the chains that bound us, to be at liberty. Our guilt and bondage to sin have been sent away from us as surely as Jesus' spirit left Him on the cross; their power has not been weakened but has gone. We are free from sin! It is this meaning that we must insert every time we read of His forgiving us.

FORGIVENESS OF OUR SIN

We have seen that the Greek word *hamartia* describes the principle and the power of sin, which came into the race through the rebellion of Adam.

> **Therefore, just as through one man sin** *(hamartia)* **entered the world, and death through sin, and thus death spread to all men, because all sinned.**
>
> **Romans 5:12**

We have seen that *hamartia* describes the governing force behind sin, out of which comes the catalog of sins. Jesus came with the mission of releasing us from our sins.

> **And she will bring forth a Son, and you shall call His name JESUS, for He will save His people from their sins.**
>
> **Matthew 1:21**

> **The next day John saw Jesus coming toward him, and said, "Behold! The Lamb of God who takes away the sin** *(hamartia)* **of the world!"**
>
> **John 1:29**

The words "take away" mean to pick up and away from and carry away,[2] giving much the same picture as the meaning of forgiveness. The Gospel is clearly the Good News of our being set free from the power of sin through the blood of Jesus.

> **"For this is My blood of the new covenant, which is shed for many for the remission** *(aphiemi)* **of sins** *(hamartia)*.**"**
>
> **Matthew 26:28**

A literal rendering of this verse would be "...which is shed for many for the taking away of the principle and power of sin."

But if we walk in the light as He is in the light, we have fellowship with one another, and the blood of Jesus Christ His Son cleanses us from all sin *(hamartia)*.

1 John 1:7

Paul personalizes the principle of sin, likening it to a tyrant despot who would rule over the terrain of our mortal bodies; but forgiveness means that we are free from his rule and can choose to be as free from him as we truly are in Christ.

Likewise you also, reckon yourselves to be dead indeed to sin *(hamartia)***, but alive to God in Christ Jesus our Lord. Therefore do not let sin** *(hamartia)* **reign in your mortal body, that you should obey it in its lusts.**

Romans 6:11,12

Once the slaves of the tyrant, offering our bodies to him for his use, we are now the joyful slaves of the Lord Jesus, presenting our bodies for Him to express His life through.

And having been set free from sin *(hamartia)***, you became slaves of righteousness. I speak in human terms because of the weakness of your flesh. For just as you presented your members as slaves of uncleanness, and of lawlessness leading to more lawlessness, so now present your members as slaves of righteousness for holiness.**

But now having been set free from sin *(hamartia)***, and having become slaves of God, you have your fruit to holiness, and the end, everlasting life.**

Romans 6:18,19,22

And so the phrase "forgiveness of sins" is the essence of the Good News and the doorway to all the blessings of the new covenant. The ascended Jesus commanded that this be the content of the message:

Then He said to them, "Thus it is written, and thus it was necessary for the Christ to suffer and to rise from the

dead the third day, and that repentance and remission (aphiemi) of sins (hamartia) should be preached in His name to all nations, beginning at Jerusalem.

Luke 24:46,47

It was the joyful cry of triumph that echoed through the early church: **He has delivered us from the power of darkness and conveyed us into the kingdom of the Son of His love, in whom we have redemption through His blood, the forgiveness of sins** (Colossians 1:13,14).

OLD COVENANT FORGIVENESS

The Old Testament saints did not know this, for the blood of animals covered their sin; it awaited the blood of Jesus in the new covenant to send sin away from us, to effectually divorce us from the power of sin. The Old Testament vividly prefigured this in the sending away of the second goat of the Day of Atonement. But they could not know this, as we do, until Jesus rose from the dead to announce that sin had been taken away and the Spirit now witnesses with our spirits that we are free from its bondage.

That the Old Testament saints could not know the dismissing of sin from their lives, as we do, does not mean that the Old Testament is the domain of an unforgiving and angry deity. The Old Testament forgiveness, as we have seen it in the new covenant, was ineffectual and, in fact, impossible until Jesus, the Lamb of God, took away the sins of the world. **For it is not possible that the blood of bulls and goats could take away sins** (Hebrews 10:4). However, that does not mean that they did not enjoy the experience of God's forgiving and removing their sin as far as the revelation they had could take them.

The revelation of God to Moses became the foundation of the understanding Israel had of Him, and it is a revelation of a God of love and forgiveness.

> And the Lord passed before him and proclaimed, "The Lord, the Lord God, merciful and gracious, longsuffering, and abounding in goodness and truth, keeping mercy for thousands, forgiving iniquity and transgression and sin...."
>
> Exodus 34:6,7

This foundation passage is quoted again and again throughout the Old Testament. Throughout their desert wanderings, Israel experienced the covering over of their sins again and again.

> "Pardon the iniquity of this people, I pray, according to the greatness of Your mercy, just as You have forgiven this people, from Egypt even until now."
>
> Numbers 14:19

> ...But You are God, ready to pardon, gracious and merciful, slow to anger, abundant in kindness, and did not forsake them.
>
> Nehemiah 9:17

The prophets, although addressing a rebellious and sinful people moving rapidly to inevitable judgment, celebrated a forgiving God.

> To the Lord our God belong mercy and forgiveness, though we have rebelled against Him.
>
> Daniel 9:9

Isaiah described God's forgiveness by making reference to an ancient custom called "giving the double." In ancient times in Jerusalem, a person who was in debt with no hope of paying his creditors would write out on a parchment all of his debts and the persons he owed them to and hang it at the front of his dwelling for all to see. He waited for a generous rich man with a compassionate heart to come by. When such a man passed and saw the document fluttering in the breeze, he would read it and if he was financially able and had a large enough heart, he would double the parchment over, hiding the record of debts and write on the back, "Paid in full." The rich benefactor would then satisfy all of the creditors; the matter was now out of the hands of the debtor, and he was a free man.

Isaiah portrays Israel with her sins hanging out for all to see and the Lord, infinite in love and compassion and also the One they were in debt to, coming and giving them the double.

> **"Speak comfort to Jerusalem, and cry out to her, that her warfare is ended, that her iniquity is pardoned; for she has received from the Lord's hand double for all her sins."**
> **Isaiah 40:2**

As glorious as those words were to ancient Israel, the revelation of their full meaning awaited the new covenant. We come out of guilty hiding into the light of God, declaring ourselves sinners before God, only to discover that the One we were in debt to has written across our bill in the blood of Jesus, "Paid in full." We have seen in a previous chapter that the cry of Jesus on the cross "It is finished" has been found written across settled accounts; it was equivalent to our "Paid in full."

The psalmists join with the prophets to praise the God who forgives:

> **You have forgiven the iniquity of Your people; You have covered all their sin.**
> **Psalm 85:2**

> **As far as the east is from the west, so far has He removed our transgressions from us.**
> **Psalm 103:12**

> **But there is forgiveness with You, that You may be feared.**
> **Psalm 130:4**

The declarations and promises of God's forgiveness in the Old Testament sprang from the heart of the God who is everlasting, unconditional love. He did not begin to be a loving and forgiving God after Jesus died, as if that event changed His mind. The issue of forgiveness was settled in the heart of God from before the creation of the earth when the Trinity committed to the ultimate sacrifice of God the Son for the salvation of sinful men and women. The cost of that forgiveness given before time is manifest in time space history in Jesus' death and resurrection. The decision to create us in the light of what we would do is God's telling us that He would rather die than live without us.

The Old Testament knew of His forgiveness and praised and proclaimed Him as the forgiving God, but the people of its time could never dream what that actually meant or the cost to God in achieving it. They caught a hint in the bloody sacrifices that went on continually in the temple, and on the Day of Atonement, but none could dream of the pain in the heart of God that to Him was worth the fellowship of men and women. They lived in the predawn light of God's heart revealed; Jesus is the sun risen in full strength and glory.

> **By Him everyone who believes is justified from all things from which you could not be justified by the law of Moses.**
>
> **Acts 13:39**

REMEMBERED NO MORE

The language of the prophets as they anticipated the new covenant is extravagant; they tell us that God remembers our sin no more, that He does not bring our sins to mind, that He has forgotten them.

> **I have blotted out, like a thick cloud, your transgressions, and like a cloud, your sins. Return to Me, for I have redeemed you.**
>
> **Isaiah 44:22**

> **I will cleanse them from all their iniquity by which they have sinned against Me, and I will pardon all their iniquities by which they have sinned and by which they have transgressed against Me.**
>
> **Jeremiah 33:8**

Sin Is Remembered No More

> I, even I, am He who blots out your transgressions for My own sake; and I will not remember your sins.
>
> Isaiah 43:25
>
> ...But You have lovingly delivered my soul from the pit of corruption, for You have cast all my sins behind Your back.
>
> Isaiah 38:17

In the blood-shedding of the Lord Jesus, sin has been dealt with finally and forever. The term of the covenant says, "Remember no more," which means sin is no longer on God's agenda because it has been completely dealt with. The doctor who sees an improvement in a patient does not say that he will remember this person no more! If my house is burning, I do not want the fireman to walk away and forget my house when he has put out the fire in the living room, leaving the rest to burn.

Something that is remembered no more has been fully handled and dealt with and there is no more work that needs to be done. The patient whose disease has been completely healed is "remembered no more" by the doctor. When the fire is fully out and the embers are cold, the firemen go away to "remember it no more." God does not "remember our sin no more" until it is fully and forever dealt with and the guilt is fully gone.

There are two well-known stories that Jesus told which show us what God means by the word "forgiveness." In Matthew 18:23-35, we have the parable of the king who forgave his servant's debt. A king decided it was time to settle all accounts payable. His servants were brought in one by one to pay off their debts. It is a mystery how the servant of this story came by such a debt. Such an astronomical sum as the books showed he owed would hardly have been borrowed in a legal fashion. The king had the books open, and the ledger told the story of his debts. In today's currency, his debt would take ten lifetimes to repay, assuming that all his paychecks went in total to paying off the debt. Jesus was portraying a man with an impossible debt that was earning interest and getting larger every minute and was beyond the man's capability to pay back.

The servant did not seem to understand the enormity of his debt. He fell down before the king and asked for an extension of time so that he could pay back what he owed. The request was ludicrous.

Then the king acted in a way that we cannot expect any king of a loaning institution to act. He closed the ledger and the accounting department and dismissed his accountants. He was no longer dealing with the servant in the light of the ledger or debts, but on another basis entirely. He was moved with compassion. He freely forgave the man the entire debt; he removed the debt out of his life.

The true meaning of the word "forgiveness" is embodied in this act of the king. The man was released from the debt so that the debt was no longer a burden on the shoulders or a ball and chain around the ankle. The debt would never be associated with the servant again. The king would never deal with this man in reference to his debt. He was no longer confined, defined, or determined by his debt. He was free to get on with his life with a clean slate.

The servant was free, leaping and dancing down the road, but freedom for the servant had been a costly action for the king. Astronomical debts, or little ones for that matter, do not disappear into thin air! For the servant to be forgiven, the king had experienced an inner death; he had died to the right to expect any repayment of what was owed to him. In sending the debt away from the servant, he had to receive it in full. Moved with compassion, the king came from his accounting ledger to join the servant in his debt, assume it, and pay it off by canceling it.

The old covenant of the law was necessary, for it was a time when men and women must face the debt to God that each one owes. But the heart of God is love, not the accounting office. He comes where we are and joins Himself to us; He assumes our debt and absorbs it Himself. He declares a divine amnesty that He has made possible in the blood of Jesus.

> **Now all things are of God, who has reconciled us to Himself through Jesus Christ...God was in Christ reconciling the world to Himself, not imputing their trespasses to them....**
>
> **For He made Him who knew no sin to be sin for us, that we might become the righteousness of God in Him.**
>
> 2 Corinthians 5:18,19,21

We were the enemies of God, and He came to us where we were and achieved our reconciliation so that He is "not imputing their trespasses to them." *The New American Standard Bible* gives a clearer translation: **not counting their trespasses** (verse 19). He is not the accountant adding figures and counting debts; He is the king moved with compassion and declaring us free from all debts.

Hear the Gospel, and know why it is called the Good News. Our slate has been wiped clean of all sin, the guilt and shame gone. But our sins did not dissolve into thin air! He achieved this for us in Christ, who came where we were in our sin and became sin for us that we might become the righteousness of God in Him. The law condemns us, but He has taken our sin and there is nothing left to condemn.

> **There is therefore now no condemnation to those who are in Christ Jesus, who do not walk according to the flesh, but according to the Spirit.**
>
> Romans 8:1

On one occasion Jesus said, **"Assuredly, I say to you, all sins will be forgiven the sons of men, and whatever blasphemies they may utter"** (Mark 3:28). Such a statement leaves us speechless with joy and wonder: "All sins, whatever they are, will be sent away, be dismissed, leave you in a state of freedom and liberty" is our expanded translation.

The second parable that portrays His forgiveness is of the lost son. Jesus tells the story of two sons. The younger of them insolently demanded of his father that he divide the inheritance between the children even though the father was still alive. The law of that day said that the inheritance should be the parent's to use until death, but the son was saying in effect, "I cannot wait for you to drop dead; give me the money now!"

The father sold off one-third of the farm to give the younger one his one-third share of the inheritance, leaving the remaining two-thirds for the firstborn. It is obvious from the end of the story that the father forgave the young man for his rejection and actions even as the son was insulting his father and demanding the money. But the boy knew neither his father's love nor that he was forgiven; in fact, it does not appear that he even thought about the need to be forgiven. He squandered the money and in days of famine became a pig herder, which for a Jew was to become an abomination. Hunger finally made him think of home and returning to his father for a good meal. He had no sense of needing the father's love; he only wanted an act of charity that would make him a hired servant.

Day after day and month after month, the father scanned the horizon at the place where he had last seen the son. Now he saw the familiar figure, though only a silhouette against the sky. He ran to where the young man was and burst unannounced upon him, embracing him, kissing him repeatedly, and refusing to hear any talk of the son's becoming a hired man. He had servants bring his own best robe and shoes, while he put his own signet ring on the man's hand. The calf fattened for such an occasion was killed and roasted; the band was called in for dancing and universal celebration.

The words "forgiveness" and "reconciliation" are not mentioned in the story, yet it is obvious that the father accomplished in history what he had actually accomplished in his heart when the young man had left. At that time, he had released the young man of any moral, filial, or familial debt, and now his repeated kissing and crushing embrace announced that fact to the son. He was free from his debt of sin to his father; he was returned to the family table and proclaimed by his father as his son.

The father expressed it by saying, "He was dead and is alive again; he was lost and is found." He was referring to the dismal journey the son had taken when he had been lost from his father's love and without a map in life. In such a condition, he was dead; that is unaware, deaf, and unresponsive to his fathers' love.

As in the previous story, one received a free, unconditional forgiveness; but another inwardly died to give it. When the son asked for the money and headed for the far country, the father died to any expectancy of repayment on his rejected love. When the son returned, the father died to receiving back the years of lost love; he died by accepting the shame the young man had brought to his name. His love for the young man caused him to die to the respect of the village. It was counted as a shame for an old man to gird up his loins and run, as he had done when he'd seen his son. He would also have lost their respect and gone through an inner death when he had not handed his son over for the punishment the law demanded for sons who dishonored their father and mother.

His inner death was swallowed up by his love for the returning son as he flung his arms around the young man, embraced him, and gave him one of his own festive robes, his own shoes, and his own ring. His love continued to swallow death and become resurrection at a public feast of ecstatic joy, where he made it known that the past was not to be discussed; that this was his son once lost to him but now found, once dead to his love but now alive.

In the same way, the Triune God forgave us totally, wiped the slate clean, and robed us with His own righteousness. But to do so, He died in the heart of His Triune Being. He died before the rebellion and consequent sin of the man and the woman and a sinful race had come into being. Jesus, the Son of God, is described as being slain before the foundation of the world, before it became manifested in history at Golgotha.

In these stories, Jesus showed the overwhelming desire of God to forgive. He described Him as excited, hurrying to bestow forgiveness as one who delights in giving and cannot wait to see the joy on the recipient's face when he or she receives.

The elder brother in the parable of Luke 15 wanted to remember sin and condemn and punish the younger brother. The father was not interested in knowing any of the sins the returning son had been involved in; he was consumed with the desire to celebrate the return of his son with an extravagant party. When we feel condemned over our past sin, we must at that point deliberately join the party and dance to the tune of His grace and love.

Our repentance does not move an angry and insulted God to grant us forgiveness. Rather, we are greeted by intense and passionate love that ambushes us, to which we respond in repentance. We can give our lives away to such love.

Jesus emerged from death our new covenant Head, having secured our pardon, and the words of Isaiah were fulfilled.

> "I have blotted out, like a thick cloud, your transgressions, and like a cloud, your sins. Return to Me, for I have redeemed you."
>
> Sing, O heavens, for the Lord has done it! Shout, you lower parts of the earth; break forth into singing, you mountains, O forest, and every tree in it! For the Lord has redeemed Jacob, and glorified Himself in Israel.
>
> Isaiah 44:22,23

Chapter 13

I IN YOU, YOU IN ME

In understanding the covenant, there are two phrases that are of supreme importance. The first is the expression "in Christ"; it is a phrase that indicates that we are vitally in and part of the historical events that took place, and it is a phrase that indicates that by the Holy Spirit, we have actually been joined and made one with Jesus Christ so that His history has become our history. We are vitally one with Him in all that He has accomplished and all that He is now in the heavens.

The second phrase that we find throughout the New Testament is "in the Spirit"; it indicates the dynamic experience of the power of the Spirit actually joining us to Christ and His work and making it real in our lives. What originated in eternity in the loving heart of God the Father was effected in history by the death and resurrection of Jesus Christ the Son and is received and experienced by the people of God through the work of the Holy Spirit.

The problem in the church today is that we tend to focus on one of the phrases to the exclusion of the other. On the one hand, the work of Christ is studied objectively, out there in history, with little or no sense of the Spirit's making that work effective in our lives today. On the other hand, many are fascinated by the Spirit's power with little or no interest in understanding what happened in the historical work of Christ in His making the new covenant. The two phrases belong together; the Spirit is the presence of our covenant God in power making real and vital in us all that has been accomplished by Christ.

I cannot emphasize strongly enough the place of the Spirit in the covenant. Apart from the Holy Spirit, there is no new covenant. The lifestyle of the men and women in the new covenant is that of loving even as they are loved by God; that is an impossible goal apart from the work of the Spirit. The supernatural gifts of the Spirit are part of the dynamic of the covenant people and are totally the work of the Spirit.

The old covenant that Israel lived under was one of shadows, promises, and hope. The new covenant, called a "better covenant," is founded on the work of the Lord Jesus and is primarily the covenant of fulfillment, of power, in which God and His people are dynamically joined as one in the work of the Spirit.

The covenant seeks for union of two parties, something that the old covenant, although revealing the presence of God dwelling in the people's midst in a very real way, could ultimately only point to, anticipate, and wait for. Ezekiel saw clearly that the Holy Spirit living within the believer would accomplish this union. He looked for the day when God would dwell not merely with but within His people.

> **"Then I will sprinkle clean water on you, and you shall be clean; I will cleanse you from all your filthiness and from all your idols. I will give you a new heart and put a new spirit within you; I will take the heart of stone out of your flesh and give you a heart of flesh. I will put My Spirit within you and cause you to walk in My statutes, and you will keep My judgments and do them."**
>
> **Ezekiel 36:25-27**

Both Ezekiel and Jeremiah saw it as the day when the law would be not an exterior command but an interior bent of life.

I In You, You In Me

> "But this is the covenant that I will make with the house of Israel after those days, says the Lord: I will put My law in their minds, and write it on their hearts; and I will be their God, and they shall be My people."
>
> Jeremiah 31:33

"The heart" in Scripture is understood to be the source and life spring of behavior:

> **Keep your heart with all diligence, for out of it spring the issues of life.**
>
> Proverbs 4:23

The law would no longer be a list of exterior commands but would arise from within; it is no longer "This is what you must do" but is "This is what I want to do." Behind all of God's commands is one command—to love as He loves—and the new covenant joins us to the love of God by the Spirit, who is the driving life force and ability to live such a life.

The new covenant goes far beyond the demands of the old, which was summed up as "Love your neighbor as yourself." Under the new covenant, the Spirit coming within the believer pours out the divine love at the center of being. Romans 5:5 tells us, **...the love of God has been poured out in our hearts by the Holy Spirit who was given to us.**

This means that the command of Jesus becomes possible:

> **"A new commandment I give to you, that you love one another; as I have loved you, that you also love one another. By this all will know that you are My disciples, if you have love for one another."**
>
> John 13:34,35

All the prophets saw that the new covenant would be a covenant of the Spirit, when He would indwell God's people; and from that presence, the heart of the law would be a natural direction the heart would go. When speaking of coming to Christ, the evangelist will call people to "receive Jesus" or "let Jesus come into your heart." Although that is true, the New

Testament never speaks of salvation in that way. Always the New Testament speaks of being a Christian as one's receiving the Spirit and the Spirit's dwelling within the person. It is through the Spirit that Jesus dwells in us.

Paul is adamant that if the Spirit does not dwell within us, then we are not Christians at all! By describing our conversion as receiving Jesus, we then believe that the Spirit reception comes later and is for an above average Christian, a spiritual elite. But the Scripture is plain; no one can belong to Christ without having the Holy Spirit. Nor can we know that God is our dear Father and we His sons and daughters apart from the work of the Spirit.

> **But you are not in the flesh but in the Spirit, if indeed the Spirit of God dwells in you. Now if anyone does not have the Spirit of Christ, he is not His.**
> **Romans 8:9**
>
> **And because you are sons, God has sent forth the Spirit of His Son into your hearts, crying out, "Abba, Father!"**
> **Galatians 4:6**

THE BEAR HUG OF GOD

The very first blessing the Father would bestow upon the believer is the gift of knowing the Spirit, through whom he or she has come to know the covenant. Leaders of the earliest church of the first centuries laid hands on the new believer still soaking wet from the water of baptism and prayed they would receive the Holy Spirit. The Spirit had wooed them and brought them to Christ to confess Him as Lord and had brought about the miracle of their being joined to Christ. Now they prayed that the Spirit they lived in would be fully known to them.

> **For by one Spirit we were all baptized into one body—whether Jews or Greeks, whether slaves or free—and have all been made to drink into one Spirit.**
> **1 Corinthians 12:13**

I In You, You In Me

The Spirit is the One who puts us into the body of Christ, and we then drink deeply of Him. One description of the Spirit's relationship to a believer is in the phrase "to fall upon."

> **While Peter was still speaking these words, the Holy Spirit fell upon all those who heard the word.**
>
> **Acts 10:44**

The expression "fell upon" is an old English expression that means "to give a bear hug, embrace fervently."[1] It is used in Luke 15:

> **And he arose and came to his father. But when he was still a great way off, his father saw him and had compassion, and ran and fell on his neck and kissed him.**
>
> **Luke 15:20**

It describes the outpouring of the passionate, unconditional love of the father toward his returning son. It is significant that Luke wrote the Acts as well as his gospel, and so there is no doubt as to what he meant by this phrase. The first experience of the believer is meant to be a bear hug given by God the Holy Spirit welcoming the new believer into the family of God.

When we are given a bear hug, or a fervent embrace, all the ideas associated with love move from an intellectual concept to the actual experience of being loved. When we say that God loves us, we must never think of that in terms of a cold statement of doctrine; we must understand that the Holy Spirit is God in the act of loving us, embracing and enfolding His arms about us. The Holy Spirit is God running to us, flinging His arms around us, and passionately loving us. It is the quantum leap between knowing about a position in Christ, our representative, and actually experiencing the covenant in the bear hug of God the Spirit.

In the 1970s I was invited to address the students at a large and prestigious theological seminary concerning the Charismatic renewal and the experience of the Holy Spirit. I spoke to the entire seminary and then a smaller class. They gave me respectful attention, and after I had finished my lecture to the smaller class I opened the floor for questions. They plied me with questions for some forty-five minutes, and I realized it was degenerating into a tedious theological debate. I held up my hand and said, "I believe I have shown you from Scripture and church history that the new covenant is the covenant of the Spirit, and we can experience Him in our lives today as they did in the New Testament and early church. Now it is time to move from discussion to letting Him come into our lives as we have not done before, and I would ask for the privilege of laying hands on you and praying for you." The classroom was empty in two minutes!

It saddened me to think of those who could debate theology but were terrified of having a close interaction with the God they studied. It reminded me of the scientist dissecting a frog to analyze its parts, never having sat by a lily pond at night to be serenaded by a frog choir! Those people are ministers in large churches today, terrified of the Holy Spirit who alone makes this new covenant the reality we see reflected in the pages of the New Testament.

Without the Spirit, all that we are describing here is beautiful theory but is totally beyond the realm of reality. The love of God is not a theory that theologians debate, but it is communicated to us by the Spirit. The covenant is not the world of theory and study from which the believer must make trips into the "real" world of his own weakness, helpless struggles to be like Jesus and to face the confusions of life in the present darkness.

The Spirit dynamically connects us with the covenant made in history; He is God with us to make real and vital the incredible promises of the new covenant. He joins us to the life of the ascended Jesus and is the enabling power to live His life day by day. The Holy Spirit inducts us into the world of the new covenant called "heavenly places," which is now our real world; we live and work in this passing phony world, but we are not of it, for by the Spirit we are living moment by moment in Christ.

THE DWELLING OF GOD

The new covenant describes a union between God and man so complete as to be paralleled to the glory of God dwelling in the tabernacle and the temple of the old covenant. The bodies of men and women have become the dwelling place of the Holy Spirit. The Greek word that described the entire temple area is *hieron*,[2] but the word for the inmost shrine of the temple, the dwelling of God's glory in the midst of His people, called the Holy of Holies, is naon.[3] Speaking to the believers in Corinth, Paul describes each one of them as the *naos:* the Holy of Holies filled with the divine presence.

> **But he who is joined to the Lord is one spirit with Him.**
>
> **Or do you not know that your body is the temple** *(naos)* **of the Holy Spirit who is in you, whom you have from God, and you are not your own? For you were bought at a price; therefore glorify God in your body and in your spirit, which are God's.**
>
> **1 Corinthians 6:17,19,20**

A man or woman could not imagine such a privilege under the old covenant; the glory of God lived in a tent and later a house that they went to; to say that the glory was within them would be beyond comprehension. In all that we do, in all our relationships, we are the bearers of the divine presence. We must never think of ourselves apart from our absolute unity with the Spirit of Christ.

It is by the presence of the Spirit within us that our relationship to Jesus is made real.

> "And I will pray the Father, and He will give you another Helper, that He may abide with you forever—the

Spirit of truth, whom the world cannot receive, because it neither sees Him nor knows Him; but you know Him, for He dwells with you and will be in you. I will not leave you orphans; I will come to you.

"At that day you will know that I am in My Father, and you in Me, and I in you.

"If anyone loves Me, he will keep My word; and My Father will love him, and We will come to him and make Our home with him."

John 14:16-18,20,23

Our covenant relationship to God hinges on the Holy Spirit's being given to dwell within us. Jesus said that the day of the coming of the Spirit would be the day of believers coming to know union. "In that day," the day of the Spirit's coming, the believers would know **"I am in My Father, and you in Me, and I in you"** (verse 20) and again, **"We will come to him and make Our home with him"** (verse 23). There is not a more intense phrase to describe our union than **"You in Me, and I in you."** Your body, mind, and emotions are the home of deity through the presence of the Spirit. Stop and let these words sink in; hold your skin and know the Spirit dwells in every cell of your body.

THE VINE AND THE BRANCHES

This intense union that we have with the Triune God is described in John 15:1-8, in the image of a vine and branches. Jesus tells us, **"I am the true vine, and My Father is the vinedresser"** (verse 1).

We are not dealing with a parable in these verses but a parallel between the relationship a vine has to its branches and the relationship we have to Jesus through the Spirit. In verse 5 He says, **"I am the vine, you are the branches."** He emphatically states that He is the Vine, we are the branches, and everything that is true of the vine's relationship to the branch is true of His relationship to believers.

I In You, You In Me

I must emphasize that He reports the Vine/branch relationship as an accomplished fact. This is where we believers now are in our relationship to Him. It is important that we see this, because there are many who would see this most intimate relationship as something the believer moves toward as a future deeper life experience. Prayers are offered asking God to help us arrive at this state. This is not an experience of a few advanced believers but the way we understand our covenant relationship to Him from the first moment of our salvation.

We do not know or understand this relationship when we are reborn, any more than a newborn baby understands what being a human is; but like the baby, we grow into what is and has been true from the moment of conception. It will take the rest of our lives to begin to fathom the depth of what this means, and we continue to ever grow in the experience of it. But we will never grow in the knowledge and experience of such a relationship until we grasp the truth that we now are in Christ. Even if, through ignorance, we have not yet lived in its power this is our address: in Christ.

He is saying to the disciples gathered around the table, "This is where you are, and you are to work life out from this basis." This is not a command to try to become a branch! It is not an appeal to our willpower; He is letting us in on the mystery of our relationship to God in the new covenant.

ABIDING IN CHRIST

It is a necessity that we learn the meaning of the words of Jesus "Abide in Me." Various translations try to capture the meaning of the phrase, translating it as "dwell in," "live in," "remain in," and "remain united to." When used of persons, the phrase describes one person persevering in remaining in union with another, to be one with the other in heart, mind, and will. It describes a very real union of fellowship and communication between two or more persons.

In understanding the phrase, it is of supreme significance to note that Jesus describes His intimate relationship with the Father as a mutual indwelling, a union, with this phrase. Abiding is translated here as "dwells."

> **Do you not believe that I am in the Father, and the Father is in Me? The words that I say to you I do not speak on My own initiative, but the Father abiding in Me does His works. Believe Me that I am in the Father and the Father in Me....**
>
> John 14:10,11 NASB

We have seen above that He has already said that at the day of the Spirit's being given, they **"will know that I am in My Father, and you in Me, and I in you"** (John 14:20). Now He uses the phrase again to describe the relationship He has with each believer.

This little phrase is at the heart of the new covenant, describing the incredible union that exists; Christ is in the believer, the believer is in Christ, and Christ is in the Father as the Father is in Him. Colossians 3:3 sums it up: **For you died, and your life is hidden with Christ in God.**

This phrase is the key to the entire Vine/branch relationship; this is how the believer receives and draws his or her life from the life of Jesus.

> "Abide in Me, and I in you. As the branch cannot bear fruit of itself, unless it abides in the vine, neither can you, unless you abide in Me. I am the vine, you are the branches. He who abides in Me, and I in him, bears much fruit; for without Me you can do nothing.
>
> "If you abide in Me, and My words abide in you, you will ask what you desire, and it shall be done for you."
>
> John 15:4,5,7

I In You, You In Me

In his first epistle, John describes a believer as one who is abiding in Christ, in God:

> **Whoever confesses that Jesus is the Son of God, God abides in him, and he in God. And we have known and believed the love that God has for us. God is love, and he who abides in love abides in God, and God in him.**
>
> 1 John 4:15,16

The Christian life is the continual act of remaining in Him, dwelling in Him, being aware of Him as our life, and persevering in this relationship. It is choosing to be present to Him who is committed to be present to us.

Faith is being present in one's spirit, one's inmost self, to God, who is love, knowing that He is the final truth and that He has spoken, as 2 John 2 tells us, **because of the truth which abides in us and will be with us forever.** In that presence, we say the amen to His will and word of truth. It is the result of our abiding in Him that we obey and live His life in our behavior.

> **He who says he abides in Him ought himself also to walk just as He walked.**
>
> 1 John 2:6

> **Now he who keeps His commandments abides in Him, and He in him. And by this we know that He abides in us, by the Spirit whom He has given us.**
>
> 1 John 3:24

JOINED TO HIM

The relationship of Christ the Vine and us believers, the branches, abiding in Him describes the extent of the unity with Christ that we enjoy. It does away forever with the notion that He is "up there" or "over there" or that we come to a meeting of the church in order to find Him. We live joined to Him as the source of our life.

The branches of the vine cannot function without being vitally united to the flow of vine sap that makes the vine a living vine. The life of the vine is the energy, the life source, that produces the fruit that is to be found on the branches. The branches produce the fruit, but they do so from the sap that is surging through them and it is natural for vine life to produce grapes; the branches do not labor at an impossible task of producing a fruit foreign to the nature of the vine.

The living of the love of God in our behaviors is not the ultimate marathon act of our willpower attempting to be like Jesus. Let us accept the fact that the life that the new covenant portrays is impossible for the unaided human to accomplish. It can only take place by Jesus Himself living in us by His Spirit; He becomes the source and the ability to live the life of divine love that is the command of the new covenant. When this is understood, the Christian life is not a labor to produce a lifestyle that is foreign and awkward to us. When the center and source of our life is the fountain of love Himself, a lifestyle of divine love is not foreign and awkward but natural.

The mark of dead religion is to be found in the dedication of the devotee to keep vows with a view to pleasing God. The Pharisees in the days of Jesus spoke of this as "taking the yoke of the law." As oxen were yoked together to pull the plow, so they saw themselves as yoked to the law, observing its every command and attempting by sheer willpower to keep it perfectly. This produced utter spiritual weariness to the point of exhaustion, a burnout of the spirit. To these intense and weary people and those who followed them, Jesus issued the invitation,

> **"Come to Me, all you who labor and are heavy laden, and I will give you rest. Take My yoke upon you and learn from Me, for I am gentle and lowly in heart, and you will find rest for your souls. For My yoke is easy and My burden is light."**
>
> **Matthew 11:28-30**

I In You, You In Me

He called them to abandon the yoke of dead commands and rules that gave no aid in keeping them and come to Him who promised to be the life within them that would fulfill all the rules that God had ever demanded. Christianity is not a list of rules that is superior to the Ten Commandments. He was not offering the latest and best update of the way of the law; He was not operating in the realm of law, but in the realm of life.

He came to bring the new covenant. The word used in the Greek language for "new" is not the word used to describe the latest model in a series, as one would describe a new car. In that sense, "new" would mean the latest and improved edition of a long line of models. "New," as it is used in the new covenant, has the meaning of new in kind. Using the illustration of the new car, this would mean a new form of transport! The new covenant was not an updated rehash of religion-by-law but introduced new concepts that had never entered into the heart of humankind. This was something never conceived in the wildest dreams of prophets—not a list of rules but being joined to the life of perfect love Himself.

We cannot think of a grape-producing branch apart from the vine life flowing through it. They may be discussed separately by botanists in study and research, but in reality there is no such thing. Quite correctly grapes are called the fruit of the vine, never the fruit of the branch! Even so, a believer can never think of oneself apart from the Spirit of Christ living the life of Jesus within and through them.

The grapes are the life of the vine now translated into a form that can be eaten and enjoyed by all. So the ultimate goal of the believer's union is that the life of Christ may be released through his or her humanity to the blessing of the world.

> **"Abide in Me, and I in you. As the branch cannot bear fruit of itself, unless it abides in the vine, neither can you, unless you abide in Me. I am the vine, you are the branches.**

He who abides in Me, and I in him, bears much fruit; for without Me you can do nothing."

John 15:4,5

Maybe even more wonderful is that Christ is joined to and known by the branches. By definition, when we speak of a vine, we include the branches—we do not call a vine without branches a vine, but a stump! Vine life is expressed through the branches; the sap or life of the vine must have branches through which to express and produce the grapes. Apart from the branches, there would be no way of seeing the vine or identifying the nature of its life. We can never think of ourselves apart from our being joined to Christ; but even more amazingly, we cannot think of Jesus except as He is joined to His body, the church, through whom He lives and works on the earth today.

ONE PLUS ONE EQUALS ONE

This is how Paul explained his own life:

I have been crucified with Christ; it is no longer I who live, but Christ lives in me; and the life which I now live in the flesh I live by faith in the Son of God, who loved me and gave Himself for me.

Galatians 2:20

Paul never spoke of his trying to be like Jesus, but of Christ Himself living in and through him.

He based his teaching concerning the Christ-like lifestyle of the believers in Philippi on this reality:

Therefore, my beloved, as you have always obeyed, not as in my presence only, but now much more in my absence, work out your own salvation with fear and trembling; for it is God who works in you both to will and to do for His good pleasure.

Philippians 2:12,13

They had to work out, or literally bring to harvest, their salvation and do so with great awe and seriousness, but they could only accomplish this because God the Spirit was the One within authoring both the will and the actions.

Praying for the Galatians to come to maturity, Paul described his goal in prayer as Christ being formed in them: **My little children, for whom I labor in birth again until Christ is formed in you** (Galatians 4:19).

If Christ was formed in them, He was not merely beside them to comfort and advise them, nor ahead of them to be followed, a guide showing them where to put their feet; He was not in a distant heaven awaiting a long-distance call! It means that He was in them, one with their true and inmost selves.

Paul understood that his preaching was the living Christ ministering through him: **For I will not dare to speak of any of those things which Christ has not accomplished through me, in word and deed, to make the Gentiles obedient** (Romans 15:18). His ministry was not doing something for God, but Christ ministering in and through him.

Paul was jailed by the Roman authorities for his faith, and from the jail cell he wrote to the Philippians. He explained in an intensely personal passage his feelings as he sat in jail and awaited the verdict, which could mean freedom or the death sentence. He asked for their prayers and then wrote:

> **For I know that this will turn out for my deliverance through your prayer and the supply of the Spirit of Jesus Christ, according to my earnest expectation and hope that in nothing I shall be ashamed, but with all boldness, as always, so now also Christ will be magnified in my body, whether by life or by death. For to me, to live is Christ, and to die is gain.**
> Philippians 1:19-21

For him to be in the jail was for Christ to be there experiencing it in him, to the extent that onlookers would see Him in Paul's behavior and words.

This reality is very hard for us to grasp. It is much easier for us to think of Him invisibly beside us. He *is* with us, but the weight of the New Testament simply states that He is in us and we are in Him. He is in me, in you, in us, in all that we do and all that we experience. In us He acts, feels our sorrows, and knows our joy.

"For me to life is Christ" means that the experience I am going through at this moment, what I am doing, is being experienced and done by Jesus within me. It is He who is now punching the keys of this computer; it is He who is going to buy the groceries, going to the class. He has continual access to human life in and by us. Yet we are not passive robots but full participants in life, making true choices. This is the glorious mystery of the faith.

· The mathematics of the new covenant is one plus one equals one. He is one with us, experiencing the tiresome people we have to work with, for it is He working alongside them in us. He experiences the frustrating drivers in rush hour and the old ladies driving slowly on the way home from church. He laughs in your celebrations. He weeps at the graveside of your loved one, experiencing your loss. In you, He faces your temptations and pressures of life. He faces the opportunities and challenges of life, and in you He wills to accept them. And experiencing them in us, He is ever present to our inmost selves as the strength, the wisdom, and the ability to live in each situation. Our lives are not something we tell Him about in our nightly report to Him in prayer, for He has lived them in us second by second.

This life is not the domain of the hermit, so spiritual as to be lived out in a monk's cell. All the commands to love or to put away the works of the flesh are addressed to the mundane flow of life that we live in the home and at the job, surrounded by very ordinary people. It is around the dinner table that we put away anger and malice and put on love; it is on the job that in His strength within us we deal with envy and greed and magnify Him in our bodies. He listens and ministers at the coffee urn to hurting people.

But we are not His glove puppets! We are not nonparticipating robots, the ultimate ventriloquist dolls. The glorified Jesus is in us, and our walk of faith is choosing to die to the desires of the flesh that seek to live independently of Him and fulfill the lie, and instead to helplessly draw on His strength within us.

Chapter 14

THE SUMMATION OF THE CHRISTIAN LIFE

The Christian life may be summed as the consciousness that He lives within us, and we draw upon His infinite life in every situation we find ourselves in. This means that as we grow in Christ and become mature, we will have an increasing sense of our own weakness that we might no longer trust in ourselves and so proportionately live from His strength.

Paul went through a time of pressure in which he learned this lesson of knowing his weakness that Christ may be his life and strength. He recorded it in the following passage:

> And lest I should be exalted above measure by the abundance of the revelations, a thorn in the flesh was given to me, a messenger of Satan to buffet me, lest I be exalted above measure. Concerning this thing I pleaded with the Lord three times that it might depart from me. And He said to me, "My grace is sufficient for you, for My strength is made perfect in weakness." Therefore most gladly I will rather boast in my infirmities, that the power of Christ may rest upon me. Therefore I take pleasure in infirmities, in reproaches, in needs, in persecutions, in distresses, for Christ's sake. For when I am weak, then I am strong.
>
> 2 Corinthians 12:7-10

We do not know for certain what the thorn in the flesh was. It would appear to me that he was speaking of the men who followed him, seeking to smear his name and distort the Gospel he preached, the men whom he had spoken of in the previous chapters. But for our study it really does not matter what it was. Our interest is in what he did with it. It certainly was a trying time; a messenger of Satan driving a stake into your side is no small trial!

In prayer, he begged that God would take it away. The "three times" is a Hebrew way of saying "again and again." But the prayer was answered in an unexpected way. It was not taken away, but became the situation in which Paul learned the reality of Christ living in him. The Scripture tells us, **And He said to me, "My grace is sufficient for you, for My strength is made perfect in weakness"** (verse 9).

The Amplified Bible renders it, **"My strength and power are made perfect (fulfilled and completed) and show themselves most effective in [your] weakness."**

The trouble he was going through had drained him of all faith and expectancy of his own strength; the end of trust in him made him the perfect vehicle to express the strength of Christ.

We find it hard to come to that place of acknowledged helplessness. We do not believe that we are weak! We believe that if we can try a little harder, we can please God. Our prayers rarely are expressions of total weakness; most of the time, they indicate that we want God to help us by strengthening our strength, to help us where we fall short. But Paul's lesson makes it plain that His life can only be seen in and through us at the point of our utter weakness.

The pressures that make us face our weakness can be looked upon as blessings; knowing our weakness apart from Him makes it easier to let His life flow through us, as Paul notes at the end of the passage: **Therefore most gladly I will rather** boast in my infirmities, that the power of Christ may rest upon me (verse 9).

He uses an expression here that is difficult to translate into English. The "resting upon me" is descriptive of being engulfed, out of sight inside something.[1] *The Amplified Bible* renders it **"may rest (yes, may pitch a tent over and dwell) upon me!"**

It would appear that that experience was a life-changing moment in his life. It is possible he was referring to this in Philippians 4:11-13:

> Not that I speak in regard to need, for I have learned in whatever state I am, to be content: I know how to be abased, and I know how to abound. Everywhere and in all things I have learned both to be full and to be hungry, both to abound and to suffer need. I can do all things through Christ who strengthens me.

The words "I have learned" mean "I have been initiated into a secret," and I believe he learned this when he went through whatever is being referred to in 2 Corinthians 12. Being brought to total weakness introduced him to the secret of handling every situation life may throw at him. He had learned the secret of being content in every situation of life.

The word "content" means to be sufficient, to be possessed of sufficient strength, to be enough for a thing.[2] It was the favorite word of the stoics, who believed a man should be able by the exercise of his own willpower to resist the effects of circumstances and to be at peace, undisturbed and unmoved, whatever may be happening around him.[3] Paul was saying that he was initiated into true contentment, which did not arise from his own willpower or self-sufficiency but from Christ within him.

He defined the secret that was really an expansion of what he had been taught. "I can do all things through Christ who strengthens me." It is the word "strengthen" that is of interest to us. The word literally translated is "in-strengthened," maybe better rendered "to infuse with strength" or even "invigorate."[4] He was saying that he could do and face anything in the strength of Christ that infused and invigorated his whole being. *The Amplified Bible* renders it, **I am self-sufficient in Christ's sufficiency.**

I remember wrestling with these truths many years ago in England while sitting in a cafe over a cup of tea. I looked at my pot of tea and suddenly realized that the word "strengthen" was illustrated in the liquid in my cup. The British are rightly proud of the way they make tea! They preheat the full teapot, add a spoonful of tea to every cup and one to the pot, pour on scalding hot water, and wait while the tea fuses with the water. My grandmother would say that she was going to "fuse some tea."

As I stared at the teapot and my cup of tea I realized that I was not really drinking tea, for the leaves were at the bottom of the pot. I was drinking "tea-water"—the tasteless water that had been fused with the rich strength of the tea and made available for me to enjoy. So I realized that in this covenant union with Christ, I do not become Him, any more than the water becomes the leaves, and He does not become me; yet He fuses my bland, empty life with His rich, eternal life that the world might taste of Him through my life. Without Him, my life would be zero.

But again, note that in Philippians 4:11-13, Paul did not speak as a puppet. He was facing and feeling the ups and downs of life, and he was able to do whatever it took and be at perfect peace within it. But he recognized that he did what had to be done in the infused strength of Christ.

The same idea is present in Colossians 1:11, in which Paul is praying for the believers to be **...strengthened with all might, according to His glorious power, for all patience and longsuffering with joy.**

The words he uses here for power are a study in themselves. The word "strengthen" is a form of *dunamis*,[5] which means potential power, or innate ability. The phrase "all might" is another translation of the word *dunamis*, and the phrase "glorious power" is the word *kratos*,[6] which describes the almighty power of God.

"According to" could be translated as "in line with." Let us suppose I want to get to my room on the sixth floor of a hotel. I get in the elevator, and it takes me up to my floor. When the floor of the elevator is level with the sixth floor, the door opens because the two floors are lined up to each other. At that point, it could be said that the floor of the elevator is according to the sixth floor of the hotel.

Put all of this together, and it is saying that the "in-strengthening with all power" that we receive is "in line with the almighty power of God." This is the covenant union we are speaking about!

I've heard people say, "With such power within us, let us perform some miracles!" The verse goes on to tell us of the miracles that are accomplished by this power within us: **for all patience and longsuffering with joy.** The words "patience" and "longsuffering"[7] describe patience toward circumstances and people. Christ Jesus is within us to live in and as us, bringing the almighty power of His life to everything and everyone we have to deal with in the unfolding of life.

PRAYING FOR THE SPIRIT'S ACTIVITY

The Holy Spirit brings us to the covenant and makes us partakers of it, but our relationship to the Spirit must not stop there. He works in us continually to make every detail of the covenant a functional reality in our lives. The whole covenant is accomplished in Christ, and it is all ours as we are joined to

Him. But we must ask confidently for what is ours, and confidently look to the Spirit to bring it to pass.

With this in mind, we see that Paul's prayers for the various congregations scattered around the Mediterranean were bold in asking for the fullness of the Spirit, that the goal of the covenant become a lived reality. Look at one of them that he prayed for the believers in Ephesus.

> **That He would grant you, according to the riches of His glory, to be strengthened with might through His Spirit in the inner man, that Christ may dwell in your hearts through faith; that you, being rooted and grounded in love, may be able to comprehend with all the saints what is the width and length and depth and height—to know the love of Christ which passes knowledge; that you may be filled with all the fullness of God.**
>
> **Now to Him who is able to do exceedingly abundantly above all that we ask or think, according to the power that works in us, to Him be glory in the church by Christ Jesus to all generations, forever and ever. Amen.**
>
> Ephesians 3:16-21

His prayer is staggering in its requests, all of which are based on the fact that the covenant has been made. The ideas of a functional union are realized as he prays for the strengthening power of the Spirit at the core of the believers' being. He prays that they might know real union with Christ, that He might truly become the Self of their self. And then he takes them back to the source of it all, that they might know in their experience the unfathomable love of Christ.

His prayer describes them as "rooted in...love," drawing nourishment from it as a plant draws its life from the ground; as "grounded in love," as a building in its foundation.

The crescendo of his prayer is the heart of the covenant and what Christ has accomplished: **that you may be filled with all the fullness of God** (verse 19). *The Amplified Bible* translates

The Summation of the Christian Life

this, **a body wholly filled and flooded with God Himself!** It describes the complete and ultimate union of the redeemed creature with God. It is the ultimate goal of the covenant; God became as we are that we might become as He is. It is echoed by John: **...because as He is, so are we in this world** (1 John 4:17).

How could such a prayer be answered? It is beyond our creature thoughts! Anticipating such a question, Paul ends with a doxology of praise to the God who is able to do exceedingly abundantly above all that we ask or think—even more than he has just asked! Again, *The Amplified Bible* gives us the meaning of these words in the Greek language:

> ...is able to [carry out His purpose] and do superabundantly, far over and above all that we [dare] ask or think [infinitely beyond our highest prayers, desires, thoughts, hopes, or dreams].
>
> **Ephesians 3:20 AMP**

And how shall He accomplish this that is outside of the realm of our thoughts? **According to the power that works in us** (verse 20); that is, the power of the Holy Spirit. The language of the covenant is translated to our daily life and becomes our real world by the power of the Holy Spirit working in us.

THE BODY OF CHRIST

The Spirit joins us to Him in a union that is described as the relationship of the human body to the head. Paul speaks of such a relationship as the final reality of the believer's identity:

> **For by one Spirit we were all baptized into one body—whether Jews or Greeks, whether slaves or free—and have all been made to drink into one Spirit.**
> **Now you are the body of Christ, and members individually.**
> **1 Corinthians 12:13,27**

Paul is adamant: "you are the body of Christ"; he is not giving an illustration but stating that it is a parallel relationship;

Christ is our Head and we the members of Him and of one another. As a believer, you are in Christ as surely as the hands that hold this book and the eyes that scan this page are in your body and part of you.

Most of us define our Christian experience in terms of being forgiven, while the New Testament speaks of a forgiveness that cannot be separated from our being made one with Him. The two are one and never to be thought of as apart. Having declared the wonder of our total forgiveness in Romans 5, he goes on in Romans 6 to point out the utter impossibility of continuing in sin to glorify God's continual forgiveness—because we are "in" Christ, "in" His death and resurrection.

> **What shall we say then? Shall we continue in sin that grace may abound? Certainly not! How shall we who died to sin live any longer in it? Or do you not know that as many of us as were baptized into Christ Jesus were baptized into His death?**
>
> **Romans 6:1-3**

The head of the body is to be understood as more than the outer shape of the head with its eyes and mouth; he is speaking of the invisible brain within the head, from which the whole body receives its life. So Christ is our invisible Head in the heavens, and we are His visible body expressing His will on earth.

The believer and Christ are one but not merged into an indistinct blob! The believer is not Christ, nor does Christ become the believer. He is the living, ascended, glorified Lord distinct from and objective to the believer, yet by the Holy Spirit's dwelling in the believer the two become a functional one.

The head and the body share the same history. Everything my head has experienced, so has my body; everywhere my head has been, so also my body. If my head is in England, so is my body; and if my head has passed from England to the U.S., so has my body—or I am in big trouble! The two are one in every way. We abide in Him; He is in us, and we are in Him.

So Christ has died and in death has overcome sin, death, and the devil and now lives in the power of an endless life. We are literally joined to Him, and His history becomes our history. His death is ours, so that Paul could say that he was crucified with Christ, even as His resurrection is ours and we walk in the power of that resurrection. We are alive to two worlds at the same time. We live in the heavenly realm while we are also alive in the physical world. We view our world from our union with Christ; we perceive our physical world through inner eyes that have been raised from the dead. We become partakers of the divine nature; we share His eternal life and become members of the Father's family.

The Head and the body—and each of the members of that body—share equally in the same state. If the Head is rich, so is the body. He does not enjoy such riches and live in the heavenly dimension while we live in poverty locked into the material world. All the blessings that He earned by His obedience are ours because we are in Him. We have been joined to His history; we share His death and resurrection and ascension.

> **Blessed be the God and Father of our Lord Jesus Christ, who has blessed us with every spiritual blessing in the heavenly places in Christ...and raised us up together, and made us sit together in the heavenly places in Christ Jesus.**
>
> **Ephesians 1:3; 2:6**

To be in the new covenant is to be part of a community that lives day by day in a heavenly dimension, in a literal spiritual locality that is the person of Christ.

Paul again addresses this when writing to the Romans. We should remember that he had never met the Roman believers and knew nothing of their spiritual condition. He therefore writes what he believes to be true of every believer:

> Or do you not know that as many of us as were baptized into Christ Jesus were baptized into His death? Therefore we were buried with Him through baptism into death, that just as Christ was raised from the dead by the glory of the Father, even so we also should walk in newness of life.
>
> For if we have been united together in the likeness of His death, certainly we also shall be in the likeness of His resurrection, knowing this, that our old man was crucified with Him, that the body of sin might be done away with, that we should no longer be slaves of sin.
>
> Romans 6:3-6

He is speaking of what happened to them at their baptism at the beginning of their Christian life, not of an experience beyond baptism or second blessing. He does not present it as something to be prayed about or prayed for or sought after but as something that is true of every believer. He is saying, "I am talking to believers; therefore, you know what kind of people you are—those who are part of Christ and share His history."

He is reminding them of what is their status as believers and what constitutes the basic facts of their faith in Christ. The most basic fact of who they now are as believers is that they are in Christ, united to Him, and share His history; and this has been true since the first act of their faith in Him when they were baptized.

The believer is together with Christ in His history and at this and every moment is in Him sharing His life. As you sit and read this book, know that the Spirit has included you into the history of the Lord Jesus. You have died with Christ and risen with Him, and you now are seated in the heavenly realm of the Spirit. That is not something you go forward for hands to be laid on you that you might "get it" but something that is, upon which you build your life and behavior.

Many believers live in the frustration of trying to arrive at where they already are! Imagine the confusion of the person who is sitting down while continually being told to sit down! Yet in meeting after meeting believers are urged to die with Christ, and they go forward to pray and be prayed for instead of realizing that the Spirit placed them in Christ and, therefore, into His death and resurrection when they believed upon Jesus.

The knowledge that we are one with the living Christ, His body on earth, is the missing factor in the experience of many believers at the beginning of the twenty-first century. We have been taught to think of God as "up there" and "over there." Our evangelical church language is peppered with statements that back up that thinking. Enthusiastically we tell each other "God was really here today," or we are exhorted in song to "reach out and touch the Lord as He goes by" and to testify that "He touched me."

I know what the speakers and songwriters mean—they speak of special moments when the presence of the Lord is unusually felt. But we have expanded the meaning of their words to define our everyday relationship with God—a relationship in which at best we believe that He is alongside us and, for most, so far away that we have to call out to Him to come from distant heaven and solve the problems that we have. He is the specialist called in to handle the tough problem. After He has worked His wonder we thank Him, He goes back to heaven, and we get on with life.

The believers of the New Testament knew nothing of this, for as we have seen above, they were "in" Him and He was "in" them the same way each cell of one's body is "in" the body and one's life is "in" every cell of the body. They prayed and worshipped Him as objective to them at the right hand of the Father; but at the same time, they knew that through the Spirit they were united as one with Him. The language of the New Testament continually points to the union of the believer with Christ. The expression "in Christ" and its parallels "in the

Lord," "in (God's) love," and "in the Spirit" or the words of Jesus describing life in the covenant "I in you and you in Me" are to be found throughout the New Testament.

We are in Christ—the "in" of being inside something—and He is "in" us. We are immediately present to Him and He to each of us. There is never a second in which we are apart from Him. I am now "in" the atmosphere of planet Earth. In that atmosphere, I find light and life and the food to sustain the life. Likewise, we are placed in Him who is our atmosphere, our very life.

The physical cells of my body are "in" my presence, even as my presence is in them. Each cell is present to me; I am present to each and all the cells. When I leave, the body disintegrates into dust, for I am its life. So we live in Him: He is our life, and we owe our true life to Him.

IN THE WORLD, BUT NOT OF IT

One day I sat by a pond meditating on these things, and I saw a water spider clinging to a reed. Then it disappeared into the water. It had gone to its home at the bottom of the pond made of many bubbles of air that had been captured between the spider's legs and carried and lodged at the base of the reeds. It lived there in the water while breathing the air of the world above. Although it lived in the water, it was not a creature of the water; it breathed air from the world above the pond.

We are not speaking of a fantastic imagination! In His glorified humanity, Jesus is literally and truly present to us, and we actually are joined to and share in His humanity. The person who said and did all that we read of in the accounts in the Gospels is in this room with me, but more than with me—He is in me and I am in Him; we are joined as one.

In my own life, it was one of the great moments of freedom when I discovered this truth. I had struggled in many prayer meetings to die with Christ, but the more I tried to die the more alive to self I felt! Then I realized that the beginning of faith was to realize that I had been included into the covenant, into Him who is the covenant, Christ Jesus. At my new birth, I had been joined to Him; and since then, I shared His history. He lived in me, His life was my life, and all that He had achieved was mine. My problem had been that my uninformed faith was looking into the future for something to happen to me, instead of biblical faith looking back to His death and resurrection and resting in the fact that I was there.

The New Testament believer is one who looks at the whole world through the reality that he or she is in Christ. How we work out our relationships, how we face all the challenges and opportunities of life, all the way to how the believing slave works at his meaningless task—all of life is understood and accomplished because we are in Christ.

> **If then you were raised with Christ, seek those things which are above, where Christ is, sitting at the right hand of God. Set your mind on things above, not on things on the earth. For you died, and your life is hidden with Christ in God.**
>
> **Colossians 3:1-3**

The believers of the New Testament did not live by rules and laws but by His presence in and with them. He dictated their lives from within. Any law was not an imposition but arose from the life within.

LEARNING TO LIVE IN CHRIST

Jack wrote and told me what it was like for him to discover the life of faith, and I quote it here as he wrote it to me. Jack is a missionary in the Philippines. He shared with me how his life had been transformed the summer before his final year in theological seminary.

He described his Christian life up until that time as a struggle. He disciplined himself to live the life he thought of as being a successful Christian life. But his spiritual exercises were not working! His strict regime of Bible reading and prayer, his days of fasting, his list of books by spiritual giants to be read each month, left him cold and empty inside. In moments of facing the stark truth about himself, he knew that on the surface he had the appearance of spirituality; but just below the surface, he knew he was a million miles from what the New Testament demanded. He kept a strict time of prayer but knew he could not begin to keep the command of Jesus to love others as He had loved him. He could get an A+ in his examinations in theology, but if ever anyone tested his true walk with God, he would get an F.

When summer vacation rolled around, he took a job at a builders' yard assisting customers. One of his rules for his idea of a successful Christian was to listen to Christian radio, and so at lunch time he went into a nearby park and listened while munching on a sandwich. The first day, he tuned in to my daily program. He tells what happened to him:

"I don't believe I was a know-it-all, but I was head of my class in theology and believed I had a good grasp of the Gospel and the various theories of the Atonement and did not think anyone could teach me something I didn't know in that area. That day in the park, I heard that the death and resurrection of Jesus, His ascension, and His sending of the Holy Spirit, were the making of a covenant on my behalf. I had never heard it before and was stopped in my tracks. For the next six weeks, I planned my day to be in the park every day to listen and take notes.

"I was forced to confront what Jesus did on the cross in terms of what He was doing for me. In my head I knew how to describe what He did to pass an exam, but this was utterly

The Summation of the Christian Life

different—my heart was getting involved. If asked, I would have told you that Jesus died and rose again to save me from eternal death; I had made Him Lord of my life and was doing my best to obey and serve Him.

"As the days passed, I was confronted with a totally new concept: that He was my representative making a covenant with the Father as and for me. His obedience to the Father in His going to death, His rising out from death, and His return to the Father was as me: I was included in His action. I had thought that I was to produce the perfect obedience and to somehow die to my selfishness. Now I was confronted with the Gospel that said He had obeyed as me, He had died as me, and in His resurrection I had risen from the dead. It was not a matter of my trying to obey and failing, but of trusting His obedience and trusting His death for me; no longer my trying to keep a regime of spiritual exercises, but believing that He had carried me to the Father in His ascension and that I lived in the heavenly realms in the Fathers' presence.

"I realized that I thought of the fullness of my Christian life as being experienced in some act of obedience I would do some day or some experience of God that I would achieve by hitting on the right set of spiritual exercises. I believed and worked toward that "something" that would happen to me so that I would feel and act dead. It was always in the future, and I was always striving to do whatever it would take to make me dead with Him.

"Now I saw that I had been working backwards—trying to achieve what had already been done instead of moving from it as the starting point of life. I had been looking for the experience that would catapult me into an experience of God instead of realizing His resurrection and ascension had carried me into the covenant friendship of God.

"My baptism came alive to me. Prior to this, it had meant very little in my life. Now I understood that it was the physical expression of my faith in His action for and as me as the Spirit joined me to Him.

"One day it was so plain to me that I had died and risen again in my representative. It was accomplished history never to be reversed. I was dead! I had risen from the dead. I was a man who had returned from his own funeral alive in the power of an endless life. And it had all happened in my representative. I wanted to run back to tell my customers I was a resurrected person, but I restrained myself!

"I had always thought of my relationship with God as being between God and me, which made it very shaky and conditional, being dependent upon my current spiritual state. I cannot tell you what it meant to know that my relationship to God was based on and dependent upon Jesus, who was acting as me. My relationship to God, then, is as strong as that of Jesus' to the Father.

"Now my whole existence depended on Jesus. Apart from Him, I have nothing and can do nothing. Apart from Him, I have no history with God and no hope of living the Christian life in the here and now. Looking back, I realize that my Christian life was a struggle to try and fit the image of what I thought a Christian should be. Jesus was the One I tried to imitate. Now, for the first time, I understood what Paul meant when he wrote, 'For me to live is Christ.'

"As my return to seminary drew closer, I realized that a great load had been lifted from me, a load I had not realized I had until it was taken away. I had never thought of myself as a candidate for Jesus' invitation for the laboring and heavy laden to come to Him for rest; but in that six weeks I found He was talking about me, and I came to Him and I rested. I felt like laughing with relief.

"Since that time, I have learned and still am learning to stand in the truth in the daily situations of life, to face life as a man who has passed through death and now lives in the life of Jesus."

THE HIDDEN MYSTERY

That we should be united to Christ, His body living by His life, is the "wisdom" and "mystery" that Paul spoke of that was hidden from past ages but is now revealed to us by the Spirit.

> But we speak the wisdom of God in a mystery, the hidden wisdom which God ordained before the ages for our glory.
>
> But as it is written: "Eye has not seen, nor ear heard, nor have entered into the heart of man the things which God has prepared for those who love Him."
>
> But God has revealed them to us through His Spirit. ...no one knows the things of God except the Spirit of God. Now we have received, not the spirit of the world, but the Spirit who is from God, that we might know the things that have been freely given to us by God.
>
> 1 Corinthians 2:7,9-12

Apart from the enlightenment of the Spirit, the truth is more than we can take in. United to Jesus, we have been granted to share in the love relationship of the Trinity. As the Father loves the Son, so He loves us, for we are in Him. We share His glory and, therefore, are no more of the world than He is.

> "That they all may be one, as You, Father, are in Me, and I in You; that they also may be one in Us, that the world may believe that You sent Me. And the glory which You gave Me I have given them, that they may be one just as We are one: I in them, and You in Me; that they may be made perfect in one, and that the world may know that You have sent Me, and have loved them as You have loved Me.

> "And I have declared to them Your name, and will declare it, that the love with which You loved Me may be in them, and I in them."
>
> John 17:21-23,26

Many believers are so removed from the New Testament and the practice of the early church that their experience of entering the covenant spans months or even years, when it was intended and originally enjoyed at the beginning of the Christian life. Many believers come to faith and only later are baptized and then, at an even later date, experience the fullness of the Spirit. In the early church, entrance into Christ was at baptism and was attended by the convert's being filled with the Spirit, a glorious entrance with great joy into the new covenant.

But God loves us; He is on our side and is merciful to us in our confusion. This chapter is not to suggest that those who waited months or years to be baptized or who have not yet awakened to the Holy Spirit within them are not in the covenant. What I am seeking to point out is that the pattern of the New Testament is the path that brings us to the immediate and fullest understanding of the dynamic working of the covenant in our lives.

Let us not be shy! Nor let us present our unbelief as humility. All He is, all He has won, and all His authority on the earth is made manifest in and through us. He is now our sphere of living. He faces life in and through us. He responds to the challenge of the age in and by us, and we face it in and through His life.

Chapter 15

HOW TO WALK IN THE SPIRIT

But how does this actually work out in life? How do we live from Christ our lives day by day? We have seen that the believer stepping out of the baptismal waters is in a new world in Christ, with new potential that he or she has never known before. Limitations known in the old life have gone in the resurrection of Jesus; signposts that directed us in life have been removed and new ones erected. We can never think about life in the same way again.

We look at our world that has been our comfortable home since we can remember, all we took for granted as part of life—the selfishness, greed, anger, and envy—and see now that it is finished and passing away to give way to the real in Christ. We are coming alive to the new creation built on the infinite, unconditional love of God, in which all the expressions of love—the kindness and compassion, the forgiveness of our enemies—are the normal behavior. In baptism, we have been joined to this world in Christ; in the covenant meal, we are embraced and participate in Him who is the life of this new world.

ACTING AS IF...

How do we live these new behaviors and walk in this love that is alien and foreign to this world? Doing something that we have never done before, that we never thought of doing and, if we did, believed that it could not be done, is begun by acting as if it can be done. Faith has no other frame of reference, no past track record to pull from, no feeling of doing it before that we can dredge up into our consciousness. All we can do is nakedly obey God and act as if Christ lives in us and that we can live the life of the new creation.

Think for a moment of Peter in the boat on the Sea of Galilee hearing the call of Jesus to come and join Him walking on the water. When he obeyed, he did so with no past experience. In fact, he had a track record of sinking! But he proceeded to get out of the boat as if the water were solid ground.

The normal way to journey from a boat to the water is to plunge in, getting over the side in such a way as to prepare to swim. When one gets from the boat to solid ground, the approach is very different. Peter must have flung a leg over the side as if there were dry ground awaiting him.

I use the expression "acting as if" to describe acting without reference to feelings. Unbelief holds a committee meeting with feelings to see if they approve of what He has said. Our feelings scream and howl, telling how foolish we are to proceed with the harebrained plan to obey God. Faith disregards feelings and acts as if God's Word is true. Abraham acted as if God had spoken when he packed his house and left the land of his fathers.

Exodus 14 tells the story of Israel's being pursued by the Egyptian army, with the Red Sea in front of them, and accusing God of abandoning them in the desert. The Israelites were abiding in the presence of the Egyptian army; they were practicing the presence of the Red Sea! Moses practiced the presence of God and heard His voice telling Him what to do.

And the Lord said to Moses, "Why do you cry to Me? Tell the children of Israel to go forward. But lift up your rod,

> and stretch out your hand over the sea and divide it. And the children of Israel shall go on dry ground through the midst of the sea.
>
> Then Moses stretched out his hand over the sea; and the Lord caused the sea to go back by a strong east wind all that night, and made the sea into dry land, and the waters were divided.
>
> Exodus 14:15,16,21

To human logic and feelings, the word of God made no sense. To go forward was to walk into the Red Sea! What could the lifting of a rod do to open a way through the sea? Nothing made sense—obedience to God was to go against all common sense, logic, and feelings. Moses acted out of sheer will, acting as if God's word was true even though he could not understand or be overly excited about it.

When our feelings and logic scream against the will of God, we must ask ourselves, "What would I do now if this were really true?" We then proceed to act as if His Word is true. There is nothing else to do, for we have no past history of doing anything like this; we are proceeding on the Word of God alone.

There is a sense in which faith always behaves in the "act as if" mode. If we believe our feelings that He is not with us but is an absent God who has left us alone in life, our faith in our feelings will then act as if that were true by worrying and sweating anxiety. So, when we believe His covenant Word that He is with us and in us, faith will act as if that is so.

Numbers 13 and 14 tell the story of the unbelief of the Israelites at the border of the land of Canaan at the place called Kadesh. Moses had sent into the land twelve spies, one representing each of the twelve tribes of Israel. They brought back the report of what they had seen. Ten of the spies told of the immense difficulties that awaited them in the land; two of the spies, Caleb and Joshua, brought back a report of faith that recognized the presence of God with His people. It is a lengthy Scripture passage, but read it carefully as it contains what we are looking for. The ten spies are speaking:

> **Nevertheless the people who dwell in the land are strong; the cities are fortified and very large; moreover we saw the descendants of Anak there.**
>
> **Then Caleb quieted the people before Moses, and said, "Let us go up at once and take possession, for we are well able to overcome it.**
>
> **But the men who had gone up with him said, "We are not able to go up against the people, for they are stronger than we." And they gave the children of Israel a bad report of the land which they had spied out, saying, "The land through which we have gone as spies is a land that devours its inhabitants, and all the people whom we saw in it are men of great stature. There we saw the giants (the descendants of Anak came from the giants); and we were like grasshoppers in our own sight, and so we were in their sight."**
>
> Numbers 13:28,30-33

Actually, what they said made very good common sense and was an accurate report given by the five senses. Their advice in the light of what they had seen made good sense too.

> **So all the congregation lifted up their voices and cried, and the people wept that night. And all the children of Israel complained against Moses and Aaron, and the whole congregation said to them, "If only we had died in the land of Egypt! Or if only we had died in this wilderness! Why has the Lord brought us to this land to fall by the sword, that our wives and children should become victims? Would it not be better for us to return to Egypt?" So they said to one another, "Let us select a leader and return to Egypt." Then Moses and Aaron fell on their faces before all the assembly of the congregation of the children of Israel.**
>
> Numbers 14:1-5

The ten spies, and now the people, were practicing the presence of the Canaanite giants and their own natural inability to take God's gift. There is not one mention of God in their entire report; it is, in fact, a report of persons alone and without God or covenant.

They were present to the evidence of their senses and what their senses reported. Sense evidence filled them until their bodies were racked with sobbing and their tents with panic-stricken conversation that plainly said that, in their estimation, God's covenant and promise was a foolish pipe-dream.

"Acting as if" is not to be thought of as an isolated behavior; it draws all of life into it. It encompasses how we think about a situation, how we talk about it to close friends, where we go in our imagination with it.

> **But Joshua the son of Nun and Caleb the son of Jephunneh, who were among those who had spied out the land, tore their clothes; and they spoke to all the congregation of the children of Israel, saying: "The land we passed through to spy out is an exceedingly good land. If the Lord delights in us, then He will bring us into this land and give it to us, 'a land which flows with milk and honey.' Only do not rebel against the Lord, nor fear the people of the land, for they are our bread; their protection has departed from them, and the Lord is with us. Do not fear them."**
>
> **Numbers 14:6-9**

The two spies had seen the same things as the other spies and had cowered before the sight of the great inhabitants of the land. They had seen the inhabitants of the land as they had practiced the presence of God and reminded themselves of His faithfulness to His covenant promises. They talked and acted as if the Lord was with them as their covenant partner. They gave the barest reference to the land and its inhabitants, for the evidence they found in the presence of God canceled out the evidence that their eyes had seen.

Hebrews 4 uses the response of the ten spies and the people to illustrate hearing God's Word but not mixing it with faith.

> For indeed the gospel was preached to us as well as to them; but the word which they heard did not profit them, not being mixed with faith in those who heard it.
>
> **Hebrews 4:2**

Caleb and Joshua saw the impossible task and mixed it with faith. The God of covenant was the starting point of their interpretation of the facts that their senses had recorded.

I WILL FEAR NO EVIL

This principle of choosing to believe without reference to feelings is seen throughout the Psalms, but nowhere better than in the words we all know in Psalm 23: **Yea, though I walk through the valley of the shadow of death, I will fear no evil; for You are with me; Your rod and Your staff, they comfort me** (verse 4).

At this point, David was peering into the future, which is when most of us collapse into anxiety, and imagining the worst thing that could happen to him. He said in effect, "If it comes to that, my worst fear, this is the action I will take: **I will fear no evil.**" He made a life choice that came up out of his inner true self, his spirit. He then gave the reason behind the choice: **...for You are with me;** he was speaking out of his practicing the presence of his covenant God. The valley of the shadow of death was a terrifying reality, but the greater reality that was his starting point was that he was present to God, who would never leave him.

PUT ON BEHAVIOR

Another way the Scripture speaks of this action of faith from the will is of putting on behavior as one would put on a suit of clothes. Do not think of this as the action of a hypocrite. This expression, which is found throughout the Scripture, describes the choice to do a behavior that reflects who we truly are. This may be illustrated from Isaiah 59:17, which speaks of God putting on His actions as a garment.

> **For He put on righteousness as a breastplate, and a helmet of salvation on His head; He put on the garments of vengeance for clothing, and was clad with zeal as a cloak.**
> **Isaiah 59:17**

He certainly is not covering who He is with an action or behavior that is hiding who He really is! The expression "put on" indicates the doing of a behavior that reflects who we really are in our inmost selves.

Or again, Isaiah 51:9 calls upon God to put on strength: **Awake, awake, put on strength, O arm of the Lord!** Very obviously, He is not putting on something that He did not have before but is bringing forth a potential action of His true self.

To "put on" a behavior that is fitting, expressing who we know ourselves to be in Christ as we abide in Him, is not hypocrisy but the act of faith. Hypocrisy is putting on a behavior, not because we practice His presence but because we want to impress, please, or deceive other people.

We put on the behavior of Christ because abiding in Him, present to Him, and seeing ourselves for who we truly are in Him, we know such behaviors to be the truth. He never asks us to be who we are not. In Scripture, the garment describes the person. We put on the garments of praise because we have been called out of the darkness to proclaim His praises. We are joined to Him who is love, and the love of God is shed abroad in our hearts, and we choose with an act of will to clothe ourselves in love behavior. In putting on Christ behaviors, we are workers together with the Spirit to do the will of the Father. The energy of the Spirit connects our behavior with our true selves and our whole beings are drawn into line.

We put on clothes that fit us, that reflect who we truly are, and at certain times that shows up more than at other times.

Joseph put on the garments of prime minister, throwing away the prison clothes, because he now was the prime minister, and it was fitting that he wear the clothes of his position. He could not have fulfilled his duties if he had insisted on wearing the prison clothes around the palace!

The prodigal threw away the garments of the far country and put on the best robe because the rags of the far country did not describe who he truly was, the beloved son of his father.

In both of these cases, the men would have had to grow into feeling comfortable in the new clothes. After prison garb and rags, it would feel odd, awkward, even embarrassing, to dress in the new clothes. These men would have had to get used to the sniggering of old friends making fun of them dressed in such an unusual way.

Likewise, we go through a period of awkwardness as we get used to the reality that we truly are not the persons we were but are new creations in Christ and, therefore, called to wear new behaviors. The pressure of the world around is to entice us, bully us, into putting on the old clothes that no longer describe who we are.

> **And do not be conformed to this world, but be transformed by the renewing of your mind, that you may prove what is that good and acceptable and perfect will of God.**
> **Romans 12:2**

Phillips' version of this reads, **Do not let the world around you squeeze you into its own mold.** I have never forgotten the pathetic sight of a grandmother in the teenage clothes department dressing herself in clothes that she had outgrown thirty years before! We are in Christ, joined to Him in covenant, and the behaviors of the flesh no longer fit; we make fools of ourselves trying to be who we are not.

Clothes do not come to our bodies; we go to the clothes closet, choose the ones that we want or need to wear, and deliberately put them on our bodies. We choose the ones that fit us, that describe who we are. As faith behaves and acts out the truth of who He is and who we are in Him, the Spirit witnesses that truth within us and draws our whole being into line with it.

This is not only true in the development of a godly life, but also the ungodly. If we assume a behavior, we will become what we have chosen to act like. A dramatic illustration of this is in Psalm 109:

> **As he clothed himself with cursing as with his garment, so let it enter his body like water, and like oil into his bones.**
> **Psalm 109:18**

This man whom David describes put on cursing his neighbor as he put on his suit of clothes in the morning. The result was that his behavior linked with his ungodly self, his behavior seeped into his body, and he became what he had assumed. This is the energy of the flesh at work—to "put on," or assume, unforgiveness by willing not to forgive—and bitterness becomes the way one is in one's deepest self.

We have seen teenagers fall in with bad company and before our eyes "put on" dresses in the behaviors of the gang. They adopt the language, music, and lifestyle of the gang, and it is only a matter of time before it has become their lifestyle; before they have become the behavior, they "put on."

PUTTING ON CHRIST

The Epistles abound in the language of putting on behavior by a willed act of faith: **But put on the Lord Jesus Christ, and make no provision for the flesh, to fulfill its lusts** (Romans 13:14).

We not only put on the behaviors of the Lord Jesus, but we starve the flesh by making no provision for its needs. This means that we avoid the places and triggers that the flesh craves, not in order to try to kill it but because that is not who we are anymore, and we neither need it nor want it. We strengthen who we truly are by faith behaviors, and we reinforce the crucifixion of the flesh by not feeding its cravings. The cries of the flesh are like the itch of an amputated toe! The toe has been cut off but the toe feelings are still there. We declare the feelings and act the truth, and we become who we are.

Our old behaviors are seen now for what they are—rags filled with the lice of lust—and we fling them away from us. We do this in baptism, but it must then be implemented in the choice of faith. Not only is this so, but the behaviors of the past are now ill-fitting; we do not look good in them anymore. In Christ, we have grown out of them and they no longer describe who we are; they are old and ready for the garbage can.

Therefore, as the elect of God, holy and beloved, put on tender mercies, kindness, humility, meekness, longsuffering; bearing with one another, and forgiving one another, if anyone has a complaint against another; even as Christ forgave you, so you also must do. But above all these things put on love, which is the bond of perfection.
Colossians 3:12-14

Notice that, first, the persons this is addressed to are identified; they are the "elect of God, holy and beloved." Because of who they are, they are commanded to put on a certain lifestyle, to do certain things. There is no mention of feelings. The lifestyle that they are to wear is essentially the love first seen on earth in the humanity of Jesus and now ours through the Spirit. It becomes functionally ours as we assume the behaviors of that love. Then the final sentence calls us to put on love as if putting on the coat that covered all the others.

I am often asked how we can love as Jesus loved, and that is an important question because He commanded us to do just that! We should not continually examine ourselves to see if we have godly feelings of love toward our neighbor because this command is not speaking of behavior arising from feeling. It calls us to will to put love on: Act as if you do! You will find that when you behave in faith as if you love someone, the Spirit will silently work within you, and you will soon come to truly love the person.

We are commanded to put on these behaviors, not to feel them. We are directed from the Word of God that we hear as we practice abiding in His presence, not from our dark flesh feelings.

> **That you put off, concerning your former conduct, the old man which grows corrupt according to the deceitful lusts, and be renewed in the spirit of your mind, and that you put on the new man which was created according to God, in true righteousness and holiness.**
>
> **Ephesians 4:22-24**

A radical change has taken place, and we must now adopt the radical behavior that goes with it. I must emphasize that we are not marionettes made to act by the Spirit's pulling strings! We act; we will choices; and our faith declares, "In Christ, this is who I am; therefore, I choose to act in accord with truth." To "act as if" is the act of faith of Christ in my life, that He is truly within. Faith says, "That being the case, this is what I can and must do." It is saying that we believe He has willed and worked within us and, therefore, we will now work out our salvation.

> **Therefore be imitators of God as dear children.**
>
> **Ephesians 5:1**

We imitate God, do His behaviors after Him; but notice carefully that this is not the old, dead-end path of the flesh trying to be like God. We imitate God "as dear children"; we have received His life, and putting on His behavior is a matter of drawing from His life that is within us and, in so doing, becoming who we are, His dear children.

I was visiting missionaries deep in the jungle of West Africa and flew from station to station in a small aircraft. As we landed on the bumpy homemade airstrips, we were greeted by the missionaries, accompanied by excited believers. On one such trip, I went down the receiving line shaking hands with each missionary and found at the end of the line a chimpanzee dressed in clothes from barrels of old clothes sent from the U.S. He stood solemnly extending his hand, which I shook. We walked back to the mission house, and the chimp followed us, hands behind his back and nodding solemnly as the head missionary was doing as he talked to me. His nearly perfect imitation of a missionary was greeted with howls of laughter from all.

I flew from there to London to be greeted by my daughter and a friend. The friend said, "Your daughter gets more like you every day." I suddenly remembered the chimp. The more perfectly he imitated a human, the more we laughed; the more my daughter became like me, the more we were congratulated. I realized that my daughter, living from my life, was imitating the behavior of that life she saw in me; when animal life tried to imitate human life, it was obviously just that—and the better it was done, the greater the laughs.

When we have received eternal life and are joined to God our Father in covenant, it is natural to adopt His behavior and walk it out from His Spirit within. But when the flesh tries to imitate the life of God, it is a shabby imitation at best, and were it not so eternally tragic, it would be the best joke in the universe.

THE PLACE OF FEELING

But, someone says, "Is the entire Christian life void of feeling? Is it all lived in cold choices and willing?" Not at all. It is quite the reverse: The Scripture abounds with words indicating strong emotion. Words like "rejoice with joy unspeakable and full of glory" or "the peace of God that passes human understanding" tell us that the believer can be caught up in ecstasy in His presence.

But the terrible possibility is that we can become addicted to the feeling of His presence and rejoice in it instead of His true presence. I know some dear believers who are consumed by spiritual lust, living for the next sensation to assure them that God is with them. They are chasing the wind and ever seeking the new thing and never knowing the satisfaction of the person of the Lord Jesus, because they are obsessed with feeling Him.

Going hand in hand with that is the belief that we live the Christian life by experiences and feelings. The feeling of His presence is given to us as His gift, in which we rejoice, but faith settles in to act as if His presence fills our lives.

Many years ago, I walked with a brother in what I believed to be a covenant relationship. We prayed together, shared the truths we found together, and tried as often as possible to minister together in conventions, complementing each other's message. What I did not know was that he was envious of me and quietly plotting the destruction of my ministry. When he finally showed his intention, it was in a large meeting; what he said and did shattered me. I knew that the lies he had announced publicly would be broadcast throughout the U.S. before midnight and by tomorrow would be accepted as truth, and my ministry would be over. But that the words had been spoken by him, my friend, left me paralyzed and numbed. I stumbled from the platform of the auditorium with every eye upon me and, like a robot, walked out of the building.

I walked for several minutes like a zombie, and then a rage exploded inside me. Feelings flamed like an inferno against him. I felt murder in my heart for the betrayal.

Deep inside me I heard the still, small voice of the Spirit, *He can never destroy you, but if you continue the way you are you will destroy yourself!* In that moment, I ceased to be present to what had happened, to my betrayer, to my hurt, and to what would happen; I became present to Christ, my life, to the love that embraced me, and I participated in and knew what I had to do.

The expression of rage that I had been entertaining was not a garment that fitted a child of God such as I knew myself to be. I knew that I had to forgive him. But in my entire being I did not have a feeling to forgive! I had never had to forgive a person for something as big as this; I had no track record, and my feelings were against the whole idea. I put on forgiveness; I acted as if I could forgive by a sheer act of willing obedience to God.

I turned in the road, pointed back to the building, and naming him said aloud, "I forgive you for what you have done, in the name of the Lord Jesus Christ. I am not your judge; I release you, and I send you to Him to deal with as He will." I had immediate peace and walked on down the road.

Ten minutes later I heard within me, *How could he have done that to you?* And every revengeful feeling, like a furnace heated seven times hotter, surged through me.

I stopped and turned again in the direction of the building and said, "Ten minutes ago, this man was released to the keeping of the Lord Jesus. He is forgiven, and I have no more say in the matter."

Throughout that night this repeated, with the time between the feelings of rage returning getting longer and longer. Then they returned maybe once a day, then once a week, until they did not return. I still did not have feelings of warmth and joy at the sound of his name, but from my position of dwelling in Christ I held to the reality that he was forgiven.

A year later he called, weeping on the phone. What he had unsuccessfully tried to do to me, someone had effectively done to him. He had lost everything and was out of the ministry, homeless and living on the street. My heart was filled with divine compassion, and I brought him into my home and ministered to him and gradually restored him to faith and ministry.

That is what I mean by "acting as if" and "putting on" a godly behavior.

OVERCOMING TEMPTATION

What of the temptations that come upon us—when like a whirlwind our feelings, thoughts, imaginations, and even our physical bodies are all swept up into the call of a sin, a habit, or lust?

We become deliberately present to God, which means that we choose not to be present to our feelings or to our circumstances or to the powers of darkness. For believers newly delivered from drug and sexual addictions, this cannot be emphasized strongly enough. Do not wait until the temptation is at full strength, but at the first thought, the first suggestive whisper, immediately be present to the Spirit of Christ. Realize that He is in you, your body is His temple, you are in Him, and He is your life and breath.

This is so important because if we do not believe it, we will believe that the churning of our flesh is our real person. Write this indelibly on your mind: "Through the blood of the covenant and by the working of the Holy Spirit, the real, true me is forgiven, washed, and cleansed; in my innermost and true self, I am hidden with Christ in God. From that position in Him, I look straight into the face of God my Father, who declares over me that I am His beloved child in whom He delights, and I respond with 'Abba, Daddy, my Father!'"

This is the first weapon in your armory combating the shame that will suffocate you if you are not sure of who you are.

This is never more true than in the shame-filled bondage to sexual addiction. A man I will call Chris shared with me how after a few days of repenting and calling on God for deliverance from pornography, the old seducing call to the magazine rack and the movies on television came as a whisper in his mind. His first reaction was shame. He told me, "I thought, *Oh no! I am just the same person I always was. The thoughts and lusts only went into hiding, and now here we go again!*" He felt deep shame and self-hatred and could not think of facing God. Because of such a mood, it was only a short time before he yielded and plunged into an even deeper self-hatred that sought medication for its pain in more pornography.

When I told him that the thoughts and lusts both in body and imagination were not the true Chris, for he was hid with Christ in God and was at that very moment the focus of His love, he was speechless. I told him, "The thoughts and physical craving are the death thrashings of your defeated enemy. Do not yield to the temptation, but do not give it your attention either; choose at that moment to deliberately abide in Christ, be present to the God who loves you, and at the same time be present to who you really are—His child. To think on your temptation, to give it all your attention in trying to fight it, is to practice the presence of the lust and be filled with shame, to not be present to God."

Our pathway to sure defeat in any area of strong temptation is to feel shame at having the tempting thoughts and then to fight them and try not to think them. That course of action inevitably fails; and as the thoughts continue to come, pictures flash on the screen of the imagination, relentlessly crushing all of our resolutions to not obey their bidding. We inevitably fall and are then plunged yet deeper into hopeless despair and shame.

We do not deny the feelings that rage within us, nor do we try not to have them. The more we wrestle with them, the stronger they get, for in so doing we are giving them status; we are calling them forth as part of the true us, as valid feelings to be confronted and fought with. They are not! They have been crucified with Christ, and the real you is being called forth by the Spirit through this situation.

I told Chris, "When the gnawing of lustful habits makes you physically restless, choose to be still within, whatever your body is doing, and realize that in this minute you are in the presence of God. Know that He does love you and is on your side against the flesh. Without the presence of shame, you can tell Him your feelings, whatever they are, share with Him what you are going through, and give Him thanks that He has made you His very own. Do it out loud to take you out of the spaghetti bowl of your thoughts. He is in the process of separating you from your past and making you whole. You are at that moment beginning to be the new person that you truly are."

Now, from that center where we have our identity as joined to Him, we choose to put on the action behavior of Christ. We put on the behaviors of Jesus, declaring that they reflect in our outer persons who we truly are in our inner persons.

USING TEMPTATION

This is the secret of using temptation. We must not see temptation as the enemy but the necessary confronting of the negative for the glorious positive of our life in Christ to blaze forth. We cannot show forth the life of Christ in a vacuum; He is seen over and against the negative of the calls of the flesh.

One day, I was talking with some people about the raising of Lazarus from the dead, and some dreamy-eyed believer said, "Oh, that would be so wonderful to be raised from the dead by Jesus!" I reminded her that before you can be raised you have to die! The power of Jesus to raise the dead can only be seen with a dead body; it cannot function in a vacuum.

If we will know the fullness of the love of God in us, we must be in the midst of people who cannot be loved by the best efforts of human love. We will discover the peace of God that passes human comprehension when we are in a situation where human flesh would be in a state of nail-biting anxiety. The joy of the Lord is best experienced when our circumstances would naturally plunge us into despair. As we have seen, Paul had to learn the lesson that the power of God is best seen in our weakness and the conundrum of the covenant is that **...when I am weak, then I am strong** (2 Corinthians 12:10).

Trial and temptation are allowed in our lives to draw out of us the fullness of the life of Christ that, but for the temptation, we would never think of drawing on, for there would be no need. We should not view temptation as an enemy but as the opportunity to live in the "act as if" and "putting on" mode and so to grow in grace where we have never grown before. James exhorts us to **...count it all joy when you fall into various trials** (James 1:2).

Temptation is the opportunity for the Spirit to produce the life of Christ in our lives. We will always fail if we approach temptation as something to be overcome by our willpower for God, instead of by the strengthening of the Spirit of Christ. Temptation is the time when we die to the pseudo strength of our flesh and enter into the resurrection life of Christ.

CHRISTINE'S STORY

Christine knew her problem: It was gossip. She could not resist the latest juicy morsel that her friends dropped in her ever-open ear. She could not resist passing it on with such an air of secrecy that the receiver felt honored to have been selected to be trusted with such a top-secret piece of information. She had been the center of more than one ugly situation in the church for the insinuations and half-truths she peddled. Then the Spirit began to convict her. She realized that she was grieving the Spirit and hurting her brothers and sisters. She knew that this was what the Spirit meant when He said, **Let no corrupt word proceed out of your mouth, but what is good for necessary edification, that it may impart grace to the hearers** (Ephesians 4:29).

The Spirit made her very aware that every time she picked up the phone a torrent of corrupt communication came out of her mouth, and she set herself to stop it. But she quickly discovered that she was powerless to stop it. When the other party said, "Have you heard…" she forgot her resolution, sucked up the information, and questioned to get the last drop out of the informer. When she put the phone down, she was heartbroken over what she had done and then disgusted with herself for not having more control. She posted notes by the phone telling her what to say when someone tried to share gossip, but given the chance she was blind to notes and forgot all promises and resolutions made to God.

Her determination to pass on only edifying and grace-imparting words didn't work either. She was drawn to gossip with her friends, however much she prayed for strength. She began her day by promising Jesus that this day would be different. Before she met with friends, she whispered to herself, "I will not be drawn into gossip. I will not. Jesus, I promise You." But before thirty minutes passed, she had forgotten all her vows.

She asked to see me after a meeting in her church. I had been speaking on the subject of our covenant union with Christ, and a ray of hope that she could overcome her sin made her seek me out. I listened to her story and then asked her, "How would you describe your approach to this temptation, Christine?"

She looked puzzled and almost annoyed: "I hate it. I don't want it, and that's why I say no to it every time I think it's coming up!"

I said, "Christine, never say no to temptation; say yes to Jesus!" She looked shocked but nodded for me to go on. I continued, "When you say no, you are drawing on your willpower, concentrating all the energy of your flesh to refuse the temptation. You are mustering all your human ability to do something to please God. But that isn't the way the Christian life is lived. That is dead religion at its best! This is your God-given opportunity to die to the flesh activity of gossip and of trying to stop gossiping, and let Christ by the Spirit live through you."

I went on to share the truths of her union with Christ and show her Colossians 3:1-3: **If then you were raised with Christ, seek those things which are above, where Christ is, sitting at the right hand of God. Set your mind on things above, not on things on the earth. For you died, and your life is hidden with Christ in God.**

The setting of the mind on Christ and our lives being hidden with Christ in God are worked out, among other things, in verses 8, 12, and 13.

> **But now you yourselves are to put off all these: anger, wrath, malice, blasphemy, filthy language out of your mouth.**
>
> **Therefore, as the elect of God, holy and beloved, put on tender mercies, kindness, humility, meekness, longsuffering; bearing with one another, and forgiving one another, if anyone has a complaint against another; even as Christ forgave you, so you also must do.**

The putting off of filthy language and the putting on of the language of love could not be achieved in isolation from the first three verses. I told her, "It is because you are now united with Christ and He is your life that you can learn the language of His love. It is not a matter of saying no to filthy language but yes to your true new self in Christ and letting His love pour through you. You are not a robot. You have a choice, a big choice, to make. But it is not the choice to try in your own strength to stop gossiping, but to yield to Christ your life, love, and strength."

My meetings had ended, and I flew out the next day. She later wrote me of the radical change that had come to her since that conversation. Beginning that same night, her whole approach to the problem had changed. Instead of focusing all her energy in promising God that she would not gossip she instead prayed, "I thank You that I am included into Christ, and His Spirit lives in me. I thank You that this is who I truly am and therefore this gossiping, corrupt language is not compatible with my true self. You are my life, Lord Jesus, and I ask that all day and every day You fill my thoughts and the words that I speak. I am helpless before this desire for filth, and I ask that the Spirit bring forth Your desire for truth and love in my mind and mouth." When she met with her friends or the phone rang, she whispered, "This is Your conversation, Lord!"

She related what happened when the phone rang that first day. The first thing she noticed was that there was not the usual tension caused by fear that she was going to fall again. There was, instead, the rest that He indeed was in her and this was His conversation; she could afford to rest and enjoy how He would handle it. As the conversation got under way, she realized that she really had a choice; she was not being swept along by the sound in her friend's voice as she prepared to divulge the latest tidbit. She was not a robot; she was choosing, yet she realized the power to choose was His gift. With the phone to her ear, she realized that she did not want to get involved in what her friend had to say and that she did not have to. Then came the words that normally would have swept all her resolves and dedications away: "You will never guess what Jane's husband did at work the other day!" There was a quiet sense of the Holy Spirit within Christine as she said, "No, Susan, I have not heard anything, and I would prefer not to. The Holy Spirit has been convicting me about the way I have been talking about people. I will pray for Jane's husband, but I do not need to know, for the Lord knows what he did." Taken aback, her friend said, "Oh!" and rapidly brought the conversation to an end.

At the next meeting at the church, her clique was looking at her strangely as she walked towards them to join them. Obviously Susan had passed along the phone conversation. Christine had prayed about this first meeting with her gossip buddies and had been urged by the Spirit to take the offensive. She began, "I just have to share what the Holy Spirit has done in my life in the last few days..." and went on to tell them of the work of the Spirit in her life in the last hours. That was the end of temptation from that direction. Some of the women later called her and told her they had been going through the same conviction and thanked her for saying what she had said.

In the next days, she was convicted that this was not merely about not gossiping but about taking the initiative of loving people. She read the text that had started it all—**Let no corrupt word proceed out of your mouth, but what is good for necessary edification, that it may impart grace to the hearers** (Ephesians 4:29)—and the passage I had shared with her:

> **But now you yourselves are to put off all these: anger, wrath, malice, blasphemy, filthy language out of your mouth.**
>
> **Therefore, as the elect of God, holy and beloved, put on tender mercies, kindness, humility, meekness, longsuffering; bearing with one another, and forgiving one another, if anyone has a complaint against another; even as Christ forgave you, so you also must do.**
>
> **Colossians 3:8,12-14**

She realized that the Spirit did not want her merely to stop gossiping but to commence an entirely new life in the way she looked at others and what she did with their problems that she may hear about. It was not merely stopping one activity but starting a new one. She prayed and asked the Holy Spirit to lead her. She realized that in some way her tongue had affected every family in the membership of the church. She took the church directory and began to pray through it, bringing each family in the church before the Lord. She realized that she had spent hours of every week either in active gossiping or finding out the details of the weaknesses and failings of others. She set aside the time now to pray and make the weaknesses she heard of the grist for her prayers. The Spirit of God within her has turned around her besetting sin to become her ministry that blesses the church.

Chapter 16

THE PEOPLE OF THE SPIRIT

The new covenant is anticipated throughout the Old Testament, and to some extent it is the subject of all the Prophets. Although there are many descriptions of what that covenant would be like, there is one phrase that is used again and again: "I will be their God, and they shall be My people."

> "But this is the covenant that I will make with the house of Israel after those days, says the Lord: I will put My law in their minds, and write it on their hearts; and I will be their God, and they shall be My people."
>
> Jeremiah 31:33

> "Then I will give them a heart to know Me, that I am the Lord; and they shall be My people, and I will be their God, for they shall return to Me with their whole heart."
>
> Jeremiah 24:7

> Moreover I will make a covenant of peace with them, and it shall be an everlasting covenant with them; I will establish them and multiply them, and I will set My sanctuary in their midst forevermore. My tabernacle also shall be with them; indeed I will be their God, and they shall be My people.
>
> Ezekiel 37:26,27

He is "our God," and this is reflected in the Psalms when the psalmist cries out, **O God, thou art my God** (Psalm 63:1 KJV). Only a people in covenant with Him can say that He is uniquely their God. A person outside of the covenant may well call on God, but would not dare to lay any claim upon Him.

We have seen that one of the major differences between a contract and a covenant is in what is being exchanged. A contract is the exchange and passing of property, possessions; a covenant is the exchange of persons. The contract says, "This is now yours," while the covenant says, "I am now yours." So God does not merely promise His impersonal blessing; His blessing is the gift of Himself in the person of the Holy Spirit.

THE NEW COVENANT TEMPLE

We cannot think of the new covenant effective in the earth apart from the Holy Spirit. The indwelling Spirit characterizes the new covenant, as Ezekiel prophesied:

"I will put My Spirit within you and cause you to walk in My statutes, and you will keep My judgments and do them" (Ezekiel 36:27).

The indwelling Spirit communicates to believers all the blessings of the covenant that have been purchased by the Lord Jesus. Apart from Him, the blessings would be beautiful but unobtainable ideas.

We have seen that the Holy Spirit takes up His abode in every believer, and his or her body becomes His dwelling place. But that is only the beginning. The Holy Spirit does not only dwell in each man and woman as an individual; He dwells in the body of believers in every locality, forming that body into the temple of the new covenant in that locality.

The temple of the old covenant was in Jerusalem, in the land of Israel; it was the place where God chose to make His name and presence known. The people of the covenant lived in that land and yearly went to worship their covenant God in Jerusalem, celebrating Him and the covenant He had given them. But in the new covenant, there is no land or place where the covenant God dwells in the midst of His people. He dwells in His church and specifically the body of believers—His people—in any given locality. It is in His people that His presence is uniquely made manifest.

We have seen that the Greek word *naos*, meaning "the Holy of Holies," is used to describe the body of every believer. (1 Corinthians 6:15.) However, although we dealt with that aspect first, the primary use of the word is to describe the gathered company of God's people. The believers in any town or city constitute His people, and they are the dwelling of God, the place where the glory of God dwells in that locality.

> **In whom the whole building, being joined together, grows into a holy temple** *(naos)* **in the Lord, in whom you also are being built together for a dwelling place of God in the Spirit.**
>
> **Ephesians 2:21,22**

Listen to the covenant language Paul uses to describe the believers in Corinth:

> **For you are the temple** *(naos)* **of the living God. As God has said: "I will dwell in them and walk among them. I will be their God, and they shall be My people."**
>
> **2 Corinthians 6:16**

> **Do you not know that you are the temple** *(naos)* **of God and that the Spirit of God dwells in you? If anyone defiles the temple** *(naos)* **of God, God will destroy him. For the temple** *(naos)* **of God is holy, which temple** *(naos)* **you are.**
>
> **1 Corinthians 3:16,17**

The coming of the Spirit in the new covenant has removed the veil separating sinful men and women from the presence, so that we can behold the glory of the Lord Himself in the face of Jesus Christ. We have entered the Holy of Holies; we live behind the veil in the very presence of God. We not only behold Him but also are being transformed into the same image from one degree of glory to another.

> But we all, with unveiled face, beholding as in a mirror the glory of the Lord, are being transformed into the same image from glory to glory, just as by the Spirit of the Lord.
>
> 2 Corinthians 3:18

The temple of the new covenant is "living stones," the people of God, God dwelling in the midst of us by the Spirit. The cornerstone, by which the whole building holds together, is the Lord Jesus. The people are not only the stones of the temple but also the priests who serve, worshipping in the power of the Spirit.

> **Coming to Him as to a living stone, rejected indeed by men, but chosen by God and precious, you also, as living stones, are being built up a spiritual house, a holy priesthood, to offer up spiritual sacrifices acceptable to God through Jesus Christ.**
>
> **But you are a chosen generation, a royal priesthood, a holy nation, His own special people, that you may proclaim the praises of Him who called you out of darkness into His marvelous light.**
>
> **1 Peter 2:4,5,9**

In the earliest church no one went to church, for it was not understood as a building on Third and Main Street that one could go to. The church was made up of believers who were the living stones or bricks making up the structure of the new covenant temple in their locality, wherein the presence of God was known and made manifest. The church was not primarily a building but people who gathered together and, having worshipped and celebrated their covenant God, became the church scattered throughout the city.

JOINED TO THE BODY OF CHRIST

The New Testament knows nothing of an isolated believer living in a private relationship to God. Each individual believer is joined to Christ and therefore to His body, the people of God.

The People of the Spirit

The covenant is not with us as individuals but with the "people" who are in Christ, with whom the covenant is made. We have an intensely personal relationship with God in Christ, but we do not have an individual relationship; it is a corporate one.

Becoming a Christian means that one has been found by Him and come to Him personally, but at the same time is plunged into a relationship to the covenant people, the body of Christ. In His parables, Jesus found the individual lost item but always with a view to bringing it back to the corporate expression. The lost sheep was returned to the flock, the lost coin was returned to take its place with the woman's nine coins; the lost son returned not only to the father but also to the family celebration.

It is the people of God that are the object of God's saving activity in Christ. God is not saving an unconnected set of individuals, each with a private, isolated relationship to Him; He is saving a company, a special people. The Scriptures tell us that He **...gave Himself for us, that He might redeem us from every lawless deed and purify for Himself His own special people, zealous for good works** (Titus 2:14).

In the Western world we think of ourselves as isolated from our neighbors, islands that live and succeed or fail with little or no reference to anyone else. It follows that salvation is seen as personal and individual, a relationship with God that is in no way connected with anyone else.

That has given us the Christian alone in front of the television, a member of the electronic church. We must understand that this scenario is unknown in the New Testament. Salvation is intensely personal, and we are drawn to Christ individually, but we are saved to become part of His corporate body. To enter the new covenant is to be joined to Christ and to His people to become the embodiment on the earth of the presence of God.

Our confusion on this point is multiplied; there are many verses in the New Testament that appear to apply to the individual, but in the Greek they are plural. In our English translation, we no longer have the plural form of "you"; the fact is that "you" is plural, but we no longer use the singular "thou." The only way we can get the true sense of this and many other verses in the New Testament is to translate them as they would say in New York, "yous," or in Texas, "y'all"! This means that the verses address and apply primarily to the people of God and then secondarily to individuals within that company. Here is an example:

> **Therefore, my beloved**(s)**, as you**(s) **have always obeyed, not as in my presence only, but now much more in my absence, work out your own salvation with fear and trembling; for it is God who works in you**(s) **both to will and to do for His good pleasure.**
>
> **Philippians 2:12,13**

Obviously this is true of every individual believer, but it is true only in the context of that believer's relating to the people of God in his or her locality. His working in our lives to bring about His will and good pleasure takes place when we interact with the other people of God, receiving their exhortation, testimonies, prayers, and ministry.

It is true to say that my life dwells in each individual cell of my body, but that is only true because each in-dwelt cell is in my body! There are many who see themselves as isolated individuals who are doing their best to hold on to their faith until they make it to heaven; to such, being a Christian is all about where we go when we die. In the New Testament, believers are always portrayed as a body of people among whom the Spirit can live and who, in their lives together, will reproduce God's life and character in their city. Here is another example:

The People of the Spirit

> You are of God, little children, and have overcome them, because He who is in you is greater than he who is in the world.
>
> 1 John 4:4

How many times have we been exhorted with these words spoken to us as individuals in a private relationship with God? We have been told that the One who lives in us is greater than the one in the world. I am sorry to disappoint you, but that is not the primary meaning of the text. Notice that it is addressed to a plurality of people called "children," and again the "you" in this verse is plural and addresses the entire body of believers in any locality. The Holy Spirit, the presence of God on the earth, is greater in the body of believers than all the powers of hell and the world put together. Only as it is true of the body of believers can it then be said of each individual member of the body. But if we are true to Scripture, it cannot be said of one isolated individual whose only contact with other believers is as a part of a television congregation.

> **God willed to make known what are the riches of the glory of this mystery among the Gentiles: which is Christ in you**(s)**, the hope of glory.**
>
> Colossians 1:27

"Christ in you." We have seen that this is true of every believer: Your body is the dwelling place of God. But the fullest application of this is that the glory of God, the divine presence that dwelt in the Holy of Holies, now dwells in the congregation of His people—both Jews and Gentiles.

THE NEW COMMUNITY

The people of God in the New Testament saw themselves as the people of the end time. By "end time," I do not refer to the fantastic prophecies involving Israel, Russia, the Rapture, and the Antichrist that are the limit of some theologies of the end. The end is signaled by the resurrection of the dead, the end of the reign of death, the consummation of the kingdom of God, the eternal reign of the Lord Jesus, the passing away of this world system, and our beholding Him face to face. The people of God have already entered into the end.

> **Whom having not seen you love. Though now you do not see Him, yet believing, you rejoice with joy inexpressible and full of glory, receiving the end of your faith—the salvation of your souls.**
>
> **1 Peter 1:8,9**

We are partakers of eternal life, which is the life of God Himself, the only life of eternity. We share in the resurrection of the Lord Jesus, and in the Spirit we are already enjoying the foyer of heaven.

> **Now all these things happened to them as examples, and they were written for our admonition, on whom the ends of the ages have come.**
>
> **1 Corinthians 10:11**
>
> **Those who were once enlightened, and have tasted the heavenly gift, and have become partakers of the Holy Spirit, and have tasted the good word of God and the powers of the age to come.**
>
> **Hebrews 6:4,5**

The New Testament believers, although living as citizens of the Roman Empire, knew that first they were citizens of the kingdom of God and that **...the form of this world is passing away** (1 Corinthians 7:31).

The company of believers are those who, although living on earth, have their true citizenship in heaven. **For our citizenship is in heaven, from which we also eagerly wait for the Savior, the Lord Jesus Christ** (Philippians 3:20).

Paul wrote to the Philippians and made reference to the status of the city of Philippi within the Roman Empire. In the interest of colonizing Macedonia, the conquering Romans chose this important city and declared it a "little Rome" in the midst of Macedonia. Although Greek-speaking Macedonians, all the citizens of Philippi were made citizens of Rome. Within the city all the laws of the city of Rome were enforced, and the manners, fashions, and habits of Rome were encouraged. The Macedonians for miles around had a living demonstration of what the capital of the Empire was like; to enter into the city of Philippi was to enter into Rome and to be exposed to what Rome was all about. The Romans knew how to colonize; it was not long before the whole area had been Romanized.

In the same way, Paul said to the Philippians, "Although you live on earth in Philippi, you are already true citizens of heaven. To come among you believers is to come into a 'little heaven' on earth, where His will is done as it is in heaven and the law of divine love holds sway. You are the living demonstration of the heart of Christ and what it means to be in Him. You are, in fact, the presence of the glory of God in Philippi."

As I have traveled the world, on occasion I have been in a country that is hostile to the West. In such a country, it is a great comfort to see the U.S. flag flying over a building. It tells me that it is the U.S. embassy, and to cross over its threshold, one enters "little U.S." where the laws of the U.S. are operative. When I enter that building I enter an outpost of the U.S. Likewise, any pagan or believer who enters a company of believers has come into heaven, on the way to heaven, to be embraced by the unconditional love of God.

But although in the Spirit the New Testament believers lived in all the powers of the end, the age to come, they yet waited for its fullness to be revealed at the Second Coming of Christ. They were people in whom the end had begun to be, while they awaited its consummation.

This understanding gave them their outlook on life, how they conducted themselves and understood what was happening.

It gave them a clear understanding of where they fit into the world that was finished and passing away.

> **Do not love the world or the things in the world. If anyone loves the world, the love of the Father is not in him. For all that is in the world the lust of the flesh—the lust of the eyes, and the pride of life—is not of the Father but is of the world. And the world is passing away, and the lust of it; but he who does the will of God abides forever.**
>
> **1 John 2:15-17**

They were forbidden a clinging to this life and its possessions, being part of this world that was passing away. They saw themselves as those who were passing-through strangers and pilgrims not caught up with a world that finds its meaning in the satisfaction of the flesh.

> **Beloved, I beg you as sojourners and pilgrims, abstain from fleshly lusts which war against the soul.**
>
> **1 Peter 2:11**

We are walking the streets of our cities, working in factories and offices, with the stamp of eternity upon us. We are strangers and pilgrims, citizens of another world.

The future heaven is as sure as the presence of the Spirit in the church. The Spirit is the seal of ownership on the believer; His presence is God's saying, "This one is Mine." He is also the guarantee of our finally receiving our covenant inheritance, which we have begun to receive in Him.

> **In Him you also trusted, after you heard the word of truth, the gospel of your salvation; in whom also, having believed, you were sealed with the Holy Spirit of promise, who is the guarantee of our inheritance until the redemption of the purchased possession, to the praise of His glory.**
>
> **Ephesians 1:13,14**

The People of the Spirit

THE COMMUNITY OF AGAPE

Such a people living in this present age in the power of the life of God, everlasting life which is agape, are going to be marked by a divine love for one another.

> **For you are all sons of God through faith in Christ Jesus. For as many of you as were baptized into Christ have put on Christ. There is neither Jew nor Greek, there is neither slave nor free, there is neither male nor female; for you are all one in Christ Jesus. And if you are Christ's, then you are Abraham's seed, and heirs according to the promise.**
>
> **Galatians 3:26-29**

In any age, the community Paul describes is a miracle! Race, status in society, and gender have been transcended in Christ so that the people truly love and accept one another. Such a community of love and acceptance can only exist because the God who is love is dynamically in the midst of the people; His love is being poured into their hearts. It is this divine love for one another that marks and defines the covenant people in the world.

> **"A new commandment I give to you, that you love one another; as I have loved you, that you also love one another. By this all will know that you are My disciples, if you have love for one another."**
>
> **John 13:34,35**

It is the Holy Spirit who pours out that love in our hearts.

> **Now hope does not disappoint, because the love of God has been poured out in our hearts by the Holy Spirit who was given to us.**
>
> **Romans 5:5**

The covenant produces a new and divine community of men and women who are literally the body of Christ on the earth. They are infused with His life, His very being, by the Spirit. This company is the dwelling of Jesus Christ on earth by the Spirit; it is among these people that His words of forgiveness are heard and received, that His healing power can be known and experienced. It is the place where God reveals Himself and His purposes.

The presence of the Holy Spirit is the badge of the covenant people of God; and where the Spirit is, there is love. Any group that does not give first place to the Spirit and allow supernatural love to reign is not an authentic expression of the church. Note this connection in 1 John 4:7-8:

> **Beloved, let us love one another, for love is of God; and everyone who loves is born of God and knows God. He who does not love does not know God, for God is love.**

John addresses the Christian community and calls them to love one another. He uses the word *agape*, which we have seen is the word to describe the unique, unconditional love of God. The rationale he gives for such a command is that love *(agape)* is of God; it finds its eternal source in God, who is love. If we are born of God, then we will be partakers of God's life that is agape and we will therefore love *(agape)* one another. That for John is the answer to the question as to who is in the community of the people of God and who is not. A person who does not love neither is born of God nor knows him.

We are the people who have come to grasp and give definition to the love of God in the act of God in Christ. A Christian can never talk about love in the abstract; love has a face in the person of the Lord Jesus. Our salvation is in our seeing and believing His love, confessing Him as the truth, saying our amen, and submitting our lives to Him. If this is the case, then it is expected that we adjust our entire lives to that love and show it in loving one another.

> **No one has seen God at any time. If we love one another, God abides in us, and His love has been perfected in us. By this we know that we abide in Him, and He in us, because He has given us of His Spirit. And we have seen and testify that the Father has sent the Son as Savior of the world. Whoever confesses that Jesus is the Son of God, God abides in him,**

and he in God. And we have known and believed the love that God has for us. God is love, and he who abides in love abides in God, and God in him.

1 John 4:12-16

He makes the amazing statement that the invisible God is beheld in the community of believers who actively love one another. As a community of people who have received His Spirit, we abide or dwell in Him and love one another. This is true of the community because it is true of each man and woman in the community. Notice it is not only the us of community but also the individual him or her.

If someone says, "I love God," and hates his brother, he is a liar; for he who does not love his brother whom he has seen, how can he love God whom he has not seen? And this commandment we have from Him: that he who loves God must love his brother also.

1 John 4:20,21

He sums up the whole of the argument, showing the absolute necessity of love in the Christian community. We are the objects of the infinite unconditional love of God; we have partaken of that love through the Spirit and love our brothers with the power of that Spirit. If not, John dismisses our claim to being part of the people of God without further discussion.

This high and lofty goal is set before us, and we move toward it. Do not be discouraged that you are not yet perfect! A little green apple is perfect for its age, and many of us are green and sour apples if compared to what we shall be when He is finished with us.

Know and believe that the love of God to us transcends any human love of a parent. The little babe stumbles and falls, but the parents are delighted at any indication that steps are taken. There is celebration and records are made when the first stumbling step is taken in the midst of many sprawls on the floor. Likewise, there is celebration in heaven over the most awkward and immature attempts of the believer to walk in love and show any indication that Christ lives within. Do not focus on your faults and imperfections, but give glory to God and share in the celebration when you take a step that manifests Christ your life. You will fall, but you know who lives within you; pick yourself up and move on more aware of your weakness and, therefore, trusting in Him more deeply.

YOUR PLACE IN THE CHURCH

Someone asked me if the church I have attempted to describe here really exists on the planet! The most common questions that come to me by letter and fill my e-mails are questions concerning the church. They ask, "Where do I find a local church that even remotely fits the New Testament model?" I find countless thousands of people burned out on the local church; they love the Lord but have given up on His people. They are tired of a church that is run like a Fortune 500 company, where the main reason to go on Sunday is to give in the omnipresent offering plate. Others are exhausted from a weekly diet of condemnation. Where do we find the people I have described in this chapter?

There is no question that the church at the beginning of the twenty-first century is in a pitiful condition—from apostasy at one end of the spectrum, to spiritual lust after supernatural experience that at best is flesh and sometimes borders on witchcraft at the other end. How shall a believer go about coming to the kind of gathering of believers described here?

Let me be frank with you who ask these questions. I have noted in talking with many believers concerning their involvement in a local church that they approach the matter almost entirely from the perspective of what they are going to get out of the arrangement. Finding a church has degenerated into a social context; it is understood as joining an exclusive club of like-minded people, where there will be lectures and entertainment provided each week. Church is understood as joining together to fulfill common goals and share common interests and have our children involved in a clean and safe environment, where they will also find their entertainment and social life. There is no awareness of being joined by the Spirit to a supernatural company of people to bring about the agape community of the covenant.

The believer gathers together with those in the locality who have received the same grace gift of eternal life as he or she has and together with them seeks to give visible form to the community of agape in the area of town in which he or she lives. The believer along with all the others in that church will be the body of Christ in that neighborhood of the city.

I often tell those looking for the perfect church, "You will find that the people in the church are probably not qualified to serve you, any more than you are ready or qualified to serve them. You are joining yourself to a group of very imperfect people who are at various stages of their growth in Christ. They will make many mistakes as they move toward loving one another as Christ has loved them. You will join yourself with them because they are your covenant brothers and sisters in Christ, and you too are a mistake-making, imperfect brother or sister, learning how to love."

The churches we know of in the New Testament were far from perfect, and Paul was aware that he was dealing with imperfect, immature believers who were liable to act in the most unchristian fashion at times. To discover how he handled those churches will help us as we settle into our imperfect, immature group.

SPIRIT-DIRECTED IMAGINATION

Paul had what we might call a Spirit-directed imagination; he saw believers as they truly were in Christ and how they would be when He had finished with them. He thought of them and addressed them in that fashion. The church in Corinth was in many respects a spiritual disaster, a zoo of conflicting voices fragmented around various leaders. In writing to them, Paul addressed them according to his Spirit-inspired imagination.

> **To the church of God which is at Corinth, to those who are sanctified in Christ Jesus, called to be saints, with all who in every place call on the name of Jesus Christ our Lord, both theirs and ours: Grace to you and peace from God our Father and the Lord Jesus Christ. I thank my God always concerning you for the grace of God which was given to you by Christ Jesus, that you were enriched in everything by Him in all utterance and all knowledge, even as the testimony of Christ was confirmed in you, so that you come short in no gift, eagerly waiting for the revelation of our Lord Jesus Christ, who will also confirm you to the end, that you may be blameless in the day of our Lord Jesus Christ.**
>
> **1 Corinthians 1:2-8**

That is an amazing paragraph to be written to such a church! It is only because he has thus seen them that he can confront them in all of their problem areas. As you look at the body of believers that you are bound up with in being the body of Christ, learn to deliberately see them as they, as you, are in Christ. Let your faith see you with them as you will be when He has done His perfect work in you.

SPIRIT-DIRECTED PRAYER

But then, Paul prayed that the body would grow and mature. His prayers are to be found throughout the Epistles. Ephesians 1:16-21, 3:14-21, Philippians 1:9-11, and Colossians 1:9-12 are the major ones. In these prayers, he prays for them—believers—to come to know by experience who they really are in Christ.

In the early 1960s I was a rookie pastor in Northern Ireland trying to bring my flock of Irish farmers to maturity in Christ, with little success. Then I realized that these prayers scattered through the New Testament were given to us by the Spirit, giving us a model for our prayers. I began to pray them for myself, and then for each member of the congregation, adjusting the prayers to their specific needs. Within months, a transformation had come to all of us. Daily pray these prayers for your pastor and the congregation, and you will see miracles take place before your eyes.

Surrender to the Spirit, asking Him to show you what your place is in the body of believers, where you fit in bringing to pass this community of *agape*. Above all, remember that this is a covenant community and, therefore, *hesed* is the way the fellowship works. Toward every member, act in steadfast, loyal, covenant love. Put aside gossip and all malice, and speak only words of love to them and about them.

Chapter 17

THE FRIEND OF GOD

After addressing pastors in a meeting in Brazil, a young pastor shared his testimony. In broken English, he told me how he surrendered his life to God to preach the Gospel. He left a successful, blossoming business career, and his denomination sent him, along with his wife and baby girl, to a remote village in the region of the Amazon. They threw themselves into the preaching of the Gospel with zeal and excitement. He prayed and employed all his strength in the attempt to fill the little church with converts.

But nothing happened. The people did not come, and the few Christians who were there when he arrived did not share his excitement. He worked in the stifling humidity, watching his personal funds gradually drain away. Tithes from his tiny congregation were paid in vegetables. The weeks passed into months, and he watched in mental agony his wife and children living on a starvation diet. His denomination assured him that they would send money, but it rarely came. He felt disillusioned and abandoned by God and humanity.

One night, lying awake sweating in the stifling heat, he felt his discouragement take over. He woke his wife and told her that he had decided they would leave and return to Rio Janeiro, where he would resume his business career. But before leaving, he knew he had to process his anger toward God.

"He brought us up here and dumped us. He doesn't care whether we live or die, and I have to tell Him how I feel," he angrily told his wife. He left her to pack their few possessions while he went to spend time in a remote shack on the edge of the jungle to pour out his angry and confused heart to God.

The first morning in the tiny shack, the dam of his pent-up emotions burst. He railed and raged at God for bringing them to such a place, expecting him and his family to serve Him under such impossible conditions. He shook his fist and shouted, "Did you bring us here to starve us to death?" and then wept at his own disappointment in God.

In the early afternoon, he sensed the presence of God filling the cabin and a great stillness came upon him. He heard God speak clearly and distinctly in his heart:

Above all, I desire your friendship. If serving Me interrupts and disrupts our friendship, I would rather you go back to your business and continue to be My friend. Your friendship is more important to Me than all your acts of service.

He dissolved into tears and wept in wonder and joy the remainder of the afternoon. Those few words had turned his whole concept of Christianity on its head. A God who wanted his intimate friendship more than his service was a concept that he had never considered in his craziest dreams. He had been reared to think of God as a kind Master to be served. He now realized that his whole Christian life had been an attempt to work for God rather than live out a relationship of love and friendship. He remembered his denominational leaders had sent him on his way with the words "Go and do a work for God!" and he knew that phrase had encapsulated his whole Christian life. The thrust of his being a Christian was to work for God;

even his prayer time was a "to-do list" of things needed in the activity of being a Christian and serving God. To be God's friend! To be with Him to love and be loved! These were concepts that he had never given a moment's thought to. Now the concept danced in his head as he wept for joy at the prospect of such a life

The next day, he ran back to share the new understanding with his wife. They did not leave the little church but set a new priority. It was as though he had heard the Gospel for the first time and with it a revolutionary new calling. He now saw that his priority calling was not to serve God but to revel in His love, pursue His friendship, and enjoy intimacy with Him. He reveled in the God who loved him limitlessly and let the relationship dictate his service. He moved from doing for God to being in Him.

His preaching changed, reflecting his new understanding of the Gospel as a call to union with the God of unlimited love. The little church began to fill up and flourish, and he was still there when he told me his story.

The revelation that Brazilian pastor had received was one of the promises of the covenant:

"No more shall every man teach his neighbor, and every man his brother, saying, 'Know the Lord,' for they all shall know Me, from the least of them to the greatest of them, says the Lord."

Jeremiah 31:34

This is not speaking of knowing a creed or being intellectually convinced of the existence of God; it describes a firsthand knowing of Him. This term of the covenant is the pouring out of the yearning love of God that reaches out to us to include us into His circle of intimate friends.

THE ULTIMATE FRIENDSHIP

It is the covenant that fulfills the longing of God, granting men and women the gift of His life so that in this present time they live the life of the age to come. This gift makes them His children, giving them the unspeakable privilege of enjoying intimate friendship with Him.

> **The secret of the Lord is with those who fear Him, and He will show them His covenant.**
>
> **Psalm 25:14**

This may be one of the most amazing verses in the Bible, putting into one sentence the incredible plan God has purposed for humankind. The union described by the Hebrew word for "secret" is paralleled in the same verse with "covenant." The uniting of God and man in the strong bond of friendship is achieved by the covenant God has made with us.

"The secret of the Lord"[1] is a translation of a rich Hebrew word that takes many words and ideas to translate into English. The word portrays persons who have their heads close together in private sharing, a tight-knit group of intimate friends. It speaks of friends with a life-and-death commitment to one another, in an atmosphere of unconditional trust in each other; a place where it is safe to share one's weaknesses and sorrows as well as strengths and victories, knowing that one is not rejected but loved and given the strength of the group in the day of weakness. It speaks of faithfulness, loyalty, and enduring friendship.

It is wonderful enough when such a relationship is found among humans, but this verse is speaking of the relationship of men and women to the Lord God! God loves the world, but believers are His circle of intimate friends with whom He shares His heart. Every believer has been called to such a relationship with God in Jesus Christ and in the empowerment of the Holy Spirit. It is this kind of friendship with Him that is potential in our new birth. We were saved from sin for such a relationship. We have been saved out of the world to become friends of God, part of His inner circle of intimates. The new covenant makes it possible to live on the earth as those whose true center and sphere of life is heaven.

"The secret of the Lord is with those who fear Him." This close circle of friendship is for those who fear Him. That sounds strange when we are speaking of friends who delight in each other in a place of safety! We must understand what the Bible means by the phrase "the fear of the Lord," for it does not mean that we are terrified of Him and tiptoe around Him! It describes those who have entered the circle of His intimate friendship.

The word "fear"[2] means to stand in awe of, respect, expect of, honor, and submit to. It is a phrase that in the Old Testament describes the character of the faith we have in God. We stand in awe of Him, giving Him honor and respect, and in obedience submit to Him. It also carries the idea that we trust Him and expect Him to keep His word to us. The Bible knows nothing of faith being a formula whereby we can extract something from God. Faith is our response of trust to the revelation God has given us of Himself.

Sinful fear is when we transfer our fear from God to another human, to humans, or to the demonic. We then give to them the respect and awe and submissive expectancy that belong only to God, and we tremble before them. We fear them; that is, we believe in their power to do us harm instead of believing in and submitting to, that is fearing, the love of God that is greater than all designs against us.

KNOWING THE LORD

If the heart of the covenant is to be united as one to Him by the Spirit, the goal of the covenant is to know Him. The word "know"[3] is a rich word in both the Hebrew and the Greek. In the Hebrew the word is *yada* and describes the knowledge that comes by observation, intimate knowing, uniting knowing; it is knowledge gained by experience with the senses, by investigation and proving, by reflection and consideration; it is firsthand knowledge. The opposite of this word is to know about, to know by secondhand information. It is the difference between a student's relationship to the material he or she studies and the relationship between husband and wife.

Yada[4] is the word of intimacy, of covenant union. It is consistently used to describe marriage, the most sacred covenant among humans. It is the knowing of the whole person. It is also referred to as uncovering the nakedness of another, the ultimate covenant act of having no secrets and nothing held back. Such is the relationship we are called to with God through Jesus Christ. *Yada* could well sum up Moses' life in one word.

> **So the Lord said to Moses, "I will also do this thing that you have spoken; for you have found grace in My sight, and I know you by name."**
>
> **Exodus 33:17**

> **But since then there has not arisen in Israel a prophet like Moses, whom the Lord knew face to face.**
>
> **Deuteronomy 34:10**

The Old Testament prophets continually referred to the relationship of Israel to the Lord as marriage, and in the New Testament Christ is described as being married to the church.

Yada describes experiential knowledge, in which the one knowing has actual involvement with or in the object of the knowing. Potiphar "did not know" what was in his house because he had no contact with it. (Genesis 39:6.) To know God is to have intimate and experiential, hands-on knowledge of Him.

Yada is not sentimental but is the expression of the faith that obeys the Lord. The pharaoh of the Exodus refused to let Israel go because he said,

> **Who is the Lord, that I should obey His voice to let Israel go? I do not know the Lord, nor will I let Israel go.**
>
> **Exodus 5:2**

He meant that, although he certainly knew of the Lord intellectually, he did not recognize His authority over him in his personal life or the decisions he made as the pharaoh.

Solomon was exhorted to know the Lord, which entailed serving Him with loyal heart and willing mind:

> **"As for you, my son Solomon, know the God of your father, and serve Him with a loyal heart and with a willing mind...."**
>
> **1 Chronicles 28:9**

There is no greater description of the meaning of *yada* than that given by Jesus in the Upper Room when He spoke of the most intimate knowing and abiding in the love of the Triune God. But He made it very plain it was not a sentimental feeling of romantic love but a union expressed in keeping His commands.

> **"He who has My commandments and keeps them, it is he who loves Me. And he who loves Me will be loved by My Father, and I will love him and manifest Myself to him.**
>
> **"If anyone loves Me, he will keep My word; and My Father will love him, and We will come to him and make Our home with him. He who does not love Me does not keep My words; and the word which you hear is not Mine but the Father's who sent Me.**
>
> **John 14:21,23,24**

The intimacy with God that the Word speaks of is linked with the revelation of His purposes.

> Now Samuel did not yet know the Lord, nor was the word of the Lord yet revealed to him.
>
> 1 Samuel 3:7

The New Testament word is *ginosko,*[5] meaning to understand completely; to be taking in knowledge; to come to know, recognize, and understand. The word indicates that who or what is known is of great value or importance to the one who knows and, hence, a relationship is established. It is the definition Jesus gave us of eternal life when He said, **"And this is eternal life, that they may know You, the only true God, and Jesus Christ whom You have sent"** (John 17:3).

Eternal life is not merely going to heaven when we die; it is the beginning of heaven in the here and now in that we share the divine life, everlasting life, and, in that, are caught up into the intimate fellowship of the Trinity.

Ginosko confronts us with the love God has for us, for we know Him only because He has set His love upon us, known us from before the creation of the universe. Our knowing Him is our response to His first knowing us.

His intimate knowledge of us is described in Psalm 139. In verses 1-3, the word translated "know" is *yada.*

> O Lord, You have searched me and known me. You know my sitting down and my rising up; You understand my thought afar off. You comprehend my path and my lying down, and are acquainted with all my ways.

This is not God knowing us, because God knows everything, but God knowing and delighting over us in love. The psalm goes on to explore this thought. In verses 13-16 He is portrayed caressing the child in the womb, infinitely loving us before we were born.

The word is used to describe His love knowledge of us in salvation:

The Friend of God

But if anyone loves God, this one is known by Him.

1 Corinthians 8:3

But now after you have known God, or rather are known by God....

Galatians 4:9

Nevertheless the solid foundation of God stands, having this seal: "The Lord knows those who are His," and, "Let everyone who names the name of Christ depart from iniquity."

2 Timothy 2:19

"I am the good shepherd; and I know My sheep, and am known by My own.

"My sheep hear My voice, and I know them, and they follow Me."

John 10:14,27

Notice the progression in these verses. He knows us with the knowing of love. We then respond to His love and come to know Him. Dwelling in such knowledge, we hear His voice, love and obey Him, and are thus identified as being known by Him.

As with *yada*, this is not a sentimental feeling but love that acts. His knowing of us took Him to the cross, and our love for Him is expressed in the joyful doing of His will. We obey Him not to gain this divine knowledge but because it is ours, and we now delight to do His will as a result of the love relationship.

Now by this we know that we know Him, if we keep His commandments. He who says, "I know Him," and does not keep His commandments, is a liar, and the truth is not in him. But whoever keeps His word, truly the love of God is perfected in him. By this we know that we are in Him. He who says he abides in Him ought himself also to walk just as He walked....

1 John 2:3-6

Beloved, let us love one another, for love is of God; and everyone who loves is born of God and knows God. He who does not love does not know God, for God is love. And we

> have known and believed the love that God has for us. God is love, and he who abides in love abides in God, and God in him.
>
> 1 John 4:7,8,16

I cannot emphasize strongly enough that He first loved and knew us; it is out from His love initiative that we come to know and love Him and to walk in love. Our first steps of love and obedience will be stumbling and very far from perfect, but the life of God has been born within us and the process of bringing our entire being into the obedience of love has begun. This knowledge of Him knows continual growth.

> **But grow in the grace and knowledge of our Lord and Savior Jesus Christ. To Him be the glory both now and forever. Amen.**
>
> 2 Peter 3:18

TAUGHT OF GOD TO KNOW HIM

How do we attain such an intimate knowledge of God? We do not look for this knowledge in Bible study, which can become arid and lifeless. We are seeking to know Him, not merely know about Him; we are not filing Him in neat categories of theology, but growing in a love relationship with Him.

Nor should we feel that this is for a small, elite group within the body of believers. He delights to give this knowledge to all His children; as we have seen, this is the essence of eternal life. The promise of the covenant clearly states that it is for everyone in the covenant:

> **"No more shall every man teach his neighbor, and every man his brother, saying, 'Know the Lord,' for they all shall know Me, from the least of them to the greatest of them, says the Lord."**
>
> Jeremiah 31:34

The Friend of God

The "all" begins with the least and moves to the greatest, as if He would encourage the newest believer and the one who still feels unworthy. This knowledge of God is for you!

Both *yada* and *ginosko* speak of the knowing as a lover and friend. It is a shock to many who would settle for a life of serving God that, above all else, He fervently desires our friendship. He desires us infinitely more than we desire Him. The Gospel calls us to the giddy heights of a relationship of love, living in the embrace of God, who calls us His friend. At the beginning of the twenty-first century, many have settled for a withered and shrunken theology that reduces the Gospel to the way to escape an angry God and hell.

It may help us to think about the cry of a human after God and then hear the same words coming from the heart of His infinite love:

> **As the deer pants for the water brooks, so my soul pants for You, O God. My soul thirsts for God, for the living God. When shall I come and appear before God?**
>
> **Psalm 42:1,2**

So wrote the psalmist of his own heart cry, but what if we hear it as the cry of God? "As the deer pants for the water brooks, so My heart pants for you, My child. My whole Being thirsts for you, My child. When shall the longing of My heart be satisfied?" When God in Christ hung on the cross and cried, "I thirst," He was longing for more than water: He thirsts for your love and friendship; He would rather die than not have you with Him. This is the wonder of the message of covenant.

Each of us has been called to intimate friendship with Him, a union that is lived out in our homes, in our classrooms, on the factory floor, and in the office. We do not have to leave society and become religious to enter into intimate relationship with God. In the middle of the daily grind with all its demands and responsibilities and activities, we are called to walk with God.

Our friendship with Him becomes the center from which all of life flows in harmony.

Abraham was called the friend of God. He was certainly not a hermit or recluse! Genesis portrays him as a desert sheik ruling over his tent kingdom, a rancher and astute businessman having 300 men in his employ. In raising his cattle, sheep, and camels and making his business deals, he was the friend of God walking through life learning to trust Him.

Remember that this is His covenant promise and, therefore, is backed by the oath of God. This is not an add-on to life, an extra for the really enthusiastic, but the promise of the covenant ratified by the blood of God. He takes it upon Himself to bring us to know Him. This knowledge is given by the operation of the Holy Spirit and does, as we have seen, grow throughout our lives.

> **"Then I will give them a heart to know Me, that I am the Lord...."**
>
> **Jeremiah 24:7**
>
> **At that time Jesus answered and said, "I thank You, Father, Lord of heaven and earth, that You have hidden these things from the wise and prudent and have revealed them to babes. Even so, Father, for so it seemed good in Your sight.**
>
> **Matthew 11:25,26**

The "wise and prudent" might be better understood as the "clever"; and the "babes" are the untaught, ignorant, unskilled, or even childish. Notice the two key points in the text: On the one hand, He has hidden from the clever; on the other hand, He has revealed to babes. The more we try to know God by stuffing our heads with religious facts, the further we are from knowing Him; conversely, to come to Him admitting our helplessness makes us candidates for His implementing the covenant promise.

The Friend of God

The old covenant had mediators: the priests, by whom the people approached God, and the prophets, through whom they heard from God.

"No more shall every man teach his neighbor, and every man his brother, saying, 'Know the Lord,' for they all shall know Me, from the least of them to the greatest of them, says the Lord."

Jeremiah 31:34

In the new covenant, we do not have earthly mediators but know Him and approach Him directly.

Let us therefore come boldly to the throne of grace, that we may obtain mercy and find grace to help in time of need.

Hebrews 4:16

In whom we have boldness and access with confidence through faith in Him.

Ephesians 3:12

In both of these texts, the words "boldly" and "boldness" are the same. These were strong words for the person who knew only the old covenant in which only in the representative high priest, and that but once a year, did a human enter the holiest of all. The meaning of the word "boldly" is very strong. It is to be filled with confidence and without fear; to come with freedom of speech. In England, we have an expression that sums up its meaning: "with a brass neck"!

This does not mean we do not need instruction; He has set in the church pastors and teachers. But the teacher must be very aware of his or her total reliance upon the Spirit. The audience will not understand the teacher unless the Holy Spirit is applying the promises of the covenant. It is the work of God to cause His people to know Him. The teacher of truth has been taught of God, and the same Spirit is teaching those he or she now teaches. Both teacher and student must rely heavily on the Spirit to teach the heart. If teaching the Scripture is in the same category as teaching mathematics, then all we have is an amassing of facts, with the end result of being intellectually bloated. If the Spirit teaches, then we are enlightened in our hearts to be drawn into a closer friendship with God and further conformed to the image of the Son of God.

This is knowledge of God that is not located in the head but in the heart. There is a feeling to this knowledge that is not the satisfaction of the head that comes from understanding a theological problem, but a direct and immediate knowing, an inner knowing which is independent of study or instruction by man that brings with it a certainty and familiarity with God. First John 5:10 describes it as the believer's having the witness of the Spirit within.

This, of course, is my biggest problem! I am a bookish chap; I love to study. I might even be addicted to sniffing the smell of a library! I ever return to this truth, knowing that I balance on the edge of losing the knowledge of Him in the knowledge about Him.

I might add that this is not the theoretical knowledge that we may receive by attending Bible conferences or Sunday school, dependent on the communication and instruction of a person. It may well be given during such times of instruction, but it is different. Instruction, like personal Bible study, builds fact on fact; whereas this knowledge is an impartation of grace, arriving in the consciousness full-grown and convincing.

BEING OR DOING

Tragically, we have settled for a lot less than such covenant intimacy. In the parable of the lost son in Luke 15, Jesus described him making the decision to return to the vicinity of his old home because of the miserable state his sin had reduced him to. He could not imagine his father loving him and restoring him to the place of a beloved son in the home. He prepared his speech that outlined a business proposition in which he proposed that he would become as a hired servant in his father's employ.

> "I am no longer worthy to be called your son; make me like one of your hired servants."
>
> Luke 15:19

A hired servant was what today we would call a temporary employee. Servants lived on the property and were looked after throughout the year, whether there was work to be done or not. Hired servants, on the other hand, were hired by the day when there was too much work for the servants to do, usually during the planting season or when the harvest was to be brought in. Early in the morning the rancher would go to the marketplace, where the unemployed would gather, and pick the men he needed, agree on fair pay for a day's work, and take them back to the farm.

When the lost son proposed that he be made a hired servant, it would be assumed that he would live away from the father's property and join the unemployed in the early hours of the morning to be chosen by his father whenever he needed extra help. It described an arm's-length relationship with his father and was the best he could imagine, considering his track record.

Jesus then described the father as seeing the vagabond man when he was still a great way off from the farm. He recognized him as his son and ran to him, embraced him, held him close, and covered him with kisses. The amazed young man ambushed by love hardly knew what was happening to him. Incredibly, he was determined to go through with his speech asking for temporary employment a few times a year! But the father refused to let him finish his speech, cutting him off before he could make his proposal. The father did not want another employee! This man was his beloved son to be robed and shoed and ringed and celebrated with the fattened calf.

In the mad frenzy of doing for God that passes as dedicated Christian living in many churches, we need to ask ourselves a question. Did we come to God to serve Him from a fearful distance or to be the object of His delight and to discover our true identity in His love?

It would appear that in many cases the more involved in the church we become, the further away we go from the glorious calling that we were saved to pursue to its fullest potential. The higher we rise in leadership within the church, the more immersed we become in its business, in programs and promotion. The pastor of a large church on the West Coast in the U.S. confided in me, "I left everything to give myself to God and serve Him, but I realize today that I have become a booking agent for the best charismatic acts that are passing through town!" Another, having built the largest church building for miles around, on the night of the dedication sat white-faced and fearful in his office and said to me, "Is this it? Is this what I have given my life to? This building has meant my life for years, and now I am already bored with it."

The crying need of pastors, priests, and congregations is to realize that Christ died to bring us into an intimate covenant relationship with the Triune God. While we are in a frenzy of doing for Him, we are in grave danger of missing the whole point of the Gospel—which is being with Him.

We do not have to be in the ministry to face the same problems the young Brazilian pastor faced. How do you define your relationship to God? Is it to be likened to an employee answering to a master? Or is it a daily responding to His love, delighting in Him as dearest friend? Is it doing for Him or being in His love?

He has many servants but few friends!

The Friend of God

The Spirit calls us, nudges us with those inner longings after the knowledge of God, but we must respond by positioning ourselves where the Spirit can bring us to know Him.

Let us know, let us pursue the knowledge of the Lord. His going forth is established as the morning; He will come to us like the rain, like the latter and former rain to the earth.
Hosea 6:3

The word "pursue" is a strong word and would better be understood as "run after with zeal and excitement." The prophet not only urges us to pursue such knowledge, but assures us that He will be found—as surely as the dawn breaks and the rains come in their season.

It is significant that many of the prayers of Paul for his converts centered on this idea. He wanted them to move beyond an intellectual knowledge, a studying of a subject, a knowing about, to this knowledge of intimate experience. We can do no better than to take one of his requests and make it our life prayer:

[That you may] **know the love of Christ which passes knowledge, that you may be filled up to all the fullness of God.**
Ephesians 3:19

AFTERWORD

We have journeyed together through the wonders of the new covenant, and we are about to part company. But the question hangs, "What shall we now do?"

We must understand the nature of the body of truth that we call the new covenant. The events it reports are rooted in history—the blood of God was shed as the clock was marking off minutes and hours—but it must never be approached as ancient history. The Gospel is God's speaking to us right now, His words coming to us fresh from His mouth, as new as the day they were first spoken; the events are present to us in the fullness of the infinite power released the first second they took place.

Because these words and events are the report of true history we can think about them, discuss them, and understand them at an intellectual level. But they are the announcement of the action of the living God; and we must go beyond objective debate and believe them, trusting our very lives to the Lord Jesus, who is the covenant.

The Gospel of the new covenant is in the eternal present tense: In all its fullness it *is*, now. There is nothing to be added to it, and there is no cause to be achieved in me to make me worthy of it. It is a pure gift to be received now, this instant.

We must be aware that this is life-threatening to the flesh, the false self. To say yes to the pure gift of God and receive it means that I am in the position of the helpless recipient in the hands of Another and no longer in control of my salvation or the living of the Christian life. Independence, self-sufficiency, and control of my salvation are the life energy of the flesh; to receive as a gift what cannot be earned and over which I have no control is certain death to the flesh.

To realize that the new covenant, the free gift of God, is pressing upon us in this moment, complete in its fullness, waiting to be taken, is a flesh emergency! The moment we discover the awaiting gift, we are also aware of the energy of the false self urging us to flee from any response in this moment. It seeks to stop us on two fronts. First, it urges us, "Study more; you do not understand it yet—be worthy of receiving it by perfect knowledge!"

Study, discussion, and debate that go on unendingly without having any effect on our lives and behavior is one of the first lines of defense of the flesh. Keep getting more knowledge, but do not receive the gift! Belief to such defensive flesh means believing *about* but does not include trusting or bringing life and behavior into alignment with what is now "believed."

Tragically, there are countless believers who study the truths of the Gospel as a hobby with no serious plan to implement it in their lives and behavior. Such information becomes an end in itself; it knows a matter simply in order to know; this is, in fact, nonsense knowing to be likened to $2 + 2 = 0$! It is an activity of religious flesh void of divine life, without Holy Spirit enlightenment, and producing no love but instead fueling pride, argument, and division.

Again and again in the New Testament, we are called to believe in the sense of trusting our entire person to the object of faith. Such belief moves from an intellectual exercise and

Afterword

becomes the energy of life. We study, think about, and discuss divine truth but with reverence, knowing that our study must be with the enlightenment of the Spirit and leading to further trust in Him.

Who can study and come to know the love of God? The human brain is too small and limited to take in the infinite love of God! Such love can only be known through the Spirit's revelation and in the leap of faith in which we trust ourselves to Him. So with every facet of the new covenant, we can only study up to a point and then commit ourselves to the living Lord of the covenant and let Him work it into us and transform our lives.

The flesh has a second front to stop us from accepting the gift now; it will accept—*but with conditions*. It must have time to make itself ready with dedications, promises to be godlier and disciplined—all of which will be in place tomorrow or next week. In so doing, the flesh will have produced a cause for receiving the promises of the covenant by a process in which it is still very much in control, determining when we are ready and when we are worthy to receive the covenant.

Religious flesh must stay in control at any cost. To confront the reality of the unconditional love of God that has given all in Christ means death to the flesh. The pharaoh of the Exodus walked through a carpet of croaking frogs, slept with their slimy bodies squatting on his bed, and endured their leaping across his royal table as he ate. It is amazing that when Moses announced that the plague was over and the frogs would leave whenever the pharaoh said so, he opted for the following day, not able to accept that the plague was now over and the frogs could leave that instant. Such immediate action left him without control over the situation and dependent in the hand of God. He preferred to share his bed with the living carpet of frogs for another night to prove that he was still in control and they would go when he said so!

I once spent a weekend presenting these truths to a congregation, and the pastor brought the meetings to a close by calling the people to come forward and "pay the price" in order to receive the blessing I had spoken of! I had to gently correct him and assure the congregation that there was no price to pay, that the gift was without cause in them and without any process that they must pursue before they could receive!

The response of faith to the gift of the covenant is to surrender, *now,* in this moment, giving all that we know of ourselves to all that we know of Him. We know little of ourselves and even less of Him, but as we surrender we shall know more. And surrender is not complicated but is in the yes breathed from the heart; yes with no promises, only giving thanks for His gift. In such a posture of receiving, we give room then for the Holy Spirit to work His miracles.

We go on to define ourselves by the surrender to the truth that is contained in the covenant. The flesh will always define us by our past, but faith surrendering to Him defines us by the covenant gift. We see and call ourselves by who we are in the light of the gift of love:

"I am limitlessly and unconditionally loved. Yes, I am!

"I am now in covenant with God through the Lord Jesus. Yes, I am!

"I have been included into Christ and am now alive in Him. Yes, I am!

"The Spirit is within me, pouring out the love of God in my heart. Yes, He is!

"My body is the dwelling of the Spirit. Yes, it is!"

From such a posture, we shall go on to grow in grace and in the true knowledge of the Lord Jesus.

ENDNOTES

Chapter 2

1. Vines Expository Dictionary of Old and New Testament Words, s.v. "new."
2. "Covenant and Creation: A Theology of Old Testament Covenants," by W.J. Drumbrell, Paternoster Press, page 16.
3. Webster's Universal Encyclopedic Dictionary, 2002 Edition, Barnes and Noble; Webster's New College Dictionary, Houghton Mifflin Co., 1995, s.v. "represent."
4. Webster's Universal Encyclopedic Dictionary, 2002 Edition, Barnes and Noble, s.v. "contract."
5. Vines Expository Dictionary of Old and New Testament Words, s.v. "lovingkindness."

Chapter 3

1. Vines Expository Dictionary of Old and New Testament Words, s.v. "live."
2. Vines Expository Dictionary of Old and New Testament Words, s.v. "life."
3. Vines Expository Dictionary of Old and New Testament Words, s.v. "sin."

Chapter 4

1. Vines Expository Dictionary of Old and New Testament Words, s.v. "lovingkindness."
2. Strong's, "Hebrew" entry #1984, s.v. "halal." Vines Expository Dictionary of Old and New Testament Words, s.v. "Praise."

Chapter 5

1. Vines Expository Dictionary of Old and New Testament Words, s.v. "love."

² Strong's, "Hebrew" entry #3045, s.v. "yada." Vines Expository Dictionary of Old and New Testament Words, s.v. "to know."

Chapter 6

¹ Vines Expository Dictionary of Old and New Testament Words, s.v. "mediator."

² Webster's Universal Encyclopedic Dictionary, 2002 Edition, Barnes and Noble, s.v. "intercede"; Strong's, "Hebrew" entry #5241, s.v. "huperentugchano."

³ Complete Word Study Dictionary, New Testament, Spiros Zodhiates, TH.D., AMG Publishers, Chattanooga, TN, #1834, s.v. "interpret."

⁴ Dictionary of Ecclesiastical Latin, s.v. "ecce," and "homo."

⁵ Complete Word Study Dictionary, New Testament, Spiros Zodhiates, TH.D., AMG Publishers, Chatanooga, TN, #3860, s.v. "paradidomi."

Chapter 8

¹ Encarta World English Dictionary, s.v. "ratify."

Chapter 9

¹ Vines Expository Dictionary of Old and New Testament Words, s.v. "faithfulness."

² Vines Expository Dictionary of Old and New Testament Words, s.v. "faithfulness."

Chapter 10

¹ Complete Word Study Dictionary, New Testament, Spiros Zodhiates, TH.D., AMG Publishers, Chattanooga, TN, #3340, s.v. "repentance."

Chapter 11

¹ Kittel Theological Dictionary of the New Testament, Volume 1, page 348ff.

[2] Webster's Universal Encyclopedic Dictionary, 2002 Edition, Barnes and Noble, s.v. "symbol."

[3] Vines Expository Dictionary of Old and New Testament Words, s.v. "communion."

[4] Vines Expository Dictionary of Old and New Testament Words, s.v. "eat."

Chapter 12

[1] Webster's Universal Encyclopedic Dictionary, 2002 Edition, Barnes and Noble, s.v. "debt."

[2] Complete Word Study Dictionary, New Testament, Spiros Zodhiates, TH.D., AMG Publishers, Chattanooga, TN, #142, s.v. "forgiveness."

Chapter 13

[1] Complete Word Study Dictionary, New Testament, Spiros Zodhiates, TH.D., AMG Publishers, Chattanooga, TN, #1968, s.v. "epipito."

[2] Vines Expository Dictionary of Old and New Testament Words, s.v. "temple."

[3] Strong's Exhaustive Concordance, #3485, s.v. "naon."

Chapter 14

[1] Complete Word Study Dictionary, New Testament, Spiros Zodhiates, TH.D., AMG Publishers, Chattanooga, TN, #1981.

[2] Vines Expository Dictionary of Old and New Testament Words, s.v. "content."

[3] Wycliffe Bible Commentary, Electronic Database, 1962 Moody Press, s.v. Philippians 4:11-13.

[4] Complete Word Study Dictionary, New Testament, Spiros Zodhiates, TH.D., AMG Publishers, Chattanooga, TN, #1743, s.v. "endunamoo."

[5] Complete Word Study Dictionary, New Testament, Spiros Zodhiates, TH.D., AMG Publishers, Chattanooga, TN, #1743, #1412, s.v. "dunamis."

[6] Complete Word Study Dictionary, New Testament, Spiros Zodhiates, TH.D., AMG Publishers, Chattanooga, TN, #2904, s.v. "kratos."

[7] Complete Word Study Dictionary, New Testament, Spiros Zodhiates, TH.D., AMG Publishers, Chattanooga, TN, #5281, s.v. "patience."

Chapter 17

[1] Vines Expository Dictionary of Old and New Testament Words, s.v. "secret."

[2] Vines Expository Dictionary of Old and New Testament Words, s.v. "fear."

[3] Vines Expository Dictionary of Old and New Testament Words, s.v. "know."

[4] Vines Expository Dictionary of Old and New Testament Words, s.v. "know."

[5] Complete Word Study Dictionary, New Testament, Spiros Zodhiates, TH.D., AMG Publishers, Chattanooga, TN, #1097, s.v. "ginosko."

REFERENCES

Vine, W.E.; Unger Merril; White, William. Vines Expository Dictionary of Old and New Testament Words, Nashville, TN: Thomas Nelson Publishers.

Webster's Universal Encyclopedic Dictionary, 2002 Edition, Barnes and Noble.

Strong, James. Strong's Exhaustive Concordance of the Bible. "Hebrew and Chaldee Dictionary", "Greek Dictionary of the New Testament" Peabody, MA: Hendrickson.

Zodhiates, Spiros, Complete Word Study Dictionary of the New Testament, Chatanooga, TN, AMG Publishers.

Steltin, Leo, Dictionary of Ecclesiastical Latin. Peabody, MA, Hendrickson Publishers.

PRAYER OF SALVATION

God loves you—no matter who you are, no matter what your past. God loves you so much that He gave His one and only begotten Son for you. The Bible tells us that "...whoever believes in him shall not perish but have eternal life" (John 3:16 NIV). Jesus laid down His life and rose again so that we could spend eternity with Him in heaven and experience His absolute best on earth. If you would like to receive Jesus into your life, say the following prayer out loud and mean it from your heart.

Heavenly Father, I come to You admitting that I am a sinner. Right now, I choose to turn away from sin, and I ask You to cleanse me of all unrighteousness. I believe that Your Son, Jesus, died on the cross to take away my sins. I also believe that He rose again from the dead so that I might be forgiven of my sins and made righteous through faith in Him. I call upon the name of Jesus Christ to be the Savior and Lord of my life. Jesus, I choose to follow You and ask that You fill me with the power of the Holy Spirit. I declare that right now I am a child of God. I am free from sin and full of the righteousness of God. I am saved in Jesus' name. Amen.

If you prayed this prayer to receive Jesus Christ as your Savior for the first time, please contact us on the Web at **www.harrisonhouse.com** to receive a free book.

Or you may write to us at

Harrison House
P.O. Box 35035
Tulsa, Oklahoma 74153

ABOUT THE AUTHOR

Malcolm Smith was born in London, England. He came to the United States in 1964. While the pastor of a church in Brooklyn, New York, his ministry was radically changed by the revelation that the heart of the gospel was found in the unconditional love of God, expressed to mankind through Jesus Christ in the covenant. He became involved in teaching the charismatic renewal in the 1960s and 70s and was known throughout the world to many thousands on radio, TV, and through seminars and retreats.

Today, Malcolm ministers extensively throughout the United States and the mission field of the world.

To contact Malcolm Smith, write:

Unconditional Love Ministries
P.O. Box 1599
Bandera, TX 78003

www.malcolmsmith.org

*Please include your prayer requests
and comments when you write.*

Fast. Easy. Convenient.

For the latest Harrison House product information and author news, look no further than your computer. All the details on our powerful, life-changing products are just a click away. New releases, E-mail subscriptions, Podcasts, testimonies, monthly specials—find it all in one place. Visit harrisonhouse.com today!

harrisonhouse

THE HARRISON HOUSE VISION

Proclaiming the truth and the power
Of the Gospel of Jesus Christ
With excellence;

Challenging Christians to
Live victoriously,
Grow spiritually,
Know God intimately.